W9-CGV-346

Global Governance:
An Architecture
for the World Economy

Springer
Berlin
Heidelberg
New York
Hong Kong
London
Milan
Paris
Tokyo

Horst Siebert (Ed.)

Global Governance:
An Architecture
for the World Economy

 Springer

Professor Horst Siebert
President
Kiel Institute for World Economics
D-24100 Kiel
http://www.ifw-kiel.de

ISBN 3-540-00439-4 Springer-Verlag Berlin Heidelberg New York

Cataloging-in-Publication Data applied for
A catalog record for this book is available from the Library of Congress.
Bibliographic information published by Die Deutsche Bibliothek
Die Deutsche Bibliothek lists this publication in the Deutsche Nationalbibliografie;
detailed bibliographic data is available in the Internet at <http://dnb.ddb.de>.

This work is subject to copyright. All rights are reserved, whether the whole or part of
the material is concerned, specifically the rights of translation, reprinting, reuse of illustrations, recitation, broadcasting, reproduction on microfilm or in any other way, and
storage in data banks. Duplication of this publication or parts thereof is permitted only
under the provisions of the German Copyright Law of September 9, 1965, in its current
version, and permission for use must always be obtained from Springer-Verlag. Viola-
tions are liable for prosecution under the German Copyright Law.

Springer-Verlag Berlin · Heidelberg · New York
a member of BertelsmannSpringer Science+Business Media GmbH

http://www.springer.de

© Springer-Verlag Berlin · Heidelberg 2003
Printed in Germany

The use of general descriptive names, registered names, trademarks, etc. in this publication
does not imply, even in the absence of a specific statement, that such names are exempt
from the relevant protective laws and regulations and therefore free for general use.

Hardcover-Design: Erich Kirchner, Heidelberg

SPIN 10911228   42/3130-5 4 3 2 1 0 – Printed on acid-free paper

CONTENTS

Preface

Stones in Seattle, Molotov cocktails in Prague, and gunfire in Genoa – in recent years, every annual meeting of the international financial institutions and every major political summit had to be held under the siege of violent anti-globalization activists. These protests are only the most visible sign that the public perception of globalization has gone sour. Large parts of the population entertain suspicion or even hostility towards engaging in an ever-deepening international division of labor and increasingly close financial relations across borders. They fear that with globalization the world economy is going down the wrong way. Against this background, the 2002 Kiel Week Conference on "Global Governance: An Architecture for the World Economy" provided economists and representatives of nongovernmental organizations with a forum to discuss the new globalization-induced challenges to the world economy. Is globalization *angst* justified and how can it be relieved? What maneuvering space remains for national governments and what policies should they pursue to reap the benefits from the international division of labor? What global institutional framework does the world economy need and how can it be implemented?

The first paper lays out the benefits from opening up to international trade and capital mobility: scarce production factors are employed more efficiently, consumption and investment frontiers shift outwards, and technological progress and economic growth accelerate. For these benefits to materialize, however, countries have to adapt flexibly to changing economic conditions, to pursue a credible monetary and fiscal policy backed up by sound regulatory and supervision mechanisms of the domestic financial markets, and to compete for internationally mobile production factors. In a globalized economy, a multilateral order for the international division of labor gains greater importance. In the areas of international trade, finance, and environmental goods, nation-states have to renounce part of their sovereignty and bind themselves to a system of international rules in order to avoid strategic behavior of individual countries and to reduce negative external effects. Popular measures such as the Tobin tax or target zones for the exchange rates of major currencies, however, are often not implementable or are even counterproductive. Instead, countries should build upon the existing international institutions and treaties.

Jagdish Bhagwati explores the reasons why anti-globalization protests have gathered considerable momentum in recent years. He argues that the anti-globalization movement is very heterogeneous. At the one end of the spectrum, there are those who wish to engage in a constructive dialogue with policy makers. But there is also the "trilogy of discontents", i.e., activists with an anti-capitalist, anti-globalization, or anti-corporation mindset, who have found a new target for their un-differentiated and inconsistent criticism. He emphasizes that the public – and to a certain extent also the academic – debate on the virtues and vices of globalization is overlaid and overwhelmed with two fallacies. First, globalization is a highly multifaceted phenomenon, embracing international trade, foreign direct invest-ment, multinational corporations, and short-term capital flows, to name but a few. Yet, in the debate on globalization the lines between the different dimensions tend to be blurred. Second, far from being monolithic – as portrayed in the media – the anti-globalization movement is a fragile coalition of disparate groups unified only by a negative agenda. In order to refute the fears and follies that animate anti-glo-balization protesters, it is important to get across that globalization itself has a hu-man face and that globalization is part of the solution, not part of the problem, if you are interested in improving social outcomes.

Pranab Bardhan assesses the widely held belief that globalization is causing hardship for the poor. In the first part of his contribution, he focuses on the poor in their capacity as wage earners and as recipients of public services. He identifies six transmission mechanisms through which international trade affects the abso-lute level of the real wage of unskilled workers. Taken together, the net distribu-tional effect of international trade is almost always context dependent, belying any oversimplified statements for or against globalization made in the opposing camps. Turning to public services in developing countries, he argues that recent budget cuts in basic services like health and education, which are often blamed on globalization, are to a large extent attributable to domestic institutional failures. In the second part, he analyzes the ways in which policies meant to relieve the eco-nomic conditions of the poor are curtailed by global constraints. He shows that while globalization can constrain some policy options, domestic vested interests are the main culprit for socially damaging policies.

The question of whether national governments lose their fiscal maneuvering space in the era of locational competition is addressed by *Oliver Lorz*. Drawing on several theoretical models, he demonstrates that fiscal competition (a) may in-crease the elasticity of the tax base, primarily, but not only, with respect to interna-tionally mobile production factors, (b) may change the level and composition of government consumption and transfers, and (c) may have consequences for the employment of immobile production factors. The policy implications that follow from the theoretical models on locational competition are less clear. In models with welfare-maximizing governments, fiscal competition can lead to inefficien-cies with respect to the level and composition of taxes and public expenditure. When political economy aspects are incorporated into the models, positive and negative welfare effects of fiscal competition are not exclusive but coexist. The empirical support for the theoretical models is at best mixed. Although some tax and expenditure changes have taken place, a collapse of the welfare state has not occurred and mobile production factors still contribute substantially to the financing of the welfare state.

In her analysis of the role of civil society in global governance, *Ann Florini* starts by outlining why NGOs and other advocacy groups have recently become so prominent in the globalization debate. Rising education levels and living standards have enabled more and more people to participate in civil society networks. The information revolution has provided the means to collaborate across borders and to disseminate their message to a greater audience. Global integration itself and the efforts to govern it through international institutions such as the World Bank, IMF, and WTO have created targets against which advocacy groups can mobilize and focal points around which they can coalesce. She argues that it is neither possible nor desirable to exclude civil society from the decision-making process. NGOs can give a voice to the politically marginalized and speak for the global public good. More importantly, ignoring civil society could generate a backlash against global governance. Hence, the question is now not so much *whether* civil society groups should be participating, but *how*. More transparency and forthcoming disclosure would be a first step towards more inclusion.

Sylvia Ostry starts her contribution by discussing three new challenges to the World Trade Organization. First, the number of member states has increased rapidly, thereby making it more difficult to reach unanimous decisions. Second, the WTO agenda has been burdened with "new issues" which are far more intrusive into domestic sovereignty than previously agreed-upon accords. In the Uruguay Round, agriculture, trade in services, intellectual property rights, and foreign direct investment were put on the negotiation table. Doha further added environmental and development goals. Third, the WTO became one of the prime targets of anti-globalization activists. As a result, the institutional infrastructure of the WTO has been stretched to the limit and is in dire need of reform. She then goes on to sketch two suggestions for overhauling the WTO. To avoid the paralysis of consensus, the day-to-day management of the WTO should be delegated to an Executive Board, as proposed in the former ITO Charter. As concerns the issue of civil society involvement in the decision-making process, the WTO should follow the example of the OECD by increasing external transparency.

Barry Eichengreen gives an overview of the state of the art in predicting and preventing financial crises. He argues that crises have multiple causes rooted in the interaction of market fundamentals and investor psychology. In addition, they are contingent on the domestic, foreign, and international policy responses to growing financial pressure. For these reasons, crisis prediction will always be imperfect. But it is still possible to limit the incidence and severity of financial crises. The key to crisis prevention is to increase transparency on the part of the borrowers, lenders, and international financial institutions so that markets begin to take corrective actions before things go out of hand. He then offers an in-depth discussion of six steps to achieve this goal. Strengthening the regulation and supervision of financial institutions, and rationalizing the exchange rate regimes should be top on the agenda. Finally, he gives two hypotheses for why contagion of the Argentinean crisis was initially milder than expected. On the one hand, since the Asean crisis in 1998, leverage in the international financial system had declined, its transparency had increased, and Chile, Brazil, and other neighboring countries had adopted more flexible exchange rate regimes. On the other hand, the Argentinean crisis was long anticipated. Discriminating empirically between these hypotheses will be crucial to determining whether contagion in general has diminished.

The next two contributions concern the link between globalization and environmental problems. *Jason F. Shogren* and *Stephan Kroll* explore the microeconomic foundations of global climate policy. Using the Kyoto Protocol as point of reference, they stress two prerequisites for any international environmental agreement: the contract must be self-enforcing and the burden sharing between developed and developing country must be equitable. To get the incentive structure right, several issues have to be taken into account in the negotiation process. First, linking climate protection with social issues might backfire because not only does it make the negotiations more complex, but it also invites opposition that might not appear if the environmental issue were negotiated alone. Second, when opting for emission trading, the seller country, rather than the buyer country, should be held responsible for overselling permits beyond quotas. It is also important to consider that in competitive emission markets, the prices for permits do not equate marginal abatement costs, since they do not reflect the ancillary benefits of reduced local environmental pollution. Finally, policy makers have to address the problem that the risk of climate change is both ambiguous and endogenous so that individual behavior towards this risk is distorted.

The link between globalization and biodiversity is analyzed by *Geoffrey Heal*. He briefly outlines the benefits of biodiversity. Access to genetic diversity stored in wild races of plants and animals has helped to raise the productivity of commercially valuable species and to provide insurance against attack by pathogens. Natural organisms have also inspired the development of new products, especially in the pharmaceutical industry. He then argues that biodiversity loss is a global problem but not a problem of globalization. It is occurring globally and has global consequences, but it is not driven by the expansion of international trade, investment, and capital flows. Globalization has rather the potential to help the conservation of biodiversity. The fact that many of the services of biodiversity are public in nature does not rule out using market mechanisms for its support. Using the examples of ecotourism and certified sustainably logged timber, he shows that bundling biodiversity with private goods can be an effective way of internalizing some of the external effects of biodiversity conservation by channeling willingness-to-pay from rich to poor countries.

In the final contribution, *Gary C. Hufbauer* takes a look thirty years ahead in global governance. Drawing upon economic history, he stresses the overriding importance of the security context in shaping the global economic and political landscape. He predicts that the early 21st century will resemble the Concert of Europe following the Congress of Vienna of 1815. Global powers, among them the United States, China, the European Union, and possibly Japan and Russia, will agree on basic security principles to avoid confrontation between them. However, this arrangement does not rule out wars between secondary powers nor worldwide terrorist attacks. As concerns the global economic order, he identifies five issues that will compel the greatest attention in the next thirty years – global warming, poverty, oil politics, financial crises, and trade and investment – and speculates on the institutional framework needed to handle them. He envisages increasing polarization around the global powers as countries affiliate their trade, investment, and currency regimes with regional economic blocs. Global governance will mainly be conducted through loose arrangements between the global powers. International organizations such as the World Bank, IMF, and WTO will focus on mediating between the economic blocs and on dealing with those countries left outside.

The Kiel Institute for World Economics is indebted to the participants of the 2002 Kiel Week Conference for having presented interesting and challenging papers, and for having conducted stimulating discussions. The Institute gratefully acknowledges the financial support of the Fritz Thyssen Stiftung. It would also like to thank Deutsche Bank, Dresdner Bank, and Landesbank Schleswig-Holstein for their hospitality. Julius Spatz organized the conference, Ingrid Lawaetz provided efficient secretarial assistance, and many members of the Institute's technical and administrative staff ensured the successful realization of the conference. The conference volume was prepared for publication by Dietmar Gebert and Paul Kramer.

Kiel, March 2003   Horst Siebert

I.
Fears and Benefits
of Globalization

Horst Siebert

On the Fears of the International Division of Labor: Eight Points in the Debate with Anti-Globalizationers

Globalization has given rise to many fears among important groups in Western societies. These fears are forcefully and sometimes militantly expressed by the NGOs. The fears have many faces. People are worried that welfare is not enhanced but seriously impaired when countries engage in the international division of labor with respect to trade and capital flows. One fear is that developing countries will lose because of the international division of labor, that their terms of trade will deteriorate, and that their per capita income will be lower after engaging in trade and after allowing capital to come in. Another fear is that industrial countries will lose in welfare. People are afraid that jobs will be destroyed in the industrialized countries, that real income will fall, and that unemployment will be the result of the international division of labor. They are afraid that all countries face additional constraints through trade and are losing maneuvering space. There are strong voices that developing countries – the emerging markets – will be destroyed or seriously impaired by speculation in the financial markets, leading to currency runs with sizable devaluations of the national currencies and to a decline in economic activity as a result of these financial crises. People are terrified that countries will lose their autonomy and their identity, that the nation state is constrained in its maneuvering space and that governments, states, and policies will be marginalized.

At the same time people are demanding that worldwide considerations such as the protection of global environmental media and the conservation of biodiversity be taken into consideration. All these fears and demands, often expressed emotionally and sometimes voiced with rage and hate, have to be taken seriously. Fear, rage and hate, however, are not good advisers. And ideas based on them are not a counter-paradigm to the idea of the international division of labor. It is the role of this conference to discuss these issues.

In order to lay the ground for the discussion, I want to elaborate eight central points of the international division of labor which the anti-globalizationers cannot ignore and deny.

1   Each Economy Can Gain through Trade

The fundamental idea of the international division of labor has been developed in over more than two hundred years of economic thinking. If a country specializes in the production and export of a good in which it has a comparative advantage due to its demand and production conditions relative to the rest of the world, it can obtain products from abroad at lower costs than it can produce the goods for at home. The economy can reach a consumption space that lies outside the transformation space. The enhanced consumption possibility, represented by the budget line BB (which is determined by the world market price) in Figure 1 indicates the potential area of gains from trade outside the transformation curve TT. In order to reach the higher consumption point C, resources are reallocated from the autarky point A to the production point P; the sector of import substitutes shrinks and the export sector expands, generating welfare gains for the country as a whole.

The exchange between countries is not a zero-sum game in which a country can only gain if another loses. Trade is a positive-sum game in which every country benefits. One indicator of gains from trade is that the terms of trade, defined as the ratio between the export price index and the import price index, improve after trade takes place. For instance, for industrial countries it pays to produce more capital-intensive or human-capital-intensive products, for the developing countries to produce more labor-intensive goods. Free trade is beneficial for an individ-

Figure 1: Production Possibility Space and Consumption Space of an Open Economy

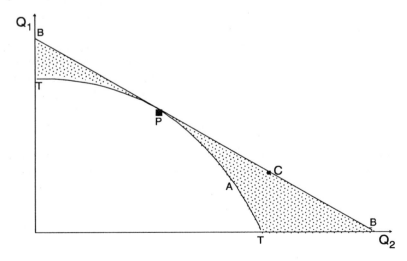

ual country even if all other countries are protectionist (free-trade-for-one theorem) because the consumption space becomes larger.

Some may be more persuaded by another idea, namely, that for a country participating in the international division of labor, new markets are opened up for its products. For instance, the developing countries can sell their goods in the industrialized world, and the industrialized countries have an additional market in the developing countries. The limit of market size has less relevance for open economies. For instance, roughly 10 percent of German exports went to Central and Eastern Europe in 2001.

Additionally, the hypothesis of *intra*sectoral trade raises hopes. In *inter*sectoral trade, i.e., exchange of different products like European investment goods against Asian textiles, a country – though gaining from trade – has to accept that the sector of import substitutes with a relative price disadvantage shrinks (for instance, textiles in the industrialized countries). In contrast, intrasectoral trade means that customers love variety and that similar goods are exchanged between countries, e.g., European cars for Korean cars. This implies that the same sector can expand in different countries when the international division of labor intensifies; albeit it expands in different product segments so that there is a vertical structure in intrasectoral trade. The world trade nowadays is overwhelmingly intrasectoral trade. This holds for the exchange between the industrialized countries, but it will also hold more and more for the newly industrializing countries in the course of economic development.

In comparison to the comparative static welfare gains, dynamic effects are more important. Open economies deliberately expose themselves to competition and use other countries as a benchmark. Competition is a discovery process in the sense of Hayek for firms and states, and in this process new technological and organizational solutions can be found. Open economies have a strong incentive and impulse for innovation; a strong export expansion is associated with a higher growth rate and higher benefits.

Many of the anti-globalizationers will probably not be convinced by such fundamental considerations. And many will not be induced by the more than two hundred years of economic thinking to revise their extremely pessimistic position. Importance should, however, be attached to the fact that the historical development gives ample proof that an open economy can draw substantial benefits from the division of labor. This holds especially for Germany, which has benefited from openness since its breakdown in 1945, openness both with respect to Europe and with respect to the world as a whole. Countries that have not dared to open up, such as the Comecon countries and countries in Latin America, with their policy of import substitution, have failed.

A realistic evaluation of the relevance of openness is necessary with respect to globalization fears. Smaller countries can gain relatively more from openness than larger nations. Their export ratios (exports to GDP) are relatively high, for instance, for the Netherlands more than 50 percent. The larger countries or regional integrations of the world like the United States, Japan or the European Union, however, have export ratios of a little bit over 10 percent, so that 90 percent of GDP relate to the internal sector. Neighborhood effects are important; regional integrations like the European Union strengthen these effects (Rodrick 1997; Wade 1996).

2   Developing Countries as a Whole Have Increased Their Welfare as a Result of the International Division of Labor

It is heavily questioned by the NGOs that third world countries have benefited from the international division of labor and it is postulated that the economic situation has worsened for third world countries. In order to shed some light on that question, different aspects can be studied: first, to what extent developing have integrated into the world economy, and second, whether per capita income has increased.

As concerns the participation of developing countries, they have succeeded in increasing their share in world trade in the last 25 years. In the period 1975–1998, the non-oil-exporting developing countries increased their share in world exports from 18 percent (1975) to 30 percent (2000). Without parallel is the success of the four Asian tigers (Hong Kong, Singapore, South Korea, and Taiwan), who raised their share from 3 percent to around 10 percent of world exports – after it had caved in during the currency crises of 1997. Quite a few developing countries have mutated into newly industrialized countries with exports in which industrial products dominate. For instance, industrial exports of Hong Kong, Mexico, South Korea, and Singapore account for 85 percent and more of their total exports; for Brazil it is 55 percent. On the whole, the developing countries have succeeded in integrating themselves into the international division of labor.

With respect to evaluating per capita income, two different criteria can be used.[1] First, whether per capita GDP or GNP has increased in absolute terms and, second, whether the relative position in per capita GDP or GNP to the industrial countries, especially the United States, has improved. In order to make a comparison in time and between countries, a common measuring rod has to be applied. This may be either constant dollars, where for international comparisons market

---

[1]   A different problem is that changes in the standard of living are not only linked to the international division of labor but are influenced by quite a set of factors, including purely internal conditions of a country.

Figure 2: Per Capita[a] GNP of Latin American Countries (Panel a) and Asian and African Countries[b] (Panel b), Absolutely and Relatively to the United States, 1975 and 1998

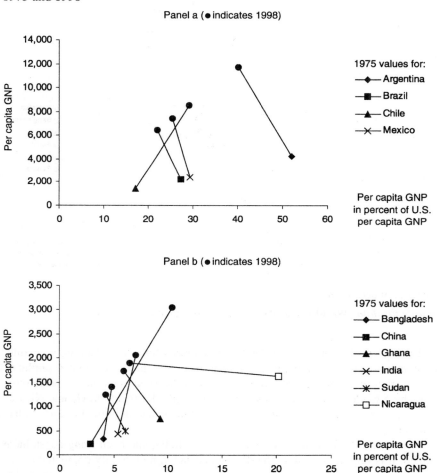

Panel a (● indicates 1998)

1975 values for:
—◆— Argentina
—■— Brazil
—▲— Chile
—✕— Mexico

Per capita GNP in percent of U.S. per capita GNP

Panel b (● indicates 1998)

1975 values for:
—◆— Bangladesh
—■— China
—▲— Ghana
—✕— India
—✳— Sudan
—□— Nicaragua

Per capita GNP in percent of U.S. per capita GNP

[a] Purchasing power parity. – [b] Including Nicaragua.

Source for data: World Bank, *World Development Indicators 2000.*

exchange rates are used, or purchasing power parity rates. Both data sets are provided by the World Bank. Here I use purchasing power parity data because they are more appropriate for comparisons of standards of living.

Figure 3: Annual Changes in the Absolute per Capita GNP and the Relative Position to the United States between 1975 and 1998

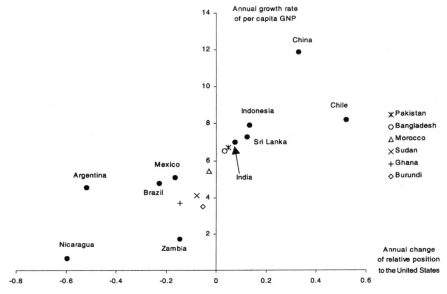

^a In terms of percentage points.

Source for data: World Bank, *World Development Indicators 2000.*

Looking at the period 1975–1998, all countries for which data are available, have improved their situation in absolute terms except the Democratic Republic of Congo (Figure 2, Panel a and Panel b, in which the 1998 position is always indicated by a circle). This also holds for countries like Bangladesh, Ghana, Nicaragua, and Sudan. Thus, it is simply not true that the situation of the third world has deteriorated.

Relative to the United States, Chile, China, India, and even Bangladesh have gained. It is important to note that China and India, both highly populated countries, have improved their situation. These countries exhibit β-convergence. Argentina, Brazil, and Mexico, however, have lost relative to the United States, reflecting the "lost decade" for Latin America. Nicaragua has lost strongly relative to the United States,[2] as have Ghana and Sudan. The latter three countries are all countries that have been affected by war and internal turmoil.

---

2   This corresponds to the Barro results that for a large group of 98 countries there is β-divergence (Barro and Sala-i-Martin 1991). The larger the sample, the more countries that experienced a relative decline are included, for instance, from sub-Saharan Africa.

Depicting the average annual rate of increase of the absolute GNP level per capita on the vertical axis and the change in position relative to the United States in terms of percentage points on the horizontal axis between 1975 and 1998, the countries can be arranged in two quadrants with the winners in both accounts in the right quadrant and the losers in the relative position in the left quadrant (Figure 3) (Siebert 2002c).

China, Chile, Indonesia, Sri Lanka, India, Pakistan, and Bangladesh gain on both accounts. Countries like Argentina, Nicaragua, Brazil, Sudan, Ghana, Burundi, Zambia, and Mexico, while gaining in absolute terms, lose in their relative position.

If industrial countries really want to foster the welfare of developing countries, there is a rather traditional message: They should open up their markets where they are still closed, i.e., markets for agricultural products, textiles, and other labor-intensive commodities such as steel to which antidumping measures are applied. The agricultural policy of the EU and the now increasing supports for agriculture in the United States stimulate overproduction that destroys opportunities for the developing countries.

3   For Workers, Trade Offers the Opportunity for Higher Real Wages

A large concern is that the integration of highly populated countries in Central and Eastern Europe and of China into the international division of labor will have negative repercussions for the real income and employment of workers in the industrial countries. It is true that the existence of benefits for a country does not imply that all factors of production will gain. The real income of that factor will increase that will be used more intensively after opening up to trade. And it is also true that in a thought experiment, the labor supply of the world effectively increases. If we imagine a world labor market, the effective integration into the world economy of China will augment global labor supply by one-fifth. In a Heckscher–Ohlin model, real wages in the industrial countries will consequently decline (in the case of incomplete specialization).

In contrast to these model results, however, labor is in reality not a homogenous factor. Workers in the industrial countries are equipped with better technology and more efficient physical capital and they are better qualified, so that they have a much higher labor productivity. If we distinguish traditional labor and qualified human capital, the real wage of human capital in the industrial countries will rise due to an intensified division of labor, since the production of human-capital-intensive products will be increased. Consequently, human capital will be used more intensively and its price will rise. In addition, the real wage will increase because importables can be obtained at a lower price. A given nominal wage, thus, represents a higher real wage. This idea was basic to the repeal of the Corn Laws in the United Kingdom in the 19th century. By abolishing the protection of agriculture, the industrial workers in the cities could be better supplied with articles of food and their real wage increased.

It is also important that intrasectoral trade does not have the same implications for labor as intersectoral trade, since sectors will not have to shrink and since workers will not have to be set free during the adjustment to changed conditions. It should also be taken into consideration that a country like China actually has a world market share of 3 percent and even if China forces other labor-intensive suppliers like Taiwan or South Korea into higher-grade production activities, the quantitative impact on the labor markets of industrial countries would be small. It also has to be taken into account that not all workers are engaged in the production of tradable goods – either exportables or import substitutes. Workers in the non-tradable area are not directly linked to the international division of labor although the demand for them depends on the income that is created in the tradable sector.

Empirically, pressure on the wages of industrial countries caused by trade with developing countries cannot be established unambiguously. It is, however, undisputed as an empirical phenomenon that the structure of demand for labor has changed in the industrial countries to the disadvantage of the less qualified. This can be observed in all industrialized countries, in Europe as well as in North America. For instance, demand in Germany for the less qualified in manufacturing and construction has decreased by 1.8 million in the last 20 years, whereas the demand for the qualified has increased by 0.4 million (Siebert 2002a). The qualified are much less affected by the decrease in labor demand. In the service sector, the demand for the qualified has increased by 2.8 million, for the less qualified only by 0.8 million. This means that the qualified are favored by the increase in demand. In the economic literature, labor-saving technical progress has been identified as the driving force for this shift in labor demand. A direct link with the international division of labor has not been established, although it cannot be ruled out that trade with highly populated countries is an incentive to look for labor-saving technological progress in the capital-rich countries.

In no case can it be argued that workers both in the industrial countries and in the developing countries will lose in terms of real income. The demand for workers in the developing countries will increase and their real income rises. Therefore, the fears of NGOs with respect to the situation of workers in the developing countries is inconsistent and not justified. Processes inherent in the international division of labor have a positive impact on their real wages there.

Anti-globalizationers demand that developing countries apply the same labor norms and social security norms as in the rich industrial countries. The demands do not relate to minimal standards to which most nations of the world have agreed in the multilateral contract of the International Labor Organization (ILO), for instance, with respect to child labor or the right for trade unions to organize. The demands relate to social norms that go beyond the minimum standards. Such norms, however, would be extremely unfair. Workers in the developing countries with a relatively low productivity have to compete with workers in the industrialized nations equipped with a lot of physical capital, up-to-date technology, and a high level of human capital. If worldwide norms were established, developing countries would not have a chance to compete. It would be as if someone required developing countries to pay the same wage as industrial countries. Unemployment in the developing countries would shoot up tremendously. In that sense, it is hypocritical of people in the rich countries to require better working conditions in China, and it should not be surprising that the demand for harmonizing labor norms is not accepted by the Third World. Even in the European Union, a harmonization of standards pertaining to the labor market and social insurance systems cannot be realized due, among other things, to diverging labor productivities and different preferences. It does not make sense to harmonize away differences in the factor endowments of countries. The international division of labor is rooted in the differences between these endowments. Harmonization would only serve to protect the rich countries; it would not serve the interests of the developing countries.

4   Beyond the Exchange of Goods, There Are Benefits to Be Derived from the International Division of Labor if Countries Succeed in Attracting Mobile Factors of Production

Countries can enjoy benefits if they attract mobile factors of production, thereby increasing the productivity of their immobile factors. This is the concept of locational competition (or competition between governments), which is so difficult to explain to our colleagues from the Anglo-Saxon world. Countries compete for mobile physical capital, for mobile technical knowledge, and for mobile, highly qualified workers. Countries can thus shape their comparative advantage for the exchange of commodities.

The world economy is now characterized by the increased mobility of factors of production. Foreign direct investments have grown three times as much as world exports, which increased twice as much as the rate of production (Siebert 2002c). Portfolio capital has become more mobile worldwide. It can be adjusted instantaneously, at the push of a button, and can be shifted from one country to the other.

The advantage of a capital import is that a country can accumulate its capital stock much more quickly and does not have to give up consumption. Thus, there is an intertemporal welfare gain that, as a first step, lifts the period restriction that national investments have to be financed by national savings. Moreover, developing countries have a chance to find quick access to new technologies. Thus, the Central and Eastern European transformation countries succeeded in financing a sizable part of their gross investment through foreign direct investment; for instance, Poland financed 15 percent in the period 1995 to 1999. The development of North America in the 19th century was made possible by sizable capital imports.

The flip side of capital imports is the necessity to pay a premium to the imported capital. In real terms, capital imports only pay off if the marginal productivity of capital is larger than the price that has to be paid for having that capital. According to this long-run optimality condition, it is important that a country does not slide into a situation in which in later periods the productivity of capital can no longer pay the price for having that capital. A capital import would shift the budget line upward in the period when debt is taken up; more commodities can be imported in that period. If these imports are used for investment, the production space will shift outward so that later on foreign currency earnings from additional exports can be used to repay the credits.

Capital can be attracted in different forms, namely as foreign direct investment, equity, bonds, bank credits, or other portfolio flows in favor of firms, banks, or the government. Besides the intertemporal gain, there is an improved risk allocation. The condition that there must be a positive marginal productivity of capital that allows the interest rate to be paid and the imported capital to be repaid will not always be satisfied, for instance, when the government incurs debt abroad in order to finance governmental consumption or social programs. In these cases, the intertemporal budget constraints will bite later on. The other side of today's consumption financed from new debt is a repayment obligation tomorrow, i.e., additional foreign currency has to be earned from exports; and these currency earnings cannot be used to finance imports. Then earlier capital imports prove to be a chain which restricts the maneuvering space of the economy later on. From the point of view of developing countries, foreign direct investment has priority in the pecking order of capital flows, since it is characterized by a more direct linkage between marginal productivity and the reimbursement of the capital owner, because it is less volatile and because it brings with it new technical knowledge.

How capital imports are evaluated varies for many with respect to time. When capital has not yet been imported, one would like to have it, and even NGOs would plead for a more gracious supply of capital. When capital is imported and when it is in place, many request a debt reduction. To view things this way is not adequate because importing capital and repaying it are indissoluble actions. Whoever does not repay will find it difficult to attract fresh capital. Therefore, there should be a difference between requesting debt reduction for the poorest countries and making debt reduction a general guideline for the international capital markets. Such a guide line would cut countries off from new capital. Last but not least, whoever wants to help the developing countries should woo the governments of industrial countries to increase their development aid.

Capital mobility, however, should not be overestimated. In real terms, a country's investments are overwhelmingly financed from national savings. Capital imports, as measured by the capital account, normally amount to only a small percentage of GDP, on the order of three to four percent, in rare cases more. In real terms, capital mobility nowadays is not any higher than at the beginning of the 20th century.

5   For a Country to Benefit from the International Division of Labor Certain Conditions Must Be Met

The international division of labor can overcome constraints such as the production possibility frontier of an economy or the financing constraint that national investments must be supported by national savings in each year; it thus creates a larger consumption and investment space. However, it would be naïve and illusionary to believe that economic constraints can be defined away altogether. Another constraint has to be taken into account, namely the intertemporal budget constraint. A country cannot import more in value terms than it exports unless it has accumulated currency reserves, unless it has accumulated foreign wealth, or unless it has accumulated debt for the future. Debt allows a higher consumption space now, but debt will have to be repaid later on. The consumption space will then be reduced. People may or may not like it: Economics is the discipline of shortage and scarcity, and this also holds for a globalized world. We cannot get rid of a budget constraint of an economy, no matter how much we would like to have that emotionally.

Beside the budget constraint there are other conditions that have to be met for benefits to arise from the international division of labor. These conditions have been discussed extensively in the development economics literature. An important aspect is that a country can adjust to changed economic conditions and develop new export products. If it does not, it faces the risk that its most important export good will be substituted for by the invention of a new product in the world market. Then the terms of trade will deteriorate. Similar problems arise in the case of monocultures or of an excessive export specialization on natural resources whose international prices vary considerably. Further, the export sector may not carry over to the rest of the economy (export enclave, dual economy). Countries may be locked in to their given situation in a vicious circle, so that a significant push for a takeoff is needed. Moreover, growth and development processes are path-dependent; economic structures that are given at a specific moment of time will influence or even determine future development. Finally, convergence processes in which poor countries can catch up need a lot of time. Whereas according to empirical studies the convergence rate between industrial countries is roughly one percent a year, including development countries in a large sample of 98 economies even shows divergence (Barro and Sala-i-Martin 1991) (see Section 2). This result depends very much on the sub-Saharan African countries. Historically, nations have fallen back in the ranking of economic well-being, for instance, Argentina, which belonged to the ten richest countries of the world around 1900.

Generalizing the conditions, there are three central conditions for benefits from openness to arise. A first condition is stable institutional arrangements conducive to growth. Warlike internal conflicts, but also abrupt changes in the institutional order are detrimental to economic development. The fact that sub-Saharan Africa is the poor house of the world is caused by the lack of a stable environment, among other factors. A second condition is that long-run constraints cannot be sacrificed on the altar of populism. To use the printing press in order to finance governmental budget deficits, to run a high governmental debt, and to have a large external debt imply a form of hyperinflation, financial instability, and quite an amount of currency reserves from exports needed in order to pay the interests on debt. The fact that Latin America experienced a lost decade in the 1980s, in which per capita income shrank by 1 percent a year, has one of its causes in this lacking condition. A third condition is an orientation towards competition as practiced by the Asian countries. The strategy of import substitution followed by Latin America from the 1950s up to the 1990s to protect the domestic sector has clearly failed. The sealing off of the Comecon region from the world economy and its internal division of labor planned from above was a failure as well. If there is a lesson from history, it is this: it pays to have an open economy.

6   Financial and Currency Crises Can only Be Prevented by a Credible Stabilization Policy

So far, we have looked at the real economy; now we are going to look at monetary-financial conditions, as these may also cause disruptions. For instance, we are all well-acquainted with hyperinflation of the Latin American type. When the money supply of Brazil increases by 219.9 percent a year, as it did in the period 1991–

1995, one should not be surprised that the annual inflation rate lies at 223.7 percent, so that a stable money does not exist. It should also not be surprising that, as a consequence, the Brazilian currency had to be devalued. If the necessary devaluation of the home currency is retarded and the inflation differential is not sufficiently reflected in the devaluation, a currency crisis is unavoidable. The root cause of these crises lies in the lack of monetary stability. The trigger of the crisis is that participants in the international capital market lose confidence abruptly and that capital inflows dry up or capital flows reverse. A currency run follows. Without a solid national stability policy such crises cannot be avoided. This means that the central bank should not be allowed to finance the budget deficit of a government, that it should be independent in its monetary policy, and that it should have a stable money as its target. Moreover, conditions that prevent excessive governmental budget deficits and that secure the stability and solidity of the banking and financial sector are absolutely necessary.

Relative to the typical Latin American currency crises, things may even be more complicated, as the 1997 Asian crises have shown. Lacking regulation of the banking sector together with a real estate boom (as in Thailand), a somewhat unfortunate performance of exports and of the current account together with some structural weaknesses, for instance, overinvestment with temporary worldwide overcapacity (as in the high-tech sector in South Korea) or other factors (as in Indonesia), can lead to currency crises with the phenomenon of contagion. Liberalization of the capital account is not adequate, if the banking system is not sufficiently regulated and if a liberalization of the capital account leads to an unwanted expansion of liquidity. It is therefore necessary to make sure that sufficient regulation of the banking sector exists before liberalizing the capital account.

In an environment of potential contagion the requirement of stability is all the more important. Because of the threat of a potential contagion, an economy must make sure that it is sufficiently robust against external shocks and that it is sufficiently immune to what happens elsewhere. To do this, however, involves costs.

Anti-globalizationers cannot argue that countries should not worry about monetary and financial stability. This would have severe consequences in the medium run and would be to the detriment of people in those countries. Currency and financial crises would then be programmed, and the countries' real economies would eventually be affected.

Once a currency crisis has broken out, a new equilibrium exchange rate has to be found, fresh capital has to be provided, and the spread of the crisis to other countries, i.e., a systemic crisis, has to be prevented. The provision of additional liquidity by the IMF is not sufficient if monetary and financial stability will not prevail in the future. This is the reason for the conditionality approach of the IMF. This approach, however, severely interferes with national autonomy, so that quite a few have raised the issue of legitimacy of the IMF.

A basic issue regarding IMF activities lies in the moral hazard problem: sovereign states and private creditors can be tempted to rely on receiving help in the case of emergency and crisis. The ex post tools applied by the IMF contain ex ante incentives for wrong behavior. Therefore, there has been discussion about the extent to which national bankruptcy rules such as "Chapter 11" can be applied analogously in the world economy. Such an approach would define a greater responsibility of private suppliers of capital. Moreover, standards on the solidity of banks help to make national systems more robust against crises (Basel I and II). In sum, currency crises can only be made less likely if countries make sure that financial stability prevails at home.

Preventing currency crises by levying a general tax on financial transactions (Tobin tax) will not work. And such an approach would imply high opportunity costs. First, while a Tobin tax may reduce the inflow of portfolio capital somewhat, it does not prevent the outflow of portfolio when a crisis breaks out and when expectations change abruptly.[3] Such a sudden outflow, however, triggers a currency crisis. Thus, the Tobin tax will not prevent currency crises. Second, exports and imports are financed by short-term credits; a Tobin tax would thus make trade more expensive and would prevent countries from reaping the benefits from trade; it would hurt developing countries. Third, foreign direct investment and equity flows are linked to portfolio capital; a Tobin tax would prevent countries from enjoying the benefits of attracting foreign direct capital (often including technology) as a factor of production. Fourth, not all portfolio flows are speculative, quite a large part of portfolio flows means hedging and using arbitrage gains. Again, the international division of labor would be negatively impacted. Fifth, in the real world, it would be impossible to put the Tobin tax solely on the "bad" or unwanted portfolio flows and to exempt the good flows, for instance, to finance trade or foreign direct investment. Sixth, the Tobin tax requires an international agreement with a uniform tax rate for all countries. It is unrealistic that such an agreement can be reached. It is also open whether the tax is applied to outflowing or inflowing capital and which country receives the tax revenue. If the Tobin tax is applied unilaterally by one country, the tax will negatively affect the necessary real inflow of capital. For instance, Chile had to give up its deposit tax for short-term capital that remained for less than a year in 1998 when the inflow of real capital dried up. Seventh, the Tobin tax would necessitate an immense amount of controls; in the real world, it is extremely difficult to differentiate trade flows from portfolio flows; market participants will find many ways around these regulations, for instance, by overinvoicing or underinvoicing. Finally, if applied unilaterally by one country,

---

3   Compare the high interest rate of 500 percent used in Sweden in 1992 and 5,000 percent in Turkey in 2001 in order to prevent capital outflows.

the Tobin tax would be a hindrance in developing a competitive financial market in that country.

Reference zones for the exchange rates of the major currencies of the world – the dollar, the euro and the yen – have been proposed as a means of obtaining stable exchange rates and preventing exchange rate volatility. Of course, it would be desirable to have stable exchange rates, but the idea of reference zones will not work. It would require harmonizing monetary as well as fiscal policies among the major regions of the world. Moreover, wage (or income) policy would have to be harmonized in those regions where such explicit policies exist, for instance, where trade unions determine the wage rate. There are many reasons why such a harmonization will not come about. The business cycle situation may be different between countries, the political cycle may be different, even the political philosophy used may be different. Moreover, it is difficult to determine the real equilibrium exchange rate that underlies reference zones in an empirical model, not to mention a target rate determined in political bargaining. It is quite likely that international coordination would be used to shift the burden of adjustment to the other fellow. Finally, experience with this approach is negative.[4]

7   Countries Need to Reorient Themselves in Locational Competition

With the increased mobility of factors of production, a new paradigm of the international division of labor arises, besides the exchange of commodities: the paradigm of locational competition or competiton between governments. In this paradigm, it is not firms that compete on the world product markets for market share, but its states or governments that compete for the mobile factors of production on the international factor markets, i.e., for mobile capital, for mobile technological knowledge, and for mobile highly qualified workers.

When capital emigrates, countries or governments have less maneuvering space. If capital emigrates or is not attracted sufficiently, a country has a lower tax base. And workers will be equipped with machines and computers less favorably, labor productivity will increase at a lower pace, real incomes and employment will be more unfavorable. Further, it becomes more difficult to finance the systems of social security.

Where, however, countries succeed in attracting mobile factors of production there are benefits from openness. The immobile factor labor is equipped better

---

[4]   Compare the Louvre Accord and the Plaza Agreement. They have been one reason for the Japanese bubble (Siebert 2000).

with real capital and with technology, and is matched by qualified human capital, so that its productivity rises and its real income can rise. In locational competition, governments have to distinguish between the negative impact of taxes on capital – high taxes drive investments abroad – and the positive effect of infrastructure – an excellent infrastructure attracts investments. This means that the maneuvering space of countries has changed but it does not imply that countries have become powerless. They have to cope with this new phenomenon of locational competition. Locational competition does not necessarily imply that there will be a race to the bottom with respect to taxes. Firms esteem a good infrastructure financed by taxation and a well qualified labor force and are thus prepared to pay taxes. Thus, benefit taxation could be used in the context of locational competition.

Governments also compete with each other's institutional arrangements. In this process of institutional competition, it has to be proven which institutional arrangements are efficient and which have to be adjusted. Institutional competition is not only a benchmarking process in which the domestic approach is compared to international experience. It is also a mechanism that leads to first-best solutions. Institutional competition can be interpreted as a device for controlling the size of government activity. In this context, it should not be overlooked that institutional competition eventually led to the collapse of the communist systems. Communism as it existed in reality was forced to measure up to the freely organized Western societies. It collapsed when in August 1989 the citizens of the former GDR broke through the fence in Sopron (Hungary) and voted with their feet against the old system.

8   A Global Order for the International Division of Labor Gains Greater Importance

Granted that countries are competing for the mobile factors of production and that they are trying to find appropriate national institutional arrangements, there are areas in which they must develop an international rule system. In such a system, they would renounce part of their sovereignty and bind themselves to specific international rules. A promising approach would be to develop such international rules if transaction costs could be reduced in this way. Such an approach of reducing transaction costs would prevent individual countries, especially the large ones, from behaving strategically to the detriment of the other countries, especially the small ones. For instance, in trade policy it would reduce negative external effects (widely interpreted, this also means wars) and it would exploit positive external effects. The approach also includes public goods, i.e., goods that must be consumed in equal amounts by all, such as global environmental media, biodiversity, the reliability of trade rules, and the stability of a global financial system.[5] Accordingly, the international order would have to relate to the international trade order, to international competition policy, to rules for using the global environment, and to the international financial order. It is, therefore, incomprehensible why anti-globalizationers attack already developed rule systems militantly. Whoever wants to see global concerns fostered has to use the already existing international global arrangements and develop them further.

In the world trade order, 144 members of the WTO committed themselves to liberalize their trade, to extend specific liberalizations which they grant one country to all other members (most-favored-nation clause), and to abstain from protectionistic measures. For small and especially open countries, the WTO represents a safeguard against larger countries using strategic trade policy. Larger countries can be forced to obey the rules by implementing the dispute settlement mechanism. Thus, WTO is an institutional arrangement by which, albeit in a limited area of international economic exchange, conflicts are avoided. Since the WTO follows the principle "one country one vote" and aims for unanimity and since developing countries constitute the majority, the criticism of the NGOs with respect to the WTO is not comprehensible.

Since parliaments in sovereign states have committed to the WTO rules, the WTO is legitimized democratically. That national governments renounce their national sovereignty by binding their future behavior to specified rules is a meaningful form of international cooperation. It is on this principle of intergovernmental cooperation that the European Union is founded, albeit in much greater intensity. Besides the NGOs have to answer the question of their own democratic legitimacy. Historical experience with "social movements" (Michels 1915) suggests that such movements are not necessarily a guarantee for a democratic legitimacy.

A complex problem is the formulation of environmental rules. If the environment is a national good, such as a river system, demanding the harmonization of environmental norms by arguing that firms should have a level playing field in each country is wrong. The international division of labor is based on the idea that countries are differently endowed with labor, capital, technology, and natural resources. If other countries have a greater environmental abundance, they can produce with a higher environmental intensity, using the environment more strongly than other countries. And if developing countries do not have the same strong preference for the environment as industrial countries, we in the industrialized world have no right to impose our preferences on them. They have to bear the costs of better environmental quality, i.e., to forgo real income. We, therefore, should not have the right to determine how other countries produce their goods.

---

[5]   This approach could also incorporate fundamental human rights.

It is a different story when a country imports goods that contain "pollutants," for instance, toxic material or mad cow disease pathogens; then a country has a right to fix quality norms for its imports. Economically motivated protectionism should not be allowed to be the reason for an environmentally motivated protectionist measure. It also has to be recognized that fixing minimum norms for importables can quickly bring international trade to a standstill. If each importing country defines its own product norms for its imports (country of destination principle), this would open the door to discretionary decisions and arbitrariness in the international division of labor. Therefore, the rule system of the WTO is not founded on the country of destination principle but of the country of origin principle. According to this principle, the rules of the country of origin should be accepted in principle. Consequently, in the case of environmental goods that contain pollutants an international harmonization for minimal norms is required.

The issue of uniform environmental norms has to be addressed differently in the case of global environmental media than in the case of national environmental goods. The former involve such problems as global warming or maintaining biodiversity in specific regions of the earth as in the Amazon Basin. Thus, it is necessary to find a global solution to the problem of CO_2 emissions. This, however, does not imply that industrialized countries can dictate to developing countries how many CO_2 emissions they are allowed to have. On the contrary, the extent to which industrial countries are prepared to cover part of the costs for global environmental quality has to be determined. We have to look for a multilateral arrangement in which countries commit themselves to reducing their CO_2 emissions and to keeping them under control. At the root, the issue is to internationally define property rights that specify how individual countries can use the global environment in its role as a receptacle for "pollutants."

9   Concluding Remarks

The above points cannot claim to cover the complete topic of globalization angst. Three important aspects in the globalization debate, however, should not be swept under the carpet. First, the strategy of using a protectionistic approach to seal oneself off from the international division of labor implies that countries would renounce the benefits that can be derived from openness, as the experience of Latin America with a failed strategy of import substitution in the four decades since 1950 and the failure of the division of labor from above in the COMECON region show. Protectionism would mean the loss of welfare, it would start a descent into poverty. This cannot be intended. Second, anti-globalizationers have to recognize basic economic interdependencies. In closed as well as in open economies, economics is about scarcity, restrictions, competing uses, and opportunity costs. Illusions and a lot of emotions cannot make basic interdependencies cease to exist. Third, hopefully no one wants a closed society, in which, to paraphrase Karl Popper, individuals do not face personal decisions, institutions do not leave room for personal responsibility, and the critical capabilities of men and women are not set free. The anti-globalizationers have to take the responsibility for the world they want to have.

Bibliography

Barro, R.J., and X. Sala-i-Martin (1991). Convergence across States and Regions. *Brookings Papers on Economic Activity* (1): 107–158.

Michels, R. (1915). Political Parties: A Sociological Study of the Oligarchical Tendencies of Modern Democracy.

Rodrick, D. (1997). *Has Globalization Gone Too Far?* Washington, D.C.: Institute for International Economics.

Sachs, J. (1998). Unlocking the Mysteries of Globalization. *Foreign Policy* 110: 97–112.

Siebert, H. (2000). The Japanese Bubble: Some Lessons for International Macroeconomic Policy Coordination. *Aussenwirtschaft* 55(2): 233–250.

Siebert, H. (2002a). *Der Kobra-Effekt: Wie man Irrwege der Wirtschaftspolitik vermeidet.* Stuttgart: Deutsche Verlags-Anstalt.

Siebert, H. (2002b). Die Angst vor der internationalen Arbeitsteilung – eine Auseinandersetzung mit den Globalisierungsgegnern. *Aussenwirtschaft* 57(1): 7–28.

Siebert, H. (2002c). *The World Economy.* 2nd edition. London: Routledge.

Wade, R. (1996). Globalization and Its Limits: Reports of the Death of the National Economy Are Greatly Exaggerated. In S. Berger and R. Dore (eds.), *National Diversity and Global Capitalism.* Ithaca, N.Y.: Cornell University Press.

Jagdish Bhagwati

Coping with Anti-Globalization

Globalization first became a buzz word. Davos and Thomas Friedman celebrated its virtues, its inevitability. But then came the anti-globalizers. Globalization then became a more conventional four-letter word. The Ruckus Society and Pierre Bourdieu proclaimed its vices, its vincibility.

As this dialectic has unfolded, it is tempting to think that there is a primeval curse on the phenomenon. After all, if you care to count, globalization is in fact a thirteen-letter word. But, seriously, globalization has become by now a phenomenon that is doomed to unending controversy, the focal point of always-hostile passions and sometimes-violent protests. It is surely a defining issue as we enter a new century. The reasons why this has happened cry out for comprehension. Without such understanding, and then informed refutation of the fears and follies that animate the anti-globalizers, we cannot adequately defend the globalization that many of us seek to sustain, even deepen.

Though there are many who are upset with globalization, they come from many directions. Basically, there are two types of objectors, each set claiming to be the new stakeholders in the globalizing world: those who wish to drive a stake through the system, as in the Dracula movies, and those who wish to exercise their stake in the system. The former wish to be only heard, the latter want to be listened to. Many among the first set have different ideological and sociological factors animating them; and I will address these while focusing more systematically on what I think is the principal driving force: what I call a linked trilogy of discontents that take the form successively of an ethos composed of anti-capitalist, anti-globalization and an acute anti-corporations mindset. These views are interlinked because globalization is seen as the extension worldwide of capitalism; whereas corporations are seen as the B-52s of capitalism and its global reach.

But then I address the second set of stakeholders who wish to sit down with us, offer "policy briefs" and to transact changes that they believe are necessary in the global economy.

These latter groups, which are now visible at international meetings such as those of the World Economic Forum in Davos or the annual OECD Forum in Paris, are characterized for the most part by a worldview that, while economic globalization may be *economically benign* (in the sense of increased efficiency and a larger pie), it is *socially malign*. That is to say that, when it comes to social objectives and agendas such as the reduction of gender equality, removal of poverty, preservation of culture, and democratic functioning of one's society or nation, globalization fails.[1] In the fashionable language of today's politicians, globalization needs a human face. But I will contend below that globalization *has* a human face, that (economic) globalization is generally socially benign also. In short, if you are interested in improving social outcomes, (economic) globalization is part of the solution, not part of the problem.

What I propose to argue is therefore very different from what even the serious critics of globalization typically propose. It has serious implications also for policy. For, if you believe that globalization needs a human face, i.e., that it lacks one, then your mind will turn to policy interventions to stop it or to reshape it in constrictive ways. But if you think that globalization has a human face, then you will think of policy interventions to supplement and accelerate the good outcomes. The policy prescriptions will thus tend to be dramatically different! I shall therefore conclude with a sketch of what policy prescriptions would improve the outcomes that globalization generates.

1   Exaggerating the Perils of Globalization

But two questions must be faced immediately or confusion will prevail, as it indeed does in the raging debate on globalization. What does one mean by globalization? And are attitudes on its virtues and, more emphatically, its vices as monolithic as the street theater and the fascination of the media with it suggests? In fact, the answers to both questions are marred by what can only be characterized as *fallacies of aggregation*.

1.1   Different Aspects of Globalization

Globalization, even in its economic aspects (as focused upon in this book) has many dimensions. It evidently embraces trade and direct foreign investment or multinationals, and short-term capital flows whose rapidity and size have caused havoc in places ranging from Bangkok to Buenos Aires. But it also must include

---

[1]   In a book that I am completing by the end of the summer, titled *In Defense of Globalization: It Has a Human Face but We Can Do Better*, I examine a number of these social concerns such as poverty, gender issues, culture, democracy et al. and conclude that, as a central tendency, globalization is socially benign as well. I indicate the nature of some of that argumentation below, here as well.

now-sizeable migrations, legal and often illegal, across borders. And it extends to the diffusion and transfer of technology (such as AIDS-fighting drugs) among producing and consuming nations.

Yet, the popular discourse on globalization has tended to blur the lines between these different dimensions and to speak of globalization and to evaluate its merits and demerits as if it were a homogeneous, undifferentiated phenomenon. Indeed, recent years have seen many polls on attitudes to "globalization," one of which I discuss below, and practically all of them are marred by a failure to specify which aspect of (even economic) globalization they are polling the respondent about. So, we have no way of finding out what exactly the respondent has in mind when she says that globalization is good for herself or for the poor or for her country.

In fact, the rot goes even deeper. In particular, in the many popular debates that I have had with Ralph Nader and other opponents of freer trade before, during and after Seattle, the critics have invariably strayed into the financial crisis that devastated East Asia in the latter half of the 1990s, arguing as if the case for freer trade had also been exposed as illusory by this financial crisis.[2] But that is a *non sequitur.*

The case for free trade and the argument for free capital flows have important parallels. But the differences are yet more pointed. The freeing of capital flows in haste, without putting in place monitoring and regulatory mechanisms and banking reforms, amounts to a rash "gung-ho" financial capitalism that can put nation states at serious risk from the possibility of panic-fed and rapid reversals of massive short-term capital funds that will drive the economy into a tailspin.

The freeing of trade can hardly do this. If I exchange some of my toothpaste for one of your toothbrushes, we will both have white teeth; and the risk that we will have our teeth knocked by this exchange is negligible. By contrast, the proper analogy for capital flows is playing with fire. When Tarzan uses the fire to roast his kill, he feeds himself and has little to fear: a forest is hard to set on fire. But, when he returns to England as the long lost Earl of Greystoke, he can carelessly and easily set his ancestral palace on fire.

Yet, manifest as this asymmetry is to any but the most ideological economists, it is a common affliction of the untutored. Indeed, they assume that if one is for free trade, one must be for free direct investment, for free capital flows, for free immigration, for free love, for free everything else! I must confess that, while the case for free trade suffers from this fallacy, and it makes our business of defending the merits of free trade more precarious, I myself have profited from it. Thus, when I wrote of this asymmetry between free trade and free capital flows in the magazine *Foreign Affairs*, right after the East Asian financial crisis had broken

---

[2]   In fact, this confusion can be laid also at the door of a sophisticated anti-globalization economist such as Dani Rodrik of Kennedy School at Harvard University.

out, alerting all to it, I became a front-rank celebrity. That I, widely complimented and condemned, depending on your viewpoint, as the "world's foremost free trader" had "admitted" that unfettered capital flows could be dangerous was considered to be a heresy worthy of the greatest attention. While a few others such as my new (Columbia) colleague Joseph Stiglitz and my old (MIT) student Paul Krugman had also registered their reservations in their own way, I became the poster boy for many who were fearful of "globalization." And yet, in all truth, I had thought that I was saying the obvious: I had in fact never thought otherwise!

1.2   The North-South Divide: An Ironic Reversal

The debate on globalization is overlaid and overwhelmed by yet another fallacy which asserts that the disillusionment with globalization, typified by the street theater and the campus protests, is *everywhere*. But this belief is simply not true.

In fact, the anti-globalization sentiments are more prevalent in the rich countries of the North, while pluralities of the policymakers and public in the poor countries of the South see globalization instead as a positive force. This was the finding of the World Economic Forum's extensive poll on Global Public Opinion on Globalization, carried out by the Canadian polling firm, Environics International, with 25,000 urban respondents in 25 different countries, and presented at the WEF's annual meetings in New York in 2002.

I call this the "ironic reversal," since the situation was exactly the other way around in the 1950s and 1960s. At that time, the rich countries were busy liberalizing their trade, investments, and capital flows. They saw international integration as the magic bullet that would bring them prosperity; and it did produce the golden age of rising tides that lifted all boats until the OPEC-led explosion of oil prices unsettled the world economy from the late 1970s. But the poor countries were fearful of international integration.

Raul Prebisch, the Argentinian economist, talked then of the dangers to the "periphery" from the "center" in international interactions. The sociologist Fernando Henrique Cardoso of Brazil invented the "dependencia" thesis, arguing how the poor countries would wind up in the international economy with a dependent status. The Chilean sociologist Osvaldo Sunkel had the striking phrase: integration into the international economy leads to disintegration of the national economy. President Kwame Nkrumah of Ghana, whom the CIA helped dislodge, wrote of "neo-colonialism": the embrace by the former colonial powers through innocent-looking instruments such as aid that would intentionally create a crypto-colonialism.

I characterized these fearful attitudes at the time as reflecting "malign impact" and "malign intent" paradigms, contrasting with the economist's conventional thinking that international integration would benefit all, rich and poor, and was therefore a "benign impact" phenomenon, whereas aid and other assistance were "benign intent" policies (Bhagwati 1978: Chapter 1).

It turned out that many poor countries, which bought into these fearful ideas and turned away from using international trade and investment flows as opportunities to be seized, turned out to have made the wrong choices. Their failures, and the example of the success of the countries of the Far East that used international opportunities to great advantage instead, have proven salutary. The result has been a turn by the South towards more globalization. The sociologist Cardoso who warned of "dependencia" sought to take Brazil into more, not less, globalization after becoming President of Brazil. The WEF poll on globalization was simply recording this swing of sentiment.

By contrast, the fearful "malign impact" ideas have come to haunt several groups, among them the labor unions, in the rich nations. And this reversal, this contrast with the poor countries, is exactly what the WEF poll was picking up. The rich tapestry of reasons why this has happened is of both interest and concern; and it is what I address now.

But before doing that, it is worth also noting that the recent polls also show a waning, rather than an enhancement, of the acute anti-globalization of the 1990s. The WEF poll found, for instance, that the positive views of globalization (as an omnibus and ill-defined phenomenon) had become more positive in North America and Europe, even while they remained lower than those in the countries of the South, big pluralities of whom continued to express high expectations from globalization. This is also the finding from the polls conducted by the Center on Policy Attitudes of the University of Maryland. Its Americans and the World Website, reported on April 12, 2002 that "Overall, Americans tend to see globalization as somewhat more positive than negative and appear to be growing familiar with the concept and more positive about it. A large majority favors moving with the process of globalization and only a small minority favors resisting it" (http:// www.americans-world.org).

But it is too optimistic to go by these polls, which must also reflect changing circumstances of the national economic performance. Good times dampen the anti-globalization attitudes; bad times deepen them instead. The WEF poll is revealing on this: the lowest pluralities in favor of globalization among the poorer nations are Indonesia, Turkey, and Argentina, where economies have been through turmoil. And so the task of understanding the anti-globalization sentiments, and responding to them if globalization is to be successfully maintained and managed, remains pressing. To this task, I now turn, beginning with what I call a "trilogy of discontents."

2   A Trilogy of Discontents

2.1   Anti-Capitalism

As the 20th century ended, capitalism seemed to have vanquished its rivals. Francis Fukuyama's triumphalism in his celebrated work, *The End of History and the Last Man* (1992), was like a primeval scream of joy by a warrior with a foot astride his fallen prey. It was not just the collapse of communism in Europe and China's decisive turn away from it. As the energetic anti-globalization NGO, *Fifty Years Is Enough*, laments, even the Swedish model had lost its appeal. The much-advertised model of "alternative development" in the Indian state of Kerala had also run into difficulties, much as President Julius Nyrere's celebrated socialist experiment in Tanzania had run the economy into the ground. This vanishing of different possibilities has led to what I have called the "Tyranny of the Missing Alternative," provoking a sense of anguished anti-capitalist reactions from both the old and the young:

The old are fewer, and they matter less, than the young. They could be the generals in the war on capitalism but the young today are happy to be foot soldiers, fighting on their own. But they can make noise; and these days almost anyone who screams is likely to get, not just heard, but sometimes even listened to.

The old are, of course, the anti-capitalists of the postwar years, ranging from socialists to revolutionaries. They are the ones who, especially when communists or Marxists, are captive to a nostalgia for their vanished dreams.

When the Davos meeting was held by the World Economic Forum in February 2001, there was an Anti-Davos meeting held in Brazil at the same time.[3] (How many know that there is even an Alternative Nobel Prize?) The rhetoric in Brazil was one of revolution. I recall George Soros, who properly considers himself to be a radical thinker, a progressive financier, going into a debate from Davos on the video monitor with some of the Anti-Davos participants. I recall his frustration, indeed astonishment, when he realized that he was the enemy, not a friend, much like the Democrats were chagrined that Ralph Nader thought during the last U.S. election that they were not really different from the Republicans.

Soros, who had not interacted with these groups, just did not get it: as far as these anti-capitalist revolutionaries are concerned, anyone who is in stocks and bonds should be put into stocks and bonds. Indeed, these groups, who were memo-

---

3   Now, that meeting has been annualized and will run parallel to the Davos meeting each year in Porto Alegre, Brazil. Whereas Davos is organized by the World Economic Forum, the Porto Alegre organizers call themselves the World Social Forum, as if they are concerned with social issues and people, while Davos is concerned with profits and corporations.

rializing Che Guevara and listening to Ben Bella, were the exact antitheses of the Arthur Koestlers of the world who wrote of *The God That Failed*. They were working from a script titled The God That Failed but Will Rise Again; they only had to keep the faith.

But the globalizers must also confront the young. And if you have watched the streets of Seattle, Washington, Prague, Quebec, and Genoa where the anti-globalizers have congregated with increasing militancy, or if you see their impassioned protests on the campuses as I have watched the Anti-Sweatshop Coalition's activities at my own university (Columbia), there can be no doubt that we have here a phenomenon that is truly important in the public space and also more potent: the nostalgia of the fading generation cannot compete with the passions of the rising generation.

So, how is the discontent of the young to be explained? Of course, a rare few among them are like the old. Consider *Global Exchange*, an NGO that likes to describe itself as a Human Rights group – this is the "in" phrase much as Socialism was three decades ago, and its moral resonance immediately gets you on to higher ground and gives you a free pass with the media and the unsuspecting public. It professes politics that is unmistakably in the old revolutionary corner and gets endorsements from the great linguist and activist Noam Chomsky, among other left intellectuals. Quite stereotypically, it describes Israel as "an exclusionary state" that "trains other undemocratic, abusive regimes" around the world and complains that U.S. aid to Israel "maintains the military-industrial complex here in the U.S." Its pronouncements on the WTO are no less dramatic and drastic: the WTO "only serves the interests of multinational corporations" and "the WTO is killing people."

But *Global Exchange* and its radical chic are really a fringe phenomenon. There are several other explanations of what animates the young in particular: each may explain part of the reality, while collectively they provide a more complete explanation.

1. Far too many among the young see capitalism as a system that cannot address meaningfully questions of social justice. To my generation, and that of the British left-leaning intellectuals such as George Bernard Shaw that preceded it, the Soviet model was a beguiling alternative. Indeed, my much-translated 1966 book on *The Economics of Underdeveloped Countries* contains a distinct nod towards the Soviet Union: "The imagination of many ... nations has been fired, perhaps most of all, by the remarkable way in which the Soviet Union has raised itself to the status of a Great Power by its own bootstraps and in a short span of time." How appalling a misjudgment this view of the Soviet alternative seems today, and how commonplace it was then!

That capitalism may be viewed instead as a system that can paradoxically destroy privilege and open up economic opportunity to the many is a thought that is still uncommon. I often wonder, for example, how many of the young skeptics of capitalism are aware that socialist planning in countries like India, by replacing markets system-wide with quantitative allocations, worsened rather than improved unequal access because socialism meant queues that the well-connected and the well-endowed could jump, whereas markets allowed a larger number to access their targets.

2. But the anti-capitalist sentiments are particularly virulent among the young who arrive at their social awakening on campuses in fields other than economics. English and comparative literature and sociology are a fertile breeding ground.

Thus, deconstructionism, espoused by the French philosopher Jacques Derrida, has left the typical student of literature without anchor because of its advocacy of an "endless horizon of meanings." Terry Eagleton (1983), the sympathetic chronicler of modern literary theory, has written:

> Derrida is clearly out to do more than develop new techniques of reading: deconstruction is for him an ultimately *political* practice, an attempt to dismantle the logic by which a particular system of thought, and behind that a whole system of political structures and social institutions, maintains its force. (p. 148)

True, the Derrida technique will deconstruct any political ideology, including Marxist. Typically, however, it is focused on deconstructing and devaluing capitalism rather than Marxism, often with nihilistic overtones which create the paradox that many now turn to anarchy, not from Bakunin but from Derrida!

The heavy hand of Marxist texts on students of literature, on the other hand, has been beautifully captured by V.S. Naipaul (1998) in his compelling portrait in *Beyond Belief* of the Pakistani guerrilla Shabaz who went from studying literature in England to starting a revolution in Baluchistan that failed:

> There were close Pakistani friends at the university. Many of them were doing English literature, like Shabaz; it was one of the lighter courses, possibly the lightest, and at this time it was very political and restricted. It was encouraging Marxism and revolution rather than wide reading. So Shabaz and his Pakistani friends in their Marxist study group read the standard (and short) revolutionary texts, Frantz Fanon, Che Guevara. And while they read certain approved Russian writers, they didn't read or get to know about the Turgenev novels, *Fathers and Sons* (1862) and *Virgin Soil* (1877), which dealt with conditions not unlike those in feudal Pakistan, but questioned the simplicities of revolution.

As for sociology, many of its students are influenced equally by the new literary theory and the old Marxism. They stand in contempt of economic argumentation that would refute their rejectionist beliefs about capitalism by asserting that economics is about value, whereas sociology is about values. But they are wrong today on both counts.

Economists will retort that, as citizens, they choose ends, but as economists, they choose the (best) means. Moreover, accused of indulging the profit motive, they respond with the legendary Cambridge economist, Sir Dennis Robertson, that economics is addressed heroically to showing how "man's basest instincts," not his noblest, can be harnessed through appropriate institutional design to produce public good. Adam Smith would surely have died an unsung hero if he had peddled the pedestrian argument that altruism led to public good.

And, indeed, economists' policy analysis necessarily requires the use of criteria that enable one to say that one policy is "better" than another. That takes them straight into moral philosophy, of course. One could thus argue that the philosopher John Rawls' input into economic theory has been as profound as that in philosophy: in fact, he drew on the economist Nobel laureate William Vickrey's concept of the "veil of ignorance" and gave economists back the maximin principle: a fair trade, I should say!

The presumption that sociology is a better guide to ethics than economics is also misplaced. Certainly, its related discipline, social anthropology, whose many adherents now find their voice in some NGOs, foundations, and in the World Bank, traditionally leans towards *preserving* cultures, whereas economics in our hands is a tool for *change*. Fascinated by social anthropology, and deeply buried in the writings of the legendary A.R. Radcliffe-Brown and many others, when I studied in England, I still wound up preferring economics for my vocation. What other choice could really have been made by a young student from a country afflicted by economic misery? If reducing poverty by using economic analysis to accelerate growth and therewith pull people up into gainful employment and dignified sustenance is not moral, and indeed a compelling imperative, what *is*?

3. But I should add that many of these students are also susceptible to the bitingly critical view of economics brilliantly propounded by Rosa Luxemburg in her classic essay on "What Is Economics," the first chapter of a proposed ten-chapter work, only six of which were found in her apartment after her murder. She had argued that "the new science of economics," which had reached the status of an academic discipline in Germany, was tantamount to an attempted legitimation of the "anarchy of capitalist production" and was essentially "one of the most important ideological weapons of the bourgeoisie as it struggles with the medieval state and for a modern capitalist state." The "invisible hand," with its rationalization of markets, had a hidden agenda, hence it lacked veracity: a *non sequitur*, of course.

4. But I also think that an altogether new factor on the scene that propels the young into anti-capitalist attitudes comes from a different, technological source in a rather curious fashion. This is the dissonance that now exists between empathy for others elsewhere for their misery and the inadequate intellectual grasp of what can be done to ameliorate that distress. The resulting tension spills over into un-

happiness with the capitalist system (in varying forms) within which they live and hence anger at it for its apparent callousness.

Today, thanks to television, we have what I call the paradox of inversion of the philosopher David Hume's concentric circles of reducing loyalty and empathy. Each of us owes diminishing empathy as we go from our nuclear family, to the extended family, to our local community, to our state or county (say, Lancashire or Montana), to our nation, to our geographical region (say, Europe or the Americas), and then the world. What the Internet and CNN have done is to take the outermost circle and turn it into the innermost, while the same technology, as Robert Putnam has told us, has accelerated our moving to "bowling alone," glued to our TV sets and moving us steadily out of civic participation, so that the innermost circle has become the outermost one.

So, the young see and are anguished by the poverty and the civil wars and the famines in remote areas of the world but have no intellectual way of coping with it rationally in terms of appropriate action. Thus, as I watched the kids dressed as turtles at Seattle, during the riotous 1999 WTO Ministerial meeting, protesting against the WTO and the Appellate Body's decision in the Shrimp-Turtle case, I wondered how many knew that the environmentalists had won that decision, not lost it! When asked, of course, none knew what they were really protesting; and, when I mischievously asked some if they had read Roald Dahl's famous story about the boy who had freed the giant turtle and sailed away on it into the far ocean, they shook their turtle heads! It has become fashionable to assert that the demonstrating youth know much about the policies they protest; but that is only a sentiment of solidarity with little basis in fact. True, there are several serious NGOs with real knowledge and serious policy critiques; but they are not the ones agitating in the streets.

5. Overlaying the entire scene of course is the general presumption that defines many recent assertions by intellectuals that somehow the proponents of capitalism, and of its recent manifestations in regard to economic reforms such as the moves to privatization and to market liberalization (including trade liberalization), are engaged, as Edward Said (2001: 32) claims, in a "dominant discourse [whose goal] is to fashion the merciless logic of corporate profit-making and political power into a normal state of affairs." Following Pierre Bourdieu, Said endorses the view that "Clinton–Blair neoliberalism, which built on the conservative dismantling of the great social achievements in health, education, labor, and security of the welfare state during the Thatcher–Reagan period, has constructed a paradoxical *doxa*, a symbolic counterrevolution." In Bourdieu's own words, this is: "conservative but presents itself as progressive; it seeks the restoration of the past order in some of its most archaic aspects (especially as regards economic relations), yet it passes off regressions, reversals, surrenders, as forward-looking reforms or revolutions leading to a whole new age of abundance and liberty."

But, frankly, this view stands reality on its head. Of course, we have known since Orwell that words do matter; and the smart duellists in the controversies over public policy will often seize the high ground by appropriating to themselves, before their adversaries do, beguiling words such as "progressive" for their own causes. Thus, believe it or not, protectionists in trade have been known to ask for "tariff reform"; today, they ask for "fair trade," which no one can deny except for the informed few who see that it is used in truth to justify unfair trade practices. Phrases such as "corporate profit-making" and "trickle down" policies do the same for the friends of Bourdieu, creating and fostering a pejorative perception of the market-using policy changes that they reject.

It is therefore not surprising that today's reformers turn to the same linguistic weapons as the anti-capitalist forces of yesterday. But let us also ask: is it "conservative" or "radical" to seek to correct, in light of decades of experience and in teeth of entrenched forces, the mistakes and the excesses of past policies, no matter how well motivated? In fact, as reformers know only too well, it takes courage and elan to challenge orthodoxies, especially those that are conventionally associated with "progressive" forces.

As for the policies themselves, the fierce binary contrast drawn by Bourdieu is an abstraction that misses the central issues today. The debate is really not about conservative counterrevolution and the enlightened past order. It is rather about shifting the center of gravity in public action, more towards the use of markets and less towards *dirigisme*. It is not about "whether markets"; it is about where the "limits to markets" must be drawn.

The present-day turn towards reforms in the developing countries is also prompted by excessive and knee-jerk *dirigisme*. As I often say, the problem with many of these countries was that Adam Smith's Invisible Hand was nowhere to be seen! Their turn to economic reforms is to be attributed, not to the rise of "conservatism," but to a pragmatic reaction of many to the failure of what many of us considered once to be "progressive" policies that would lift us out of poverty, illiteracy and many other ills. As John Kenneth Galbraith once said about Milton Friedman, and here I take only the witticism and not sides, "Milton's misfortune is that his policies have been tried"!

2.2   Anti-Globalization

Anti-capitalism has turned into anti-globalization among the left-wing students for reasons that are easy to see but difficult to accept. After all, Lenin wrote extensively about imperialism and its essential links to capitalism; and present-day writers such as Immanuel Wallerstein have seen the growing integration of the world economy in related ways as the organic extension of national capitalism.

Lenin's views on imperialism provide an insight into a principal reason why anti-globalization is seen by those on the left so readily as following from anti-capitalism. In his famous work, *Imperialism: The Highest Stage of Capitalism*, Lenin stated that the "distinctive characteristics of imperialism" in the form of monopolies, oligarchy, and the exploitation of the weak by the strong nations "compel us to define it as parasitic or decaying capitalism." Nikolai Bukharin, for whose work *Imperialism and the World Economy* Lenin wrote a Preface, considered that imperialism with its attendant globalization of the world economy is little more than capitalism's "[attempt] to tame the working class and to subdue social contradictions by decreasing the steam pressure through the aid of a colonial valve"; that "having eliminated [through monopolies] competition within the state, [capitalism has] let loose all the devils of a world scuffle."

This notion therefore that globalization is merely an external attenuation of the internal struggles that doom capitalism, and that globalization is also in essence capitalist exploitation of the weak nations, provides not only an inherent link between capitalism and globalization. It also makes globalization an instrument for the exploitation of the weak nations. And this certainly has resonance again among the idealist young on the left. Capitalism seeks globalization to benefit itself but harms others abroad. The Lenin–Bukharin argument then leads, as certainly as a heat-seeking missile, to anti-capitalist sentiments.

2.3   Anti-Corporations

But central to that perspective is the notion, of course, that it is the "monopolies," for that is indeed how the multinationals are often described even today in much of the anti-globalization literature, that are at the heart of the problem: they do not benefit the people abroad; they exploit them instead. Indeed, this notion of globalization as an exploitative force that delays the doomsday for capitalism at home and harms those abroad has captured some of the more militant among the naive youth today.

The anti-corporation attitudes come to many others, who are not aficionados of left-wing literature, also from the obvious sense that multinationals are the B-52s of capitalism and of globalization that are the object of concern. Their proliferation has been substantial, unprecedented in history. But their strength is grossly exaggerated because few understand that they, even when huge, undercut one another in economic power because they compete against one another – economists describe this as markets being contestable – and their political power is similarly stifled by economic and national competition in many instances.

Yet others find it plausible that multinationals must necessarily be bad in a global economy because global integration without globally shared regulations must surely amount to a playing field for multinationals that seek profits by searching for the most likely locations to exploit workers and nations, thereby putting intolerable pressure on their home states to abandon their own gains in social legislation in what is feared to be a "race to the bottom." Indeed, this view is so credible that even a shrewd and perceptive intellectual such as Alan Wolfe (2001: 31), who sees through cant better than most, has recently written disapprovingly and casually of the "policies of increasingly rapacious global corporations."

But appealing as this scenario may appear, it will not withstand scrutiny. Much recent empirical work shows that the evidence for a race to the bottom is practically nonexistant. The political scientist Daniel Drezner has written a whole book showing that we have here much rhetoric by both opponents and supporters of globalization; but no empirical support. Econometricians have also found little to report. This may sound contrary to common sense; surely, these social scientists must be consultants to the corporations? They are not. There are plenty of reasons why corporations do not rush in to pollute rivers and the air simply because there are no regulations. I suspect that, aside from economic reasons for not choosing say environmentally unfriendly technology, the main check is provided by reputational consequences: in today's world of CNN, civil society, and democracy proliferation, the multinationals and the host governments cannot afford to do things beyond the pale.

So the "obvious" truth of the race to the bottom in an unregulated world turns out to be not so obvious. Economists are indeed a nuisance: they complicate analysis by telling you that your gut feelings are too simplistic. This makes them particularly unpopular with the young who want to believe what seems perfectly plain but is rarely so in truth.

And so, many of the young zero in, with a "gotcha" mentality, seizing on every misdeed of a multinational they can find, seeking to validate their anti-corporation biases. This surely accounts for the return of Ralph Nader: the great scourge of misdeeds by corporations. It has also magically transformed Julia Roberts, the passable actress whose triumph was as a *Pretty Woman*, into an acclaimed actress in *Erin Brockowich* and introduced the gifted actor Russell Crowe to celebrity on the screen in *The Insider*: both movies where a David takes on the Goliath in shape of a venal corporation.

The anti-corporation militancy that is on the rise among the young anti-globalizers is also strategic, of course. We have witnessed the brilliant way in which the anti-globalizers managed to use the meetings of the international agencies such as the World Bank, the IMF, and particularly the World Trade Organization (originally the GATT), the pride of progressive architectural design regarding the management of the world economy and the permanent legacy of legendary men of vision, to protest and profess their anti-globalization sentiments. After all, these meetings were where the world's media gathered. What better place to create mayhem and get attention from the vast multitude of reporters looking for a story? So, where the old guerrillas struck where you least expected them, these new guerrillas struck where you most expected them: at these meetings!

The same strategic sense has been displayed in going after the corporations as well. Nike and Gap, two fine multinationals, now have a permanent set of critics, with newsletters and Websites worldwide. With Nike and Gap household names and having gigantic overseas operations that cannot possibly avoid lapses from whatever is defined as good behavior (e.g., that Nike does not pay a "living wage" as *Global Exchange* would define it, for instance), they represent obvious targets in a propaganda war that is stacked against them. Naomi Klein (2001), the Canadian writer, admitted it frankly in a recent article in *The Nation* faced with the amorphous but overwhelming globalization phenomenon, the only way to get at it is to latch on to something concrete and targetable.

So, they go after the corporations that spread and constitute the globalization that is reprehensible. We then also see teenagers carrying placards outside Staples and demonstrating in front of Starbucks, while their more militant adult friends threw stones through the coffee chain's windows at Seattle. I talk with them at every opportunity; I find enthusiasm, even idealism, but never any ability to engage concretely on the issues they take a stand on. But then the Kleins of the anti-globalization movement are not fazed; it is all strategic, it is in a good cause.

2.4   Political Alliances

But the recent successes of the anti-globalization forces can also be assigned to the fortuitous alliance struck between the young agitationists and the conventional organized lobbies such as the labor unions, the new pressure groups such as the environmentalists, and movements such as those for human rights.

Seattle saw these groups merge and emerge as a set of coalitions. "Teamsters and turtles" joined the unions with the students and the environmentalists. "Green and blue" joined the environmentalists with the blue-collar unions. "Labor standards" became "labor rights," heralding the alliance of human rights activists and the unions. The Anti-Sweatshop movement on the campuses signified the return of several union-trained summer interns who would ally themselves, and align their views, with the unions.

While these alliances have made the anti-globalizers more effective to date, the alliances themselves are fragile. Thus, after Black Tuesday's attack on the World Trade Center, the alliance between the unions and the students has turned brittle as the campuses have turned against war and the unions for it. The turn to violence by the students at Seattle, Quebec, and Genoa has also prompted union misgivings: the rank and file of the unions is not sympathetic to such tactics.

The Teamsters have broken with the environmentalists over the Bush administration's decision on drilling in the Alaska Wildlife Refuge for oil. At the WTO, the environmentalists got their agenda, in some form, onto the Doha Development Round of trade negotiations; but unions did not have their way on a Social Clause, so the blue-and-green alliance is likely to have a parting of the ways much the way there is today no unified bloc of underdeveloped nations in international economic negotiations but only coalitions around different interests that often cut across the conventional North-South divide. The fissures are therefore many; and, in particular, the negative agenda of anti-globalization is unlikely to be sufficient glue when the disparate groups start on different trajectories of positive achievements.

3   Confronting Anti-Globalization: Why Globalization Is Socially Benign but Good Is Not Good Enough

But that does raise the broader question: will anti-globalization then collapse? Do not count on it. It cannot happen unless we engage the anti-globalizers on many fronts. Let me sketch some of the principal ways we must do this.

Expanding the Knowledge about the Socially Benign Side of Globalization

At the outset, we need to use reason and knowledge, in the public policy arena, to controvert the many false and damning assumptions about capitalism, globalization, and corporations that I have only sketched and which cannot be allowed to fester and turn to gangrene. It is truly astonishing how widespread is the ready assumption (that is endemic by now even in some international institutions) that if capitalism has prospered and if economic globalization has increased while some social ill has worsened as well, then the former phenomena must have caused the latter! It has almost gotten to a farcical level where if your girl friend walks out on you, it must be due to globalization – after all, she may have left for Buenos Aires!

Perhaps the chief task before those who consider globalization favorably is then to confront the notion, implicit in varying ways in many of the intellectual and other reasons for the growth of anti-globalization sentiments, that while globalization may be *economically benign* (in the sense of increasing the pie), it is *socially malign* (i.e., in terms of its impact on poverty, literacy, gender questions, cultural autonomy, and diversity et al.).

That globalization is often not the enemy of social agendas but their friend is not that difficult to argue, once we get down to thinking about the matter deeply and empirically. Take the corporations again. Have they hurt women, as some claim? I would say: far from it. Consider three examples: two from the North, the other from the South. Japanese multinationals, as they spread through the world during the years of Japanese prosperity, took the men with them but the men brought their wives with them to New York, Paris, London, cities where the Japanese housewives saw for themselves how women could lead a better life. That, among other channels of diffusion of ideas and values, has turned them into feminist agents of change. Then again, the economists Elizabeth Brainerd and Sandra Black have shown how wage differentials against women have reduced faster in internationally competing industries since they can least afford to indulge their biases in favor of men. Women in the poor countries also benefit when they find jobs in the globalized industries in export processing zones. Some feminists complain that young girls are exploited and sent back to where they came from as soon as they are ready for marriage: that they therefore pick up no skills, for instance. But ask these very girls and one finds the ability to get away for work from home a liberating experience and the money they earn gives them the "empowerment" that will not come from being confined to the home.

Indeed, the jaundiced view of corporations prevents an appreciation of their often beneficial role: familiarity breeds contempt but contempt does not breed familiarity. Thus, the young campus activists against sweatshops accuse the corporations of exploitation of foreign workers. But the available empirical evidence for some developing countries, in studies such as by Ann Harrison of Columbia School of Business, shows that, in their own factories (as distinct from subcontractors or suppliers of components and parts who probably pay the going wage instead) the multinationals tend to pay what the economics literature calls a "wage premium" of the order of 10 percent over the going wage. Is this exploitation? Yes, but only if you are smart enough to know that the English dictionary defines exploiting labor as either using or abusing it!

In fact, even as we continue to teach in the classroom about the nefarious activities of ITT in destroying Salvador Allende's elected Chilean regime or the sordid story of Union Meunière in Katanga, we must come to terms with the fact that these examples, and even lesser atrocities, have become less likely in a world where democracy – admittedly not always liberal or otherwise pleasing – has broken out in several developing nations and where again civil society and the media make retribution for misdeeds more likely.

Handling the Social Downside Using Institutional and Policy Innovation

But if the common apprehensions about globalization's social impact are mistaken in the main, we cannot retreat into the notion that "by and large," "more or less," globalization is helpful. The occasional downside needs to be addressed. This requires imaginative institutional and policy innovation. For instance, the insecurity that freer trade seems to inculcate in many, even if not justified by the economists' objective documentation of the increased volatility of employment, needs to be accommodated through provision of adjustment assistance. For poor countries that lack resources, such a program must be supported by World Bank aid focused on lubricating the globalization that this institution praises and promotes.

Accelerating the Social Good Using Moral Suasion rather than Confrontation

But we also need to recognize that, particularly with the growth of civil society, there is legitimate impatience with the speed at which globalization will deliver the social agendas. Thus, child labor will certainly diminish over time as growth occurs, partly due to globalization. Globalization is part of the solution, not of the problem. But we want to go faster. The central question before the globalizers, and their foes has to be: how do we do it?

And the answer has to be one that is different from the obsession of several lobbies and our Congress with trade sanctions, a remedy that threatens globalization by using disruption of market access and hence is fraught with temptation for the protectionists around us. In rare cases of huge moral outrage, a widespread resort to trade sanctions can work. But otherwise, suasion, especially for social agendas that appeal to our moral sense, surely has a better chance. This is particularly true now that we do have CNN and the NGOs.

Indeed, I find it ironic that many among the several serious and thoughtful NGOs today, who after all must believe that public action will follow their advocacy, are the ones who are often skeptical of moral suasion. As they search for "teeth" (in the shape of sanctions), I tell them: God gave us not just teeth but also a tongue; and today a good tongue-lashing is more likely to be effective in advancing the social agendas that we espouse and share. Indeed, teeth may not just be unproductive; they may even be counterproductive. Thus, the sheer threat to exports embodied in the proposed Harkin Child Deterrence Bill led to children being laid off in Bangladeshi textile factories and female children wound up in worse employment: prostitution! Contrast this with the International Program for the Eradication of Child Labour at the ILO, which eschews sanctions but does the heavy lifting required to reduce child labor by working with local NGOs, interested aid donors and cooperative host governments, and ensuring that children get to schools, that schools are available, and that impoverished parents who lose the child's income are financially assisted where necessary.

Indeed, a great upside of the use of moral suasion to accelerate the social good being done by economic globalization is that it joins for common good the two great forces that increasingly characterize the 21st century: expanding globalization and growing civil society. Partnership, rather than confrontation, can lead to shared success. It is worth the hassle.

Allowing Corporations to Define Social Good Differently

A final thought. We need to defend the corporations against ignorant, ideological, or strategic assault. They generally do good, not harm. Again, the question has to be: can they help us to do even more good? The purists say that the shareholders must do the social good, not the corporations. But we are well past that, certainly in the United States, when it comes to what they do at home. Nonprofit organizations such as Columbia use their student and faculty resources to assist Harlem; Microsoft and IBM assist the communities in which they function and others too.

In fact, this policy of "social responsibility" has traditionally made capitalism attractive, giving an added lie to the anti-capitalist and anti-business sentiments. When there were no modern style corporations but substantial fortunes made by individuals and their families, successful capitalism was characterized precisely by such behavior. Recall Simon Schama's Dutch burghers with their "embarrassment of riches," the Calvinists, and the Jains and Vaishnavs of Gujerat in India, Mahatma Gandhi's home state, who accumulated fortunes but spent them, not on personal indulgence but on social causes.

Corporations today need to do just that, each in its own way. Pluralism here is of the essence: no NGO, or government, has the wisdom or the right to lay down what corporations *everywhere* must do. Social good is multidimensional and different corporations may and must define social responsibility, quite legitimately, in different ways in the global economy. A hundred flowers must be allowed to bloom, so that they constitute a rich tapestry of social action that lends more color to globalization's human face.

Bibliography

Bhagwati, J. (1966). *The Economics of Underdeveloped Countries*. New York: McGraw-Hill.

Bhagwati, J. (ed.) (1978). *The New International Economic Order*. Cambridge, Mass.: MIT Press.

Bukharin, N. (1929). *Imperialism and the World Economy*. New York: International Publishers.

Eagleton, T. (1983). *Literary Theory: An Introduction*. Oxford: Basil Blackwell.

Fukuyama, F. (1992). *The End of History and the Last Man*. New York: Free Press.

Klein, N. (2001). Signs of the Times. *The Nation*, October 22.

Lenin, V.I. (1916). *Imperialism: The Highest Stage of Capitalism*. Reprinted 1997. New York: International Publishers.

Naipaul, V.S. (1998). *Beyond Belief: Islamic Excursions among the Converted Peoples.* New York: Random House.

Said, E. (2001). The Public Role of Writers and Intellectuals. *The Nation* (17/24 September): 32.

Wolfe, A. (2001). "The Snake: Globalization, America, and the Wretched of the Earth," review of *Empire* by M. Hardt and A. Negri. *The New Republic* (1 October): 31.

Comment on Jagdish Bhagwati

Kevin Watkins

Fundamentalism is the bane of our age – and nowhere more so than in debates on globalisation. Simplistic ideas purporting to explain and evaluate the phenomenon have become badges of identity for like-minded groups, each with their own favourite set of sound-bites, and each convinced that endless repetition of their favoured mantras will help the world to discover what they take to be a self-evident truth.

The view of most northern governments, the World Bank, the International Monetary Fund and the World Trade Organisation, and many economists, is that 'globalisation is good'. Integration into global markets through increased openness to trade, investment and technology transfer, has, in the words of two prominent enthusiasts for the new economic order "promoted economic equality and reduced poverty" (Dollar and Kraay 2002: 120). At risk of (slight) caricature, the received wisdom in this school is that all governments need to do is to lower barriers to trade and investment, open the door to transnational companies, adopt the legal and contractual systems of advanced economies and – hey presto – the global market will boost growth and reduce poverty, and all with minimal implications for inequality. This revealed truth is supported by a bewildering array of econometric models developed in the World Bank. On the other side of the divide stand the extreme globalisation pessimists. The view here is that globalisation is inherently bad for poor people in poor countries – and inherently good for powerful transnational companies in rich ones (see, e.g., Goldsmith and Mander 2001). Integration through trade and investment, so the argument runs, is exacerbating already extreme income inequalities, and eroding the power of governments to address the needs of their citizens. What both sides have in common with each other, is a belief in the inevitability of pre-determined outcomes, and a conviction that they have a duty to reveal to a disbelieving world the deeper mysteries behind an unfolding truth.

Public discussion of globalisation is increasingly dominated by these two extreme views, notably during set-piece occasions such as annual IMF-World Bank meetings. Those claiming membership of neither find it difficult to get a hearing. For those concerned with poverty reduction and social justice, the polarisation of the current debate ought to be a source of serious concern. Most importantly, it is deflecting attention from the national and international rules and institutions that determine the distribution of benefits from globalisation, and it fails to address what is perhaps the most important challenge of our age: how to realise the potential of globalisation as a force for poverty reduction.

Jagdish Bhagwati is no newcomer to the debate on globalisation. And the title of his paper 'Coping with Anti-Globalization' provides an admirably succinct indicator as to which side he belongs. He sets out to offer an "informed refutation of the fears and follies that animate the anti-globalizers". Dismissing the charge that the emerging global economy lacks a human face, he proceeds to subject his presumed adversary to some heavy artillery. In fact, the adversary turns out to be an unholy trinity of ideas: anti-capitalism, anti-globalisation, and anti-corporation. Bhagwati is primarily concerned with the spread of these ideas among the young, since it is the young that pose the greatest potential threat. As he memorably tells us: "the nostalgia of the fading generation cannot compete with the passions of the rising generation." In a somewhat rambling fashion, Bhagwati traces the source of anti-globalisation discontent to the writings of Noam Chomsky, assorted Marxist texts, and the deconstructionism of the French philospher Jacques Derrida.

The task of the economist, in Bhagwati's view, is to contest the simplistic views of anti-globalisers. Unfortunately, he does so with some alarmingly simplistic views of his own. His paper fires some broad salvoes in the general direction of those who believe that globalisation is a 'race to the bottom', reiterating the arguments made by Paul Krugman on increased trade as a potential win-win scenario (Krugman 1998: 80–87). Critics of transnational companies get short shrift, and Nike and Gap – "two fine multinationals" – a staunch defence of their records on labour rights. Countering the standard 'sweathshop' arguments of the anti-globalisation movement, the paper contends that the feminisation of work forces in free trade zones has led unambiguously to empowerment and improved welfare. More broadly, it forcefully argues that trade expansion is one of the most powerful motors for raising living standards in developing countries.

What are we to make of all this? And to what extent does Bhagwati's argument succeed in achieving his own goal: namely, providing argument and evidence to converting anti-globalisers to his own pro-globalisation stance?

At one level, these are hard questions to answer, and for a simple reason: Bhagwati offers an infuriatingly shallow account of what he means by 'the anti-globalisation movement'. He appears to have in mind principally groups around Ralph Nader, anti- sweathshop activists, and the teamsters, with assorted environmental groups joining on an occasional basis. Bluntly stated, this is not good enough. As another of the contributions in this volume shows, a hugely broad and diverse array of civil society groups are involved in challenging current patterns of globalisation (Florini 2003). Many would have little truck with the Nader movement's curious brand of America-first mercantilism and willingness to make political deals with right-wing anti-globalisers and assorted xenophobes such as Pat Buchanan. By the same token, the liberal financing provided for some anti-globalisation protest in Seattle by Roger Milliken, a billionaire textile magnate from South Carolina, patron of right-wing causes, and practisioner of some dubious employment practices, would leave many of the strongest critics of globalisation deeply unimpressed.[1] Such cases powerfully illustrate that anti-globalisation is not the preserve of Bhagwati's fading Marxist intellectuals and new generation of student activists, but also of deeply reactionary political forces. After all, few anti-globalisers can match the anti-WTO credentials of Jean Marie Le Pen, let alone his success in mobilising popular support.

Had Bhagwati removed his ideological blinkers he would see a very different set of ideas, actors, and alliances. Let me take one example. In Britain, Oxfam is part of an organisation called the Trade Justice Movement (TJM) – a broad alliance of non-government organisations, church groups, trades unions and concerned individuals. In mid-2001, the TJM mobilised over 30,000 in a protest march against current international trade rules and rich-country trade policies. The demonstrators shared a conviction that the benefits of globalisation are being skewed towards rich countries, not because of 'market inevitability', but because of unfair international rules, poor institutions, and political choice on the part of northern governments. The briefest check-list of their demands would include the following: an end to the subsidised dumping of agricultural surpluses by the European Union and United States, improved market access for developing countries, the reform of the WTO's intellectual property rules, a prohibition on WTO/IMF policies designed to open capital markets in developing countries, and enhanced corporate responsibility to raise labour standards in developing countries. With the exception of the latter, which of these demands would Bhagwati reject?

It has to be said that there is a certain irony in Bhagwati's paper. After all, this is the author who has very publicly – and very eloquently – challenged the patent system enshrined in the WTO, led the case *against* capital market liberalisation, and, not so long ago, joined with southern non-government organisations in calling for improved access to northern markets for textiles and garment exports from developing countries. Perhaps unwittingly, Bhagwati is an emeritus member of a movement he has not understood. The more serious point is that somebody with his ability to communicate ideas, inform debate, and change policy should use his formidable abilities for something more constructive than the Don Quixote like pursuit of imaginary foes.

Turning to Bhagwati's defence of globalisation, it is hard to see the evidence and argument presented carrying much weight with his target audience: namely, passionate but 'misguided' young people.

Consider the claim that globalisation has emerged as a powerful force for poverty reduction and equity. In recent years a small cottage industry has emerged

---

[1]   On these links, see Steger (2002: 143–144).

producing research offering either a positive or a negative assessment. According to the World Bank, absolute $1-a-day poverty numbers have started to fall, mainly because of progress in China, India, Vietnam and a small group of relatively high growth countries. Set against this, we live in a profoundly unequal world: nearly half of the world's population survives on less than $2 a day, and over one billion people on less than $1. The richest one-fifth of people control around four-fifths of global income, and the income of the world's richest 5 per cent is 114 times that of the poorest (United Nations 2002).

No doubt the debate on poverty and inequality trends will continue to rage, but in many respects it misses the central point. At the beginning of a new century, global prosperity is rising in the midst of mass poverty. And whatever the precise trend, globalisation is perpetuating obscene levels of inequality. Indeed, on one account it is becoming progressively more unequal (Milanovic 2001). Young people looking at the world at the end of what many see as the second decade of the globalised era will see a profoundly unjust economic order – and they are right to challenge it.

They might also be less impressed than Bhagwati with other aspects of the record under globalisation. The relentless marginalisation of Africa is a case in point, but it is not an isolated blemish. No region has swallowed the 'economic openness' medicine in more copious quantities than Latin America. Yet with the exception of Chile, the proportion of poor people has hardly declined. This is true even in countries such as Peru and Mexico, which sustained per capita growth rates in the 1990s of 2 per cent per annum. Moreover, one recent review of household survey data for Latin America found that no country had achieved a reduction in what are exceptionally high rates of inequality in income distribution (Birdsall and Szekely 2003).

Of course, it is not just a sense of injustice that motivates people challenging globalisation: there is a parallel awareness that many of the problems facing poor people in poor countries can be traced to policy choices in rich ones. The fact that exports from the world's poorest countries to its richest ones face trade barriers four times higher than those applied in intra-OECD trade is a visible injustice. So too is the $1bn-a-day in subsidies lavished by northern governments on farmers and agribusiness corporation. These subsidies, paid for by northern taxpayers and consumers, help finance the destruction of smallholder agriculture in developing countries. Then there is the role of the WTO in facilitating self-evidently unfair trade rules on intellectual property. Lovingly crafted by the United States pharmaceuticals industry and enforced in a manner that raises the costs of vital medicines in poor countries, these rules are the equivalent of an institutionalised mugging of poor countries by rich ones. Not surprisingly, they have driven many public health interest groups into protest. At the same time, the protracted crisis facing the world's 25 million smallholder producers of coffee has strengthened consumer campaigns for greater corporate responsibility. It is, after all, the giant roasters that benefit most from what is now the deepest and most protracted price slump since the great depression. Bhagwati may take the view that protest in this area is the product of anti-corporate sentiment. The truth is that it is increasingly moving beyond small groups of activists and the fair trade movement into mainstream consumerism. Consumers, it seems, just have an irrational, non-market aversion to participating in an exchange that leaves coffee farmers with insufficient income to meet minimum nutritional standards, or keep their children in school.

It goes without saying that globalisation is not the inherently malign force claimed by some. Many countries have benefited from integration into global markets. These cases are widely cited by globalisation enthusiasts as adverts for openness and the broad mix of neo-liberal policies advocated by economists like Jeffrey Sachs and Jagdish Bhagwati himself. Widely cited – and wrongly cited. Many of the most successful globalisers have combined relatively high levels of protection, with a slow pace of liberalisation, stringent regulation of foreign investment, and domestic reforms aimed at boosting export competitiveness. As Dani Rodrik (2001) has shown, the one conclusion that can be drawn from the evidence is that countries tend to liberalise as they grow. There is no evidence that they grow *because of* import liberalisation. Indeed if import liberalisation were a magic bullet for growth, Latin America and sub-Saharan Africa would rapidly be catching up with East Asia. All of which raises fundamental questions about the use of IMF-World Bank loan conditions and WTO rules to enforce rapid liberalisation – another concern for many people contesting our current model of globalisation. This is an area in which far more attention needs to be paid to the development of national policies and institutions that enable countries to integrate into world markets in a manner that generates economic efficiency gains, higher growth, and a wide dispersion of benefits. Sloganeering on the benefits of openness does not help.

On the subject of transnational companies, Bhagwati makes an important point – and he misses another. The argument that women workers in developing countries have not derived economic benefits from producing for export is clearly fallacious. Through sub-contracting and, to a lesser degree, direct investment in production, northern transnational companies have played an important role in generating demand for labour. In Bangladesh alone, around one million jobs have been created in the textiles and garments sector over the past decade, most of them in free trade zones. Interviews with these women reveal a sense of ambiguity about their work. Most readily acknowledge an increase in income. [2] But at the same time they point to high levels of insecurity, notably regarding a fear of being sacked in the event of pregnancy. As in many other countries, independent trade unions are not permitted in Bangladesh's free trade zones. The same is true in

---

[2]   Oxfam (2001: 194). See also Kabeer (2000).

China. Here too, women are frequently subjected to what can only be described as abusive labour conditions. The sociologist Anita Chan carried out twenty-three detailed plant level surveys, documenting practices such as forced overtime, unpaid wages, illegal deductions by employers, unsafe working conditions, long hours, and involuntary confinement (Chan 2001). The companies concerned were not northern-based, but many were linked to northern transnational companies through sub-contracting.

The feminisation of labour markets under globalisation has created new opportunities for women, along with grave threats. It has also raised important questions about human development. For those who measure development solely in terms of income gains or losses, the balance sheet is clear: there are only winners. But as Amartya Sen has argued over the past decade and more, human development is multi-dimensional. And in this context, issues such as security and vulnerability matter a great deal. So, too, do gender power relations within the household (since this influences times and income distribution) and within the workplace (since this influences opportunity). Highlighting the income dimension of development to the exclusion of all other consideration, as Bhagwati does, betrays an attachment to a particularly narrow concept of 'economic man'.

So where does this leave us in terms of the debate on globalisation? The answer, I fear, is roughly where we started. At the end of one field visit to villages in Rajhastan, India, Jean Dreze wrote a short essay commenting on the clash between the world of academic debate on the poor, and the world as experienced by poor people themselves. "Social scientists," he wrote, "are chiefly engaged in arguing with each other about issues and theories that often bear little relation to the real world." He could have been commenting on the great globalisation non-debate that Bhagwati is apparently bent on perpetuating. People trying to make sense of the complex social justice and development problems raised by globalisation do not need more rhetoric, or ritualistic exchanges between the two great camps of believers and non-believers. Perhaps there is a sense in Bhagwati and his erstwhile polemical targets deserve each other. The debate on poverty and globalisation deserves something better.

Bibliography

Birdsall, N. and M. Szekely (2003). Bootstraps not Band-Aids: Poverty, Equity and Social Policy in Latin America. Centre for Global Development Working paper. February. Washington, D.C. Mimeo.

Chan, A. (2001). *China's Workers under Assault: The Exploitation of Labour in a Globalising Economy.* Armonk: Sharpe.

Dollar, D. and A. Kraay (2002). Spreading the Wealth. *Foreign Policy* (January/February): 120–133.

Dreze, J. (2002). On Research and Action. *Economic and Political Weekly*, Bombay (2 March): 10–11.

Florini, A. (2003). From Protest to Participation: The Role of Civil Society in Global Governance. This volume.

Goldsmith, E., and J. Mander (2002). *The Case against the Global Economy.* London: Earthscan.

Kabeer, N. (2000). *The Power to Choose, Verso*: London: DATE.

Krugman, P. (1998). *The Accidental Theorist.* London: Penguin.

Milanovic, B. (2001) True World Income Distribution, 1988 and 1993: First Calculation Based on Household Survey Alone. Policy Research Paper 2244. World Bank, Washington, D.C.

Oxfam (2001). *Rigged Rules and Double Standards.* Oxford.

Rodrik, D. (2001). Trading in Illusions. *Foreign Policy* (March/April).

Steger, M. (2002). *Globalism.* New York: Rowman and Littlefield.

United Nations Development Programme (2002). *Human Development Report 2002.* New York.

Pranab Bardhan

International Economic Integration and the Poor

I believe a large part of the opposition to globalization is really about the impact of volatile international financial markets and the fragility of valued indigenous cultures in the face of the onslaught of global mass production and cultural homogenization. In this paper I shall abstract from these important issues and confine myself to trying to understand the possible difficulties poverty alleviation policies in poor countries may face from international economic integration in the sense of openness to foreign trade and *long-term* capital flows.[1]

For this understanding we need first to look at the processes by which globalization may affect the conditions of the poor, and then analyze the ways in which the policies meant to relieve those conditions are hemmed in by global constraints. I believe that globalization can cause some hardships for the poor but it also opens up some opportunities, and the net outcome is often quite complex and almost always context-dependent, belying the glib pronouncements for or against globalization made in the opposing camps.

One cliché in the literature is that globalization is making the rich richer and the poor poorer. While inequality may be increasing in many countries (on account of a whole host of factors including globalization), my focus in this paper is on the conditions of those trapped in absolute poverty (measured by some bare minimum standard) in low-income countries. It is not at all clear that the poor have become poorer everywhere in recent decades when large strides in international economic integration have taken place. A quarter of a century back, most of the world's poorest people were concentrated in East, Southeast and South Asia, sub-Saharan Africa, and Central America. Since then poverty has substantially declined in large parts of China, Indonesia, and South Asia, and there also have been significant improvements in other social indicators (like literacy or longevity) in most low-income countries, while poverty has remained stubbornly high in

---

[1] Much of the financial crisis in developing countries in recent years was initially caused by overexposure to foreign-currency-denominated short-term debts. These, everybody now recognizes, are particularly crisis-prone financial instruments. In most cases, there was too little discipline in borrowing before the crises and too much discipline afterwards. Many liberal economists now believe in the need for some form of control over short-term capital flows, though there are differences on the specific form such control should take.

sub-Saharan Africa. But correlation does not imply causation: just as a large decline in poverty in China along with globalization does not necessarily mean a causal relation, the same may be the case for the nondecline in Africa. Much of the persistence or even deterioration in poverty in Africa may have nothing to do with globalization, and more to do with unstable or failed political regimes, wars, and civil conflicts which afflicted several of those countries; if anything, such instability only reduced their extent of globalization, as it scared off many foreign investors and traders. Similarly, pro-globalizers point to the fact that wages and living standards are often better for the poor in coastal cities in China than in the remote areas in the west cut off from the international economy, on the Mexican border with the United States where the *maquiladora* are located than in the interior provinces, etc., but again one needs to spell out the causal mechanisms at work to convince anybody.

1   Causal Processes

The causal processes through which international economic integration can affect poverty primarily involve the poor in their capacity as workers and as recipients of public services. Let us first take the case of poor workers. They are mainly either self-employed or wage earners. The self-employed work on their own tiny farms or as artisans and petty entrepreneurs in small shops and firms. The major constraints they usually face are in credit, marketing and insurance, infrastructure (like roads and irrigation), and government regulations (venal inspectors, insecure land rights, etc.). These often require substantive domestic policy changes, and foreign traders and investors are not directly to blame (in fact they may sometimes help in relieving some of the bottlenecks in infrastructure and services). If these changes are not made and the self-employed poor remain constrained, then, of course, it is difficult for them to withstand competition from large agribusiness or firms (foreign or domestic). Less-constrained small farms or firms are sometimes more productive than their larger counterparts, and are also more successful in export markets. But in exports the major hurdle they face is often due to not more globalization but less. Developed country protectionism and subsidization of farm and food products and simple manufactures (like textiles and clothing) severely restrict their export prospects for poor countries. I wish the anti-globalization protesters of rich countries would turn their energies towards the vested interests in their own countries which prolong this protectionism and cripple the efforts of the poor of the world to climb out of their poverty.

Turning to poor wage earners, the theoretical literature on how international trade affects the absolute level of the real wage of unskilled workers is extremely small relative to the one on wage inequality (which, though an important issue, is not my concern here). I can think of six types of theoretical mechanisms through which this effect may be significant in developing countries.

(a) The traditional Stolper–Samuelson mechanism applied to a simple two-country (rich-poor) two-factor (capital-labor) world suggests that the workers in the poor country having a comparative advantage in products intensive in unskilled labor should benefit from trade liberalization. This is, of course, complicated by the fact that developing countries (say, Brazil or Mexico or Turkey) may import labor-intensive products from even poorer countries (say, China or Indonesia or Bangladesh), so that trade even in terms of this mechanism may lead to lower wages in the former set of developing countries (Wood 1997).

(b) If some factors of production are intersectorally immobile, and some goods are nontraded, the real wage of an unskilled worker in a poor country may not go up with trade liberalization even in an otherwise standard model of trade theory. Take a three-good model in a hypothetical African country: one is a nontradable good (say a subsistence food crop) which is largely grown by women who for various social and economic reasons cannot move to other sectors, another good (say an exportable tree crop) is produced largely by men in a capital-intensive way (maybe simply because tree crops lock up capital for a long period), and the third good is an importable (say processed food) which is somewhat substitutable in consumption for the subsistence food. In this three-sector model it is not difficult to show that the real wage of women may go down when the importable processed food is made cheaper by trade liberalization (under the condition that the elasticity of substitution in consumption of the two foods is sufficiently high).

(c) Take a two-period model where labor on a long-term contract is trained in the first period and this training bears fruit in the second period, when these long-contract workers are more productive than untrained short-contract casual laborers. If opening the economy increases competition and the probability of going out of business, employers may go more for short-contract and less productive and lower-wage laborers, bringing down the average wage. By a similar reasoning, a firm may have less incentive in an open economy to invest in developing a reputation for fairness in wage payments.

(d) On the other hand, increased foreign competition may lead to exit of old inefficient firms and entry of new more efficient firms, or a better allocation of resources within existing firms – this may lead to a rise in wages in industries that attain such productivity gains.[2]

(e) If firms facing more foreign competition and pressure to reduce costs outsource activities to smaller firms or household enterprises in the informal sec-

---

[2]   The positive link between trade liberalization and productivity has been found in Chile, Colombia, Côte d'Ivoire, Brazil, India, and South Korea. One of the most careful micro-studies on this question is by Pavcnik (2002), who finds that massive trade liberalization in Chile in the late 1970s and early 1980s led to growth of productivity at the plant level at the average rate of 3 to 10 percent.

tor,[3] the average wage (of those formerly employed in the formal sector) may go down, but this need not impoverish workers in general if the poorer informal workers get more employment this way.

(f) As foreign competition (or even the threat of it) lowers profit margins, the old rent-sharing arrangements between employers and unionized workers come under pressure. Rents decline both for capital and labor, but labor may have to take a larger cut if, as has been argued, the increase in the (perceived) elasticity of demand in the product market (due to trade liberalization) leads to an increase in the elasticity of demand for labor, lowering its bargaining power and generally weakening unions.[4] Faced with a shrinking share of the industry's surplus, unionized workers sometimes tap other sources of rent by raising barriers to entry for informal workers (through lobbying for labor regulations that make hiring and firing of formal sector workers very costly for employers).

2   Empirical Evidence

Now let me briefly discuss the empirical evidence on the effect of foreign trade and investment on the wages of unskilled labor in developing countries. The micro-evidence on this is rather limited (I am ignoring the usual, flawed, cross-country regressions). More often than not, you are cited data on correlations, not a careful empirical analysis of the causal process. For example, the critics of NAFTA will readily point to the decline in real wages of unskilled workers in Mexico in the few years immediately after NAFTA came into operation, overlooking the fact that much of the decline may be due to the peso crisis that engulfed Mexico in this period, which had very little to do with the opening of trade with North America. It is important to disentangle the effects on wages of trade reform from those flowing from macroeconomic policy changes or other on-going deregulatory reforms and technological changes.

---

[3]   Attanasio et al. (2002) find some evidence that the increase in the size of the informal sector in Colombia towards the end of the 1990s is related to increased foreign competition.

[4]   See Currie and Harrison (1997), Rodrik (1997), Leamer (1998), and Reddy (2001). The theoretical relation between product market demand elasticity and the elasticity of derived demand for labor is somewhat more complex than usual in the case of imperfect competition. The empirical evidence in developing countries on the trade-induced changes in the elasticity of demand for labor is rather scanty. Fajnzylber and Maloney (2001) use a dynamic panel model to estimate labor demand relations for manufacturing firms in Chile, Colombia, and Mexico across the periods of dramatic changes in trade regimes in the last couple of decades. They conclude that there is no strong evidence that trade liberalization leads to larger demand elasticity for labor in Chile, but in Mexico and Colombia there is some (mixed) support for this.

On the whole, evidence on the labor market effect of trade liberalization in developing countries, on the basis of the few microeconometric studies, is rather mixed and quantitatively small. Analyzing a set of 25 trade liberalization episodes in developing countries, using internationally comparable sectoral labor data, Seddon and Wacziarg (2002) come to the conclusion that trade liberalization has far smaller effects on intersectoral reallocation (even at the 3-digit level within manufacturing) than is conventionally presumed. What is more likely is that much of the structural change is intrasectoral and that some of the potential changes are neutralized by policies like exchange rate depreciation, labor regulations, and sector-specific subsidies. The micro-studies of effects of trade reform in Mexico and Morocco by Revenga (1997), Feliciano (2001), and Currie and Harrison (1997) attribute the small effect on employment to labor regulations or to the firms adjusting to trade reform by reducing their formerly protected profit margins and raising productivity rather than laying off workers.

Goldberg and Pavcnik (2001), on the basis of panel data from the Colombian National Household Survey over 1985–1994, look at the effect of trade policy on industry wage premiums, i.e., the part of wages that cannot be explained by worker or firm characteristics. They find that the two most protected sectors in Colombia were textiles and apparel, and wood and wood products manufacturing, which are relatively unskilled-labor-intensive sectors, and with industry fixed effects trade protection is found to increase industry wage premiums. This is quite consistent with traditional trade theory, particularly when one keeps in mind that such protection of labor-intensive industries in developing countries may be against imports from even more labor-abundant countries, as we have noted in our theoretical mechanism (a) above.

Even when poor unskilled workers lose from trade liberalization in such contexts, it may be possible to combine a policy of trade liberalization with a domestic policy of compensating the losers at low cost. Harrison et al. (2003) have used a computable general equilibrium model for Turkey to show with a numerical exercise that a direct income subsidy to the losers of trade reform, financed by a VAT, is quite cost-effective. The main problem, of course, is that of credible commitment on the part of the ruling politicians that losers will be compensated.

Let us now briefly turn to the case of the poor as recipients of public services. In the low-income developing countries, the poor, particularly those who are in the preponderant informal sector, do not receive much of effective social protection from the state (which make them particularly vulnerable in case of job displacement brought about by international competition), but the public sector is usually involved in basic services like education and health. Cuts in public budgets for these basic services are often attributed to globalization, as the budget cuts to reduce fiscal deficits often come as part of a package of macroeconomic stabilization prescribed by international agencies like the IMF. I agree with a common characterization of some of the IMF conditionalities on a crisis-affected

country as analogous to medieval ways of trying to cure a patient by blood-let-
ting. But one should keep in mind that the fiscal deficits in these poor countries
are often brought about in the first place more by domestic profligacy in matters
of subsidies to the rich, salaries for the bloated public sector, or military extrava-
ganza. Faced with mounting fiscal deficits, the governments often find it politically easier to cut the public expenditures for the voiceless poor, and that is
primarily due to the domestic political clout of the rich, who are disinclined to
share in the necessary fiscal austerity, and it is always convenient to blame an
external agency for a problem that is essentially domestic in origin.

The low quality and quantity of public services like education and health in
poor countries is not just due to their relatively low share in the public budget. To
a large extent, even the limited money allocated in the budget does not reach the
poor because of all kinds of top-heavy administrative obstacles and bureaucratic
and political corruption.[5] Again this is a domestic institutional failure, not largely
an external problem. The major effort required here is to strengthen the domestic
institutions of accountability.

3   Constraints on Policy Options

Finally, let me take up the general issue of possible loss of national policy options
relevant for the poor brought about by a developing country's participation in the
international economic order. First of all, I agree with the anti-globalization protesters that many of the international organizations that define the rules of this order are accountable more to the corporate and financial community of rich countries than to the poor and that the decision-making processes in these organizations
need to be much more transparent and responsive to the lives of the people their
decisions crucially affect.[6] At the same time it should be pointed out that the pro-

---

[5]   To give just one instance of a rough magnitude of the problem, the World Bank
recently estimated that of the total nonsalary budget sanctioned by the central government in Uganda for schools in the period 1991–1995 only about 13 percent actually
reached them.

[6]   The protesters' demand for the abolition of the WTO is, however, misplaced. If the alternative to a multilateral organization like the WTO is for a developing country to face the
United States in bilateral trade negotiations, the United States is likely to be much more
dominant and arbitrary in such negotiations than in the dispensations of the WTO (which
in its arbitration decisions has sometimes ruled against the U.S. position). It is also to be
noted that in the WTO, each member country has one vote (the convention is to reach
decisions by "consensus," as the protracted delay caused by one developing country in
the agreement between ministers in the recent meeting at Doha shows), whereas in the
Bretton Woods institutions voting is dollar-weighted. But there is no denying the fact that
the rich countries (and their large corporate lobbies) exercise a dominant effect on the
agenda-setting and decision-making of the WTO, as with the Bretton Woods institutions.

testers in rich countries often speak in the name of the world's poor but support policies which sometimes may actually harm them (more on this below).

Coming to the issue of a government's fiscal options in a global economy, many people are of the opinion that the scope for taxing capital to raise revenue is severely limited by the threat of capital flight in the long run, even if we ignore the problem of short-term speculative capital flows. (In fact, capital itself does not have to flee the country; quite often accounting practices, through strategic book-keeping adjustments, allow the base for capital taxes to migrate even when capital itself does not.) While this limitation can be serious, one should not exaggerate its effects. Most countries collect only a small part of their revenues from capital taxation, even in relatively closed economies. In any case there are strong arguments for funding redistributive policies through progressive consumption taxes (say VAT) rather than taxes on capital or labor. Of course, there is a need for tax coordination across countries, and there is some evidence that capital taxation is declining and also converging across countries. But again, one should not overstate this. Even in the highly integrated European Union corporate tax rates have substantially converged not to zero, as some people anticipated, but to about 35 percent. In general between two equilibria, one with high taxes and high public goods provision and the other with low taxes and low public goods, capital need not choose the latter over the former.

Serious obstacles to redistributive policies are often domestic. At the micro-level of firms, farms, neighborhoods, and local communities, there is scope for a great deal of efficiency-enhancing egalitarian measures that can help the poor and are not primarily blocked by the forces of globalization. Various asset redistribution and poverty alleviation policies (like land reform, expansion of education and health facilities for the poor, making available public works programs as a last resort for the unemployed, organizing cooperative and peer-monitored credit and marketing for small firms and farms, facilitating formation of local community organizations to manage the local environmental resources, etc.) can improve productive efficiency and expand opportunities for the poor, and yet are within the range of capability of domestic institutions of the community and the polity. The main hindrance in devoting substantial fiscal and organizational resources to these projects is the considerable opposition from domestic vested interests – landlords, corrupt and/or inept politicians and bureaucrats, and the currently subsidized rich. Closing the economy does not reduce the power of these vested interests. If anything, the forces of competition unleashed by international integration may reduce their monopoly power. Of course, large transnational companies, working through the rich country governments and with their threats of financial withdrawal, can sometimes shift the political equilibrium particularly in small countries and weak states, although crass manipulations and gunboat diplomacy of the past are getting somewhat more difficult than before.

While the transnational companies may have deeper pockets and larger political clout vis-à-vis the poor unskilled laborers of a country, there is very little evidence that the latter get lower wages and fewer jobs in the presence of those companies, compared to what they will get in their absence, other things remaining the same. Contrary to the impression created by the campaign in affluent countries against "sweatshops" run by transnational companies in poor countries, the poor are often banging at the gates of these sweatshops for a chance of entry, since their current alternative is much worse, in inferior occupations or work conditions or in unemployment. For those who complain about the exploitation of young women in the garment factories of transnational companies do not often appreciate the relative improvement in the conditions and status of these women (say in the garment industry in Bangladesh or Mauritius) compared to the alternatives otherwise available to them. This is not an argument against efforts to improve their work conditions (and certainly not in favor of the totally indefensible cases of forced labor or hazardous or unsafe work conditions[7]), but it is an appeal to look at the reality of the severely limited opportunities faced by the poor and the unintended consequences of trying to restrict rich-country imports of "sweatshop" products in terms of the harm it causes to the displaced poor workers.

A similar argument applies to the case of child labor. Simply banning imports of products that have used child labor is likely to send the children often not to schools but to much inferior occupations in the usually much larger nontraded sector.[8] (In India, for example, an estimated 95 percent of child workers are in the nontraded sector anyway.) In Vietnam, a quarter of all children work in agriculture. From 1993 to 1997 the government gradually relaxed its rice export quota, which led to rice producers getting a better price. Using the Vietnam Living Standards Survey data for a panel of 4,000 households in this period, Edmonds and Pavcnik (2001) estimate that this better price received for rice can account for almost half of the decline in child labor that took place in this period. Here is a

---

[7] Conceptually, one should distinguish between unsafe or hazardous work conditions and forced labor on the one hand and low-wage jobs on the other. Under capitalism, just as workers willing to sell themselves as serfs are not permitted, unsafe work conditions that can cause bodily injury are to be strictly regulated. That is the reason why they are part of the ILO core labor standards that have been ratified by most countries. But the case for stopping workers from accepting low-wage jobs is much weaker.

[8] In 1993, Senator Tom Harkins brought a bill in the U.S. Congress to ban imports of products using child labor. It was not passed subsequently, but almost immediately after the introduction of the bill the garment industry in Bangladesh dismissed between thirty to forty thousand children it formerly employed. In 1996, OXFAM carried out a survey to find out what had happened to these children. It was found that (with the concerted effort of some education NGOs) about ten thousand children did go back to school, but the rest went to much inferior occupations, including child prostitution.

case where increased earning opportunities from participation in the international market with a product that is intensive in child labor led to its decline. A policy of trade sanctions against Vietnamese rice, with the apparent good intention of reducing child labor in its production, could have the opposite effect.

Clearly, taking mainly a legal or regulatory approach to achieve an otherwise laudable social goal is the wrong way to go about it. Unintended consequences abound, and the solutions are often a little more complex than the simplistic remedies proposed by many activists. The widely noted program in Mexico, PRO-GRESA, of paying a subsidy to the mother conditional on her children's school attendance has made a significant dent in child labor. The program (now under a different name) has expanded substantially in Mexico, and NAFTA or global integration has not got in the way. It is also important to understand the need for coordinated action among the different parties involved. A good example is the Partners' Agreement to Eliminate Child Labor in the Soccer Ball Industry in Pakistan in the mid-1990s, by which the transnational sporting goods companies (involved in production in the city of Sialkot in Pakistan of a large fraction of the world supply of soccer balls), the local government, and some NGOs reached an agreement to eliminate child labor in that industry, provide scholarships to the displaced children, and to arrange the school facilities needed.

4   Environmental Effects

Environmentalists argue that trade liberalization damages the poor by encouraging overexploitation of the fragile environmental resources (forestry, fishery, surface and groundwater irrigation, grazing lands, etc.) on which the daily livelihoods of particularly the rural poor crucially depend. Here also the answers are actually complex and mere trade restriction is not the solution. The environmental effects of trade liberalization on the rural economy depend on the crop pattern and the methods of production. Take, for example, an African rural economy where the exportable product is a capital-intensive tree crop (like coffee or cocoa), the import-substitute is a land-intensive crop (like maize), and there is a labor-intensive subsistence (nontraded) crop (like roots and tubers). The economy may have a comparative advantage in tree crops. In this case, an increase in import substitution leads to an expansion of cultivated land under the land-intensive crop as well as a shortening of the fallow period, leading to depletion of natural vegetation and biomass. Trade liberalization in this context, through encouraging the production of the less land-intensive tree crop, can significantly improve the natural biomass, as has been shown by Lopez (2000) for Côte d'Ivoire in the latter part of the 1980s, using the data from the Living Standards Survey and some remote sensing data from satellite images.

One reason why land-intensive crops may lead to overuse of land and depletion of natural vegetation (or that expansion of the agricultural frontier in general leads to deforestation) is the lack of well-defined property rights or lack of their enforcement in public or communal land. In such cases, the private cost of expanding production is less than the social cost and there is overuse and degradation of environmental resources. If the country exports such resource-intensive products, foreign trade may make this misallocation worse. International trade theorists point out that trade restriction is not the first-best policy in this situation, correcting the property rights regime is. But the latter involves large changes in the legal-regulatory or community institutional framework which take a long time to implement, and given the threshold effects and irreversibilities in environmental degradation (a forest regeneration requires a minimum stock, for example), one may not afford to wait. In that case, some program of (time-bound) trade restriction coupled with serious attempts at the overhaul of the domestic institutional framework may be necessary. In other cases, domestic policy changes can be implemented much more quickly, and restricting trade is unnecessary and undesirable. For example, administered underpricing of precious environmental resources (irrigation water in India, energy in Russia, timber concessions in Indonesia, etc.) is a major cause of resource depletion and correcting it should not take much time. Domestic vested interests, not globalization, are responsible for the prolongation of such socially damaging policies.

In the case of some resource-intensive exports, it is difficult for a country by itself to adopt environmental regulations if its international competitors do not adopt them at the same time and have the ability to undercut the former in international markets. Here again, there is an obvious need for coordination in the environmental regulation policies of the countries concerned. Given the low elasticity of demand for many resource-intensive primary export commodities from developing countries in the world market, such coordinated policies, while raising prices and the terms of trade, need not lead to a decline in export revenue.

In general, while globalization can constrain some policy options and wipe out some existing jobs and entrepreneurial opportunities for the poor and for small enterprises, in the medium to long run it need not make the poor much worse off, if appropriate domestic policies and institutions are in place and appropriate coordination between the involved parties can be organized. This, of course, does not absolve international organizations and entities from the responsibility of helping the poor of the world, by reducing their protection on goods produced by the poor, by facilitating international partnerships in research and development of products (for example, drugs, crops) suitable for the poor, and by organizing more substantial (and more effectively governed) financial and technology transfers. The empirical evidence so far suggests that the labor market effects of trade reform have been much less than was originally apprehended. Poverty alleviation in the form of expansion of credit and marketing facilities or land reform or public works programs for the unemployed or provision of education and health need not be blocked by the forces of globalization. This, of course, requires a restructuring of existing budget priorities and a better and more accountable political and administrative framework, but the obstacles to these are largely domestic. Globalization should not be allowed to be used as an excuse for inaction on the redistributive front.

Bibliography

Attanasio, O., P.K. Goldberg, and N. Pavcnik (2002). Trade Reforms and Wage Inequality in Colombia. Unpublished. Available from http://www.econ.yale.edu/~pg87/inequality.pdf.

Currie, J., and A. Harrison (1997). Sharing the Costs: The Impact of Trade Reform on Capital and Labor in Morocco. *Journal of Labor Economics* 15(3): S44–S71.

Edmonds, E., and N. Pavcnik (2001). Does Globalization Increase Child Labor? Evidence from Vietnam. Unpublished, Dartmouth College. Available from http://www.dartmouth.edu/~npavcnik/Research_files/glob_cl.pdf.

Fajnzylber, P., and W.F. Maloney (2001). Labor Demand and Trade Reform in Latin America. Working Paper. World Bank. Washington, D.C.

Feliciano, Z.M. (2001). Workers and Trade Liberalization: The Impact of Trade Reforms in Mexico on Wages and Employment. *Industrial and Labor Relations Review* 55(1): 95–115.

Goldberg, P., and N. Pavcnik (2001). Trade Protection and Wages: Evidence from Colombian Trade Reform. Unpublished.

Harrison, G.W., T.F. Rutherford, and D.G. Tarr (2003). Trade Liberalization, Poverty and Efficient Equity. Forthcoming in *Journal of Development Economics* (June).

Leamer, E.E. (1998). In Search of Stolper–Samuelson Linkages between International Trade and Lower Wages. In S.M. Collins (ed.), *Imports, Exports, and the American Worker.* Washington, D.C.: The Brookings Institution Press.

Lopez, R. (2000). Trade Reform and Environmental Externalities in General Equilibrium: Analysis for an Archetype Poor Tropical Country. *Environment and Development Economics* 4(4): 337–404.

Pavcnik, N. (2002). Trade Liberalization, Exit and Productivity Improvements: Evidence from Chilean Plants. *The Review of Economic Studies* 69(1): 245–276.

Reddy, S. (2001). Liberalization, Distribution and Political Economy. Unpublished, Barnard College, New York.

Revenga, A. (1997). Employment and Wage Effects of Trade Liberalization: The Case of Mexican Manufacturing. *Journal of Labor Economics* 15(3): S20–S43.

Rodrik, D. (1997). *Has Globalization Gone Too Far?* Washington, D.C.: Institute for International Economics.

Seddon, J., and R. Wacziarg (2002). Trade Liberalization and Intersectoral Labor Movements. Unpublished, Stanford. Available from http://www.stanford.edu/~wacziarg/papersum.html.

Wood, A. (1997). Openness and Wage Inequality in Developing Countries: The Latin American Challenge to East Asian Conventional Wisdom. *World Bank Economic Review* 11(1): 33–57.

Comment on Pranab Bardhan

Rainer Klump

Introduction

The three main points in Bardhan's paper are the following:

- Neither economic theory nor empirical evidence show that globalization per se in the medium or long run makes the poor in developing countries much worse off.
- Effective national programs of poverty alleviation should not necessarily be blocked by the forces of globalization.
- Globalization should not be used as an excuse for inaction on the redistribution front.

I totally agree with these three points. The comments which I will present in the form of three questions are therefore of a complementary nature. They try to provide additional insight into the complex interactions between globalization, social justice, and global governance by taking recourse to three different strands of economic theory. My three questions are the following:

- Why do different people view globalization so differently?
- Why is there no unambiguous effect of globalization on poverty?
- Is poverty alleviation a national or an international task?

My answers rely on basic principles of welfare economics, on neoclassical growth theory, and on some ideas of public choice theory.

Globalization, Poverty Alleviation, and Welfare Economics

Bardhan tells us that different people view globalization differently. For economists, at least, I think it is normal to view globalization as a process which aims at a more efficient use of world resources by finding more competitive ways of production and trade, ways which include substantial flows of long-term capital. The first fundamental theorem of welfare theory tells us that competitive equilibria along a world production possibility curve are Pareto optima. I think potential efficiency gains are what most economists have in mind when talking about globalization.

Nevertheless, the second fundamental theorem of welfare theory points out that distribution issues should be strictly separated from efficiency issues. Efficient allocations on the national or the global level do not have to be considered fair. A global social optimum, where the efficient allocation of goods and resoures is also the fair one, might exist but it can only be found on the basis of a global social welfare function. So far there are no normative foundations of such a global social welfare function in sight, and this has, to my mind, created a major problem for modern economics and economists.

Since there are no generally accepted normative guidelines today, most mainstream economists have eliminated questions of social justice from their research agenda and concentrate exclusively on studies related to the efficiency aspects of globalization. Needless to say, this is also the area which is the most relevant for business interests. The ongoing specialization of economists on efficiency problems has opened the door for social scientists from neighboring sciences to fill this gap and to dominate the public discourses on social justice. This is an important observation because, at least for the majority of world citizens, social justice considerations are of course a central part of practical economic policy in all countries. Given the multitude of differing and competing concepts of what social justice could be in a global context, it is no wonder that those talking about distributional aspects of globalization do not agree with mainstream economics, but neither do they agree amongst themselves.

How could modern economics overcome this problem? First, economists should point out that insofar as underdevelopment exists in the world, the most efficient use of the world's resource has not yet been realized. As long as we still live inside the world production possibilty frontier, however, efficiency and distribution equity might be much more complementary goals of economic policy than most of the anti-globalizationers would think. I will show in the next section how modern growth theory treats these issues. Second, economics – which originally considered itself a theory of social justice – should teach other social sciences the essence of Arrow's impossibility theorem. Since in general, there is no voting mechanism that ensures that a global social welfare function could be found by aggregating somehow the multitude of social orderings proposed by individuals and scientists, the idea of a democratically controlled world government must be questioned. I will come back to this point later and tackle it from a public choice perspective.

Globalization, Distribution Dynamics, and Growth Theory

We learn from Bardhan's paper that globalization can contribute to growth in underdeveloped countries. This confirms the idea proposed in recent contributions to the theory of growth that the efficiency gains of globalization should induce growth dynamic and convergence (Ventura 1997, Klump 2001). Empirically, it is not clear however that this growth goes hand in hand with significant changes in income or wealth distribution. One way to reconcile evidence and theory might be the hypothesis that something like a Kuznets curve exists. Therefore, distribution should deteriorate in the first phase of growth and then improve again in the second phase. I do not want to repeat here the long debate on possible explanations for a Kuznets curve pattern in development. I would, rather, point out that modern growth theory has provided a new explanation for this pattern by relating the transitional dynamics of growth to the transitional dynamics of distribution in an intertemporal optimizing model with heterogeneous agents (Caselli and Ventura 2000, Glachant and Vellutini 2002).

One important result from this new discussion can be directly related to one of Bardhan's main observations. The growth model tells us that during convergence a Kuznets curve pattern is more likely the lower the domestic elasticity of substitution between factors of production is. As Klump and Preissler (2000) demonstrate, the elasticity of substitution also reflects a country's institutional infrastructure. Hence, the more institutional inefficiency reigns in a country the more likely a negative correlation between growth and distribution indicators is during the first phase of transition. Domestic institutions are therefore an important strategic element not only for efficiency but also for distribution purposes.

Since Bardhan also talks about some environmental aspects of globalization it should be worth consulting the expanding literature on environmental Kuznets curves exploring the relationship between growth and environmental quality (Bretschger and Smulders 2002). There again the elasticity of substitution between factors of production is of essential significance and again it is strongly influenced by the institutional infrastructure.

Globalization, Social Justice, and Public Choice Theory

As Bardhan convincingly shows, poverty allevation is possible in low-income countries. However, anti-globalizationers might point out that despite the achievements of national policies in favor of the poor, the global income distribution has stayed rather unequal. One of the most recent studies in this field, by Milanovic and Yitzhaki (2002), based on household income data for 111 countries in 1993, found out that the world Gini coefficient is of the order of 0.66, and this is far beyond most national values even in very underdeveloped countries. One may criticize the idea of calculating a world Gini coefficient, but, as long as the mean values of national GDP per head are as different as they are, one should not be too surprised by the result. Whether this result of a very unequal world distribution is also considered unfair now depends either on a normative value judgement – for which economists no longer have any comparative advantage – or on some public choice considerations.

Such public choice considerations may explain why strategies of poverty alleviation are important elements of national economic policy in many underdeveloped countries. Making the poor better off becomes more attractive for politicians the more the poor have the power to vote. Distribution justice from this perspective is necessary to protect the stability of the whole society. The spread of democracy among countries of the former Third World which paralleled the last wave of globalization has therefore produced positive distribution side effects. However, the essential question still is whether, in the globalized world of today, the poor in Bangladesh only compare themselves with the rich people in the same country or rather with the rich or the poor in the more developed countries. Modern ways of communication make these individual welfare comparisons very easy.

Milanovic and Yitzhaki (2002) point out that since at present all countries in the world care more about their own poor than about the poor in other countries world society has not been able to form a strong middle class of individuals or countries. Much will depend on future developments in China and India. If these two countries became members of the world middle class, there would be more stability in world society than we find today. If this does not happen, one can only speculate what the options are. One very pessimistic option expects mass migration from the poor to the rich countries. This might increase the pressure in the rich countries to make poverty alleviation a global policy task. Global governance should therefore have also an eye on global distribution indicators.

Conclusion

Economists should not be too surprised that anti-globalizationers put more emphasis on distribution than on efficiency aspects of globalization. The law of comparative advantage is also at work within the various sciences. However, economists should refrain from becoming overspecialized on efficiency aspects. Transitional dynamics in growth reveal that the world production possibilities are still expanding, and the distributional dynamics under convergence are very diverse and highly dependent on institutional infrastructures. Instead of struggling about the right normative concept of global social justice, economists should have an eye on the links between globalization, democracy, and global governance.

The lack of a world middle class and the threat of mass migration from poor to rich countries might become one of the most interesting challenges for the future of world society.

Bibliography

Bretscher, L., and S. Smulders (2002). Explaining Environmental Kuznets Curves: How Pollution Induces Policy and New Technologies. In: W. Oueslati and G. Rotillon (eds.), *Macroeconomic Perspectives and Environmental Concerns*. Cheltenham: Edgar Elgar.

Caselli, F.M., and J. Ventura (2000). A Representative Consumer Theory of Distribution. *American Economic Review* 90 (4): 909–926.

Glachant, J., and C. Vellutini (2002). Quantifying the Relationship between Wealth Distribution and Aggregate Growth in the Ramsey Model. *Economics Letters* 74 (2): 237–241.

Klump, R. (2001). Trade, Money and Employment in Intertemporal Optimizing Models of Growth. *Journal of International Trade and Economic Development* 10 (4): 411–428.

Klump, R., and H. Preissler (2000). CES Production Functions and Economic Growth. *Scandinavian Journal of Economics* 102 (1): 41–56.

Milanovic, B., and S. Yitzhaki (2002). Decomposing World Income Distribution: Does the World Have a Middle Class? *Review of Income and Wealth* 48 (2): 155–178.

Ventura, J. (1997). Growth and Interdependence. *Quarterly Journal of Economics* 62 (1): 57–84.

Oliver Lorz

Do National Governments Lose Their Maneuvering Space in the Era of Locational Competition and What Can They Do?

1 Introduction

In a world with high mobility, national governments cannot take the supply of production factors in their country as given. Instead, they must compete with governments in other countries if they want to attract factors that are internationally mobile. This situation has given rise to the concept of locational competition in the world economy.[1] The following pages deal with the effects of locational competition on economic policy. They focus on fiscal competition, i.e., competition between governments' tax and expenditure policies, and consider capital as the mobile factor of production. The central question in the paper is: How does capital mobility influence the level and composition of taxes and public expenditures and what are the welfare effects of this influence? To concentrate on this question, the paper analyzes fiscal competition in a world of full information, i.e., it does not consider competition as a preference revelation mechanism for public goods (as in Tiebout 1956) or as a discovery procedure in the sense of Hayek (1978).

2 The Theory of Fiscal Competition

Since the seminal papers on tax competition by Beck (1983), Zodrow and Mieszkowski (1986), and Wilson (1986), a substantial theoretical literature has developed dealing with tax and expenditure competition between jurisdictions caused by capital mobility. According to a central result of this literature, fiscal competition between welfare-maximizing governments can lead to inefficiently low tax and expenditure levels if governments have to rely on source-based capital taxes

---

[1]   See, e.g., Siebert (2000) for a more general exposition of the concept of locational competition.

to finance their expenditures.[2] This section derives and discusses this and some other important insights following from theoretical models on fiscal competition.[3]

2.1   Capital Tax Competition and the Supply of Public Goods

A basic tax competition model may be characterized as follows:[4] Assume the world is divided into N identical countries. In each of these countries, a homogenous aggregate consumption good can be produced by using two production factors, internationally mobile capital, and immobile labor. Capital and labor are fixed in supply, with each country being endowed with L units of labor and S units of capital. The consumption good is produced with a constant returns to scale technology, $F(K, L)$, and its price is set equal to one. Governments raise a source-based tax on capital that is proportional to the invested capital stock. A representative competitive firm determines capital and labor demand in country i ($i = 1, ..., N$) by maximizing its profit, $\pi_i = F(K_i, L_i) - t_i K_i - w_i L_i - [1 + r]K_i$, with w_i as the wage rate in country i, t_i as the capital tax rate, and r as the world interest rate. The first-order condition for the demand of capital is $F_{K_i} - t_i = 1 + r$. The first-order condition for the demand of labor determines the wage by $F_{L_i} = w_i$.

In this framework the world capital market equilibrium can be described by the following two conditions: First, the marginal product of capital net of taxes has to be equal in all countries, i.e., $F_{K1} - t_1 = F_{K2} - t_2 = ... = F_{KN} - t_N$. Second, the aggregate capital stock invested in all countries has to be equal to the world capital endowment, i.e., $K_1 + K_2 + ... + K_N = NS$. These two conditions also determine the influence of capital taxes on the international allocation of capital. Consider a marginal increase in the tax rate in country 1 starting from a symmetric allocation of capital. The following equations describe the effects of such a tax increase (see Appendix):

$$\frac{dK_1}{dt_1} = \frac{N-1}{NF_{KK}} < 0, \quad \frac{dK_{-1}}{dt_1} = -\frac{1}{NF_{KK}} > 0. \tag{1}$$

According to (1) an increase in the tax rate in country 1 causes a capital outflow from country 1 to the other countries (denoted by −1).

With this basic model of the world capital market, the effects of tax competition on equilibrium fiscal policy can be derived in the following. Assume the gov-

---

2   See Zodrow and Mieszkowski (1986) and Wilson (1986). The underprovision hypothesis was formulated earlier by Oates (1972).

3   This section is not meant to be a survey of the vast literature on tax competition. For such a survey, see, e.g., Wilson (1999) or the respective chapters in Wellisch (2000) and Haufler (2001).

4   This formulation of the tax competition model is based on Hoyt (1991).

ernment of country i uses tax income, $T_i = t_i K_i$, to finance the supply of a public consumption good, G_i. Each country is inhabited by one representative citizen with utility from private and public consumption given by $U_i = C_i + V(G_i)$, with $V' > 0$ and $V'' < 0$.[5] $C_i = S[1 + r] + w_i L$ denotes the level of private consumption and $G_i = t_i K_i$ the level of the public consumption good. Governments are assumed to maximize the utility of the representative citizen. The first-order condition for the tax rate in country 1 is $dC_1/dt_1 + V'(G_1)[K_1 + t_1 dK_1/dt_1] = 0$. In a symmetric equilibrium with identical countries all countries set the same tax rate, $t_1 = t_2 = \ldots = t_N$, and the invested capital stock is equal to the capital endowment in each country, $K_i = S$. The influence of a tax increase on private consumption in country 1 is $dC_1/dt_1 = -S$ (see Appendix). Inserting from (1) then yields the following condition to describe the tax rate in the symmetric equilibrium ($G = tS$):

$$[V'(G)-1]S + V'(G)\frac{[N-1]t}{NF_{KK}} = 0. \tag{2}$$

Setting $N = 1$ in equation (2) gives the equilibrium tax rate for the closed economy. In a closed, economy the government supplies the public good on the first-best level where $V'(G) = 1$. With capital mobility ($N > 1$) the tax rate and the level of the public good are set at an inefficiently low level, and the marginal utility of the public good, $V'(G)$, exceeds the marginal costs of 1.

The inefficiency of the tax competition equilibrium is the result of a fiscal externality (Wildasin 1989): If country 1 increases its tax rate, capital moves from country 1 to the other countries, increasing the tax base there. In the noncooperative equilibrium the government of country 1 does not take this externality on the foreign tax base into account and as a result sets the tax rate at a level below the first-best optimum.

With the specification of the tax competition model presented here, the effects of an increase in the intensity of fiscal competition can be derived by considering an increase in the number of countries competing for capital. Differentiating (2) yields $dt/dN < 0$. The underprovision problem thus becomes more severe the more countries participate in competition for internationally mobile capital (Hoyt 1991).

A straightforward extension of the basic model of tax competition also incorporates endogenous savings:[6] Assume the representative individual in country i

---

5   The assumed quasi-linear utility function simplifies more general specifications in standard tax competition models.

6   For tax competition models with endogenous savings, see, for example, Bucovetsky and Wilson (1991) or Giovannini (1991). The presentation in this paper is based on Lorz (1997).

saves S_i to maximize the two-period utility function $U_i = U(C_{1i}) + C_{2i} + V(G_i)$,[7] with $C_{1i} = Q - S_i$ and $C_{2i} = S_i[1+r] + w_i L$ as the respective consumption levels in periods 1 and 2 ($U' > 0$ and $U'' < 0$). Q denotes an exogenously given wealth level of the individual in period 1. The first-order condition for savings is then given by $U'(Q - S) = 1 + r$.[8] Adding this equation to the model of the capital market then leads to (see Appendix)

$$\frac{dK_1}{dt_1} = \frac{N - \gamma}{N \cdot F_{KK}} < 0, \quad \frac{dK_{-1}}{dt_1} = -\frac{\gamma}{N \cdot F_{KK}} > 0, \quad \text{with } \gamma = \frac{U''}{U'' + F_{KK}}. \tag{3}$$

According to (3), the capital stock is not fixed even in a closed economy ($N = 1$). Instead, an increase in the capital tax rate causes a negative intertemporal effect on domestic savings.[9] The term γ ($0 < \gamma < 1$) determines the size of this intertemporal effect. The lower γ is, the stronger the reaction of domestic savings is on an increase in the tax rate and the lower the spillover is to the other countries. However, as γ exceeds zero, the fiscal externality remains positive in the case of endogenous savings.

Other extensions of the basic model drop the symmetry assumption. Bucovetsky (1991) and Wilson (1991) analyze tax competition between countries differing with respect to their size. The smaller a country is, the more pronounced the reaction of the capital stock is on an increase in the tax rate and the lower the tax rate of this country is in the tax competition equilibrium. Because of its lower tax rate, a relatively small country attracts capital from larger countries. Asymmetric tax competition can be illustrated most easily by considering the limit case of a world consisting of a small open country with no influence on the world interest rate and a large country. Capital mobility, then, does not influence the equilibrium tax rate of the large country, whereas the small country lowers its tax rate and thereby attracts capital from the large country. Starting from this equilibrium, the small country does not benefit from a cooperative increase in its tax to the level of the large country – otherwise, it would have increased it unilaterally. The small country therefore needs to be compensated to accept a harmonization of capital taxes.

Countries may be heterogeneous not only with respect to their size but also with respect to technology or relative factor endowments. They may then use tax policy to influence the world interest rate strategically – comparable to an optimum tariff in international goods trade (Kemp 1962). In this case, capital taxes do

---

[7]   Persson and Tabellini (1992) employ this utility function in their model of tax competition and redistribution (see also Section 3 in this paper).

[8]   As the utility function is assumed to be linear with respect to second-period consumption, the first-order condition for savings is the same in all countries. The index i therefore can be dropped.

[9]   With the assumed utility function, an increase in the tax rate has no income effect on individual savings, so that the tax influence on savings is unambiguously negative.

not necessarily decline in all countries if capital mobility is introduced. Capital-importing countries may instead have an incentive to increase the tax rate.

A further reason why openness does not necessarily cause a decline in tax rates is tax exportation. Tax exportation may occur if foreigners earn rents in a certain country. The government of this country then has an incentive to tax away these rents (see Mintz and Tulkens 1996, or Huizinga and Nielsen 1997).

2.2   Tax Competition with Labor Taxes

So far it has been assumed in this paper that the source-based tax on capital is the only tax governments may use to finance their expenditures. With a fixed supply of labor, this assumption may appear somewhat arbitrary, as governments could raise taxes on labor to finance the public good without having any effects on the allocation of labor or capital. With an endogenous labor supply, however, taxes on labor are no longer lump-sum taxes and capital mobility may again influence the level of taxes and public expenditures.

To illustrate the potential implications of capital mobility for labor taxation, assume the representative individual in country i decides about the level of labor supply needed to maximize the utility function of $U_i = C_i - Z(L_i) + V(G_i)$, with $Z(L_i)$ as the disutility of labor supply ($Z' > 0$ and $Z'' > 0$). The first-order condition for individual labor supply is then given by $w_i = Z'(L_i)$. For simplicity, capital supply is assumed to be exogenous, as in the basic tax competition model. The government in country i finances the public good, G_i, using a proportional tax on the employment of labor, with τ_i as the labor tax rate. The budget constraint of the government implies $G_i = \tau_i L_i$. The profit of the firm in country i is $\pi_i = F(K_i, L_i) - \tau_i L_i - w_i L_i - [1 + r]K_i$. Having made these assumptions, the following influence of an increase in the labor tax rate on the allocation of labor and capital can be derived (see Appendix):

$$\frac{dL_1}{d\tau_1} = \frac{1}{F_{LL} - Z''} - \frac{F_{KL}}{F_{LL} - Z''}\frac{dK_1}{d\tau_1} < 0, \qquad \frac{dL_{-1}}{d\tau_1} = -\frac{F_{KL}}{F_{LL} - Z''}\frac{dK_{-1}}{d\tau_1} > 0,$$

$$\frac{dK_1}{d\tau_1} = -\frac{S}{LZ''}\frac{N-1}{N} < 0, \qquad \frac{dK_{-1}}{d\tau_1} = \frac{S}{LZ''}\frac{1}{N} > 0. \qquad (4)$$

The first term of $dL_1/d\tau_1$ in (4) shows the marginal influence of the labor tax on the supply of labor with a fixed capital stock. With the assumed utility function, this influence is negative, such that labor supply declines with an increase in the labor tax rate. In an open economy the tax also causes a capital outflow, $dK_1/d\tau_1 < 0$, that additionally lowers the quantity of labor supplied.

The government of country i sets the labor tax rate τ_i to maximize the utility of its representative citizen. Inserting from (4) and setting $w_i = Z'(L_i)$ yields the following first-order condition for the tax rate in the symmetric equilibrium of labor tax competition ($G = G(\tau)$ and $L = L(\tau)$):

$$[V'(G)-1]L + \frac{\tau V'(G)}{F_{LL} - Z''} - \frac{\tau V'(G)F_{LL}[N-1]}{Z''[F_{LL}-Z'']N} = 0. \tag{5}$$

According to (5), the first-order condition with capital mobility ($N > 1$) differs from the first-order condition in a closed economy ($N = 1$). The influence of tax competition on the labor tax rate can be obtained by deriving $d\tau/dN$ from (5). The number of countries, N, influences the left-hand side (*lhs*) of (5) according to *dlhs/dN* < 0. Assuming *dlhs/dτ* < 0 then yields $d\tau/dN < 0$.[10] An increase in the number of countries competing for capital then lowers the equilibrium labor tax rate and the supplied level of the public good.

Bucovetsky and Wilson (1991) analyze the case in which governments simultaneously decide about capital and labor taxes in a model with endogenous capital and labor supply. They show that the supplied level of the public good also remains inefficiently low in this case. In addition, if the number of countries approaches infinity, the equilibrium tax rate on capital converges to zero, and the public good is financed entirely with taxes on the immobile factor labor (see also Gordon 1986). With respect to this limit result, the tax competition model predicts a shift in the tax mix from mobile capital to immobile labor.

2.3   Fiscal Competition with Public Inputs

In the basic tax competition model as discussed above, governments provide only public consumption goods. In the real world, however, a major part of public expenditures aims at increasing the productivity of private factors of production. This part of expenditures has the characteristics of a public input rather than that of a public consumption good. Governments then decide not only about the level of public expenditures but also about its composition made up of public consumption goods and public inputs. Fiscal competition can influence this composition of expenditures, as governments may shift their expenditures in favor of public inputs to attract mobile capital (Keen and Marchand 1997). In addition, capital mobility causes a decline in spending for public inputs with respect to the absolute spending level if capital taxes are the only source of financing public expenditures.[11]

---

[10]   The inequality *dlhs/dτ* < 0 can be interpreted as a stability condition for the equilibrium (see also Dixit 1986).

[11]   For the second result, see also Zodrow and Mieszkowski (1986), Gerber and Hewitt (1987), and Matsumoto (1998).

To derive these two results, assume the government in country i provides a public input, I_i, in addition to the public consumption good, G_i.[12] The public input enters the production function according to $F(K_i, L_i, I_i)$. This production function is assumed to be linearly homogenous with respect to both private inputs, K_i and L_i, such that it exhibits increasing returns to scale with respect to all inputs, K_i, L_i, and I_i. The government decides about the level of the public input in addition to the tax rate, t_i. The budget constraint, $T_i \equiv I_i + G_i$, then determines the level of the public consumption good as a residual. The influence of the tax rate on the allocation of capital is still given by equation (1). The influence of the level of the public input is given by

$$\frac{dK_1}{dI_1} = -\frac{[N-1]F_{KI}}{NF_{KK}} > 0, \quad \frac{dK_{-1}}{dI_1} = \frac{F_{KI}}{NF_{KK}} < 0. \tag{6}$$

According to (6), the government of country 1 can attract capital from abroad by increasing the level of the public input and holding the capital tax rate fixed.

The government of country 1 chooses the tax rate, t_1, and the level of the public input, I_1, to maximize $U = C_1 + V(G_1)$ with (1), (6) and $G_1 = t_1 k_1 - I_1$. The first-order condition for the tax rate in the symmetric equilibrium is given by (2). The first-order condition for the equilibrium level of the public input is[13]

$$F_I - V'(G)\left[1 + \frac{[N-1]F_{KI} t}{NF_{KK}}\right] = 0. \tag{7}$$

In a closed economy ($N = 1$), the government provides the public consumption good and the public input on the first-best level, where $V'(G) = F_I = 1$. With capital mobility ($N > 1$), public expenditures are biased towards the public input: $V'(G) > F_I$ in (7) for $N > 1$.[14] In addition, from inserting (2) into (7) it can be shown that $F_I > 1$ for $N > 1$.[15] Public inputs are then underprovided in the equilibrium if they are exclusively financed with capital taxes.

---

[12] I_i is assumed to be a pure public input that is not subject to congestion. For the case of publicly provided private inputs, see, e.g., Oates and Schwab (1988, 1991).

[13] The influence of I_i on aggregate factor income is $dC_i/dI_i = SF_{KI} + LF_{LI}$. The property $KF_K + LF_L = F$, which follows from the assumption of constant returns to scale with respect to K and L, implies $KF_{KI} + LF_{LI} = F_I$.

[14] Keen and Marchand (1997) show that welfare could be increased without changing the tax rate if all countries spent less on the supply of the public input and more on the public consumption good.

[15] Inserting from (2) into (7) yields $F_I NSF_{KK} + [N-1] F_I t = NSF_{KK} + [N-1] F_{KI} St$. With $SF_{KI} = F_I - LF_{LI}$, this leads to the equation $NSF_{KK}[1 - F_I] = [N-1] LF_{LI} t$. For $F_{LI} > 0$, this implies $F_I > 1$.

2.4   Tax Competition and Unemployment

Governments may compete for mobile capital not only because they can use it as a tax base to finance their expenditures, but also because, in a world with unemployment, they can use capital to increase labor demand and thereby the employment level. Thus, when competing for mobile capital, governments may consider reducing unemployment an additional reason for reducing taxes and public spending.

As there are many potential explanations for the existence of unemployment, there are also many potential ways to incorporate unemployment in a tax competition framework. Perhaps the most straightforward way is to assume rigid wages that exceed the full employment level. The tax competition equilibrium is derived under this assumption in the following.[16] For reasons that will become clear below, the model of the capital market is slightly modified: First, there are only two countries in the world ($i = 1, 2$). Second, capital is assumed to be imperfectly mobile between these two countries; the representative individual in country i faces strictly convex mobility costs of investing in the foreign country (as in Persson and Tabellini 1992). For simplicity, these costs are assumed to be quadratic.

With X as the net stock of foreign investment of country 1 in country 2 ($X \geq 0$) and with c as the marginal mobility costs, the capital market equilibrium is given by $F_K(S - X, L_1) - t_1 = F_K(S + X, L_2) - t_2 - cX$. The respective wage in both countries is fixed at $\overline{w}$ on a level exceeding the full employment wage. The equations $F_L(S - X, L_1) = \overline{w}$ and $F_L(S + X, L_2) = \overline{w}$ then determine labor demand and employment in both countries. A marginal increase in the capital tax rate in country 1 influences foreign investment and labor demand according to the following equations (see Appendix):

$$\frac{dX}{dt_1} = \frac{1}{c} > 0, \quad \frac{dL_1}{dt_1} = -\frac{L}{S}\frac{dX}{dt_1} < 0, \quad \frac{dL_2}{dt_1} = \frac{L}{S}\frac{dX}{dt_1} > 0. \tag{8}$$

According to (8), an increase in the tax rate causes a capital outflow to the foreign country. This in turn increases labor demand and the level of employment in the foreign country and reduces the level of employment in the home country. The lower the marginal mobility costs c, the larger the tax effects are on capital and employment. From (8) it also becomes clear why imperfect capital mobility is assumed: With perfect capital mobility, $c \to 0$, foreign investment and labor demand react perfectly elastically on a marginal change in the capital tax rate. This is the outcome of the simplifying constant returns to scale assumption with two produc-

---

16   Beck (1983) already considered fixed wages and unemployment in his early simulation study of tax competition. A more recent contribution is Huang (1994). This section is based partly on Lorz (1997).

tion factors. Marginal adjustment costs prevent factor allocation from reacting in such an extreme manner.

The influence of the capital tax on the aggregate net factor income in country 1 is $dC_1/dt_1 = -S + \overline{w}\, dL_1/dt_1$ (see Appendix). The government maximizes $U_1 = C_1 + V(G_1)$.[17] The first-order condition for the equilibrium tax rate in the symmetric equilibrium is then given by

$$[V'(G)-1]S - tV'(G)\frac{dX}{dt_1} - \frac{\overline{w}L}{S}\frac{dX}{dt_1} = 0, \tag{9}$$

with dX/dt_1 from (8). The first two terms in (9) are equivalent to the first-order condition in the basic tax competition model. The third term represents the negative employment effect of the capital tax with capital mobility. In a closed economy with a given capital stock, this employment effect would be absent.

3   Political Economy Aspects of Fiscal Competition

The theory of fiscal competition presented in the preceding section considered competition between welfare-maximizing governments. In such a setting it may not appear overly surprising that fiscal externalities reduce welfare and that the equilibrium with fiscal competition can be inefficient compared with a cooperative solution or compared with the closed economy. This picture might change if political economy aspects are also considered. According to the political economy view, governments do not simply maximize the welfare of a representative citizen: their behavior may be influenced by factors such as redistribution conflicts, self-interest, or lobbying (see, e.g., Perroni and Scharf 1999). This section illustrates how these factors can influence the fiscal competition equilibrium.

3.1   Capital Tax Competition and Redistribution

A capital tax not only contributes to the financing of public expenditures but may also redistribute incomes between households with different capital endowments. Capital mobility then influences the redistribution effects of a capital tax, as the burden of the tax is shifted from the mobile factor capital to immobile factors. As a result, a positive capital tax raised for redistribution is lower in the tax competition equilibrium than in the closed economy. Persson and Tabellini (1992) derive

---

[17]   Concerns regarding redistribution between the employed and the unemployed are neglected here.

this result for symmetric countries in a tax competition model of redistributive capital taxation.[18]

To incorporate redistribution into the basic tax competition model, assume the population of each country can be divided into q groups of individuals that differ with respect to their individual capital endowment. Each group j ($j = 1, ..., q$) is assumed to consist of one representative individual with a capital endowment of S^j ($S^1 < S^2 < ... < S^q$).[19] Aggregate capital endowment is $S = S^1 + S^2 + ... S^q = q\bar{S}$, with $\bar{S}$ defined as the average capital endowment per head. Labor is distributed equally between the q individuals, with an individual and average labor endowment of $\bar{L}$. An increase in the capital tax rate in country 1 influences individual net factor income, $C_1^j = S_1^j[1 + r] + w_1\bar{L}$, according to the equation $dC_1^j/dt_1 = -S_1^j + [S_1^j - K_1/q] F_{KK} dK_1/dt_1$.[20] The capital market equilibrium is determined by the same equations as in the basic model without redistribution. The marginal influence of the tax rate on the capital stock in country 1, dK_1/dt_1, is then again given by (1).

The government in country i maximizes aggregate utility, $W_i = \sum_j \omega^j C_i^j + V(G_i)$, with ω^j being the weight of individual j in the objective function of the government, $\sum_j \omega^j = 1$. This objective function includes the median voter model of electoral competition as a special case (with $\omega^m = 1$ as the weight of the median voter and $\omega^{-m} = 0$). However, it may also represent other settings where non-median individuals have a positive weight in the objective function of the government.

The first-order condition for the capital tax rate in the symmetric equilibrium is

$$[qV'(G)-1]\bar{S}+V'(G)\frac{[N-1]t}{NF_{KK}}+\sum_j \omega^j[\bar{S}-S^j]\frac{1}{N}=0. \tag{10}$$

The first two terms in (10) are equivalent to the basic tax competition equilibrium without redistribution. The third term shows how redistribution influences tax policy. If governments redistribute in favor of capital-poor individuals, i.e., if $\omega^j[\bar{S}-S^j] > 0$, the redistribution term in (10) is positive. This is the case, for example, in a median voter model if the capital endowment of the median voter is

---

[18]   They also consider the case of asymmetric countries where the tax rates do not necessarily decrease in all countries. In addition, they identify a "voting effect" of capital mobility in their model that mitigates the tax competition effect.

[19]   Redistribution is considered in several tax competition models. For example, Haufler (1997) and Lopez et al. (1998) analyze tax competition with redistributive capital taxes in worker/capitalist approaches of redistribution policy. Fuest and Huber (2001) set up a median voter model of tax competition with unequally distributed capital and labor endowments. The model presented here is based on Lorz (1997).

[20]   Differentiating yields $dC_1^j/dt_1 = -S_1^j + S_1^j F_{KK} dK_1/dt_1 + \bar{L}F_{LK} dK_1/dt_1$. With $F_{KK} K/q + F_{LK}\bar{L} = 0$, the equation in the text can be derived.

lower than the average capital endowment. Capital mobility reduces the size of the redistribution term in (10).[21] With redistribution in favor of capital-poor individuals, this effect causes additional downward pressure on the equilibrium tax rate when there is tax competition.

Considering redistribution not only changes the tax rate in the tax competition equilibrium, it also gives a different picture of the welfare effects of fiscal competition: with redistribution, a decline in the tax rate caused by capital mobility does not necessarily reduce the welfare of all individuals. Instead, capital-rich individuals might benefit from the lower tax burden.

3.2   Taming the Leviathan

An alternative to the view of welfare-maximizing governments has been developed in the Leviathan model of Brennan and Buchanan (1980). They assume that governments are interested in maximizing the surplus of tax revenues over government spending. In such a setting, competition between governments caused by capital mobility may improve the welfare of citizens, as it helps to "tame the Leviathan" (Sinn 1992).

Edwards and Keen (1996) integrate the Leviathan view of the government into a standard model of tax competition.[22] The essence of their approach can be captured as follows: Assume the government in country i maximizes the objective function $Z_i = \beta U_i + [1 - \beta] \Omega_i$ ($0 < \beta < 1$), with $U_i = C_i + V(G_i)$ as the utility of the representative citizen and $\Omega_i = \Omega(R_i)$ as the utility the government derives from the surplus, $R_i = T_i - G_i$, of tax revenues over the costs of providing the public good ($\Omega' > 0$ and $\Omega'' < 0$). Inserting gives $Z_i = \beta C_i + \beta V(t_i K_i - R_i) + [1 - \beta] \Omega(R_i)$. The government determines the tax rate, t_i, and the surplus R_i. The first-order condition for t in the symmetric equilibrium is the same equation (2) as with entirely welfare-maximizing governments (with $G = St - R$). The first-order condition for R in the symmetric equilibrium is

$$- \beta V'(G) + [1 - \beta] \Omega'(R) = 0. \tag{11}$$

According to (11), governments divide tax revenues between the public good, G, and the revenue surplus, R, to equalize the marginal influence of these two ele-

---

[21]   In the limit of $N \to \infty$, the redistribution term completely vanishes from (10).

[22]   Fuest (2000) extends the model of Edwards and Keen (1996) by explicitly considering bureaucracy as an additional player in fiscal competition. He models equilibrium fiscal policy as the outcome of bargaining between the government and bureaucracy. Rauscher (1998, 2000) and Apolte (2001) consider the provision of production inputs in Leviathan-type models of fiscal competition.

ments in the governments' objective function. The number of countries does not enter the first-order condition for R directly. However, the intensity of tax competition has an indirect effect on R, as it changes the tax rate and thus also tax revenues. With the assumed objective function, both R and G are normal goods, such that governments lower R and G if tax revenues decrease. Inserting $R = tS - G$ in (11) and differentiating (2) and (11) yields $dt/dN < 0$, $dG/dN < 0$ and $dR/dN < 0$. Tax competition thus causes a decline in the tax rate and thus also in tax revenues, and this lowers both the level of the public good and the revenue surplus of the government. The total welfare effect of tax competition is indeterminate.

An alternative Leviathan model of fiscal competition has been set up by Besley and Smart (2002). In their approach, there are two types of politicians: purely self-interested Leviathan politicians and benevolent politicians. Besley and Smart (2002) consider two mechanisms to "tame" the Leviathan politicians: electoral competition and tax competition.[23] Both mechanisms interact and the welfare effects of tax competition are generally ambiguous.

3.3   Lobbying by Interest Groups

Fiscal competition and the ability of governments to tax and to redistribute incomes may also influence lobbying of interest groups. For example, it has been shown above that tax competition lowers the redistribution effects of capital taxes with unequally distributed capital incomes. Lobbying for or against this kind of redistribution then may also decrease in the case of capital mobility (Lorz 1998). In the limit case of a small open economy, redistribution conflicts concerning redistribution of capital incomes completely vanish, as capital incomes are determined by the given world interest rate and the incidence of the capital tax is shifted towards the immobile factor.

However, by the same mechanism, new redistribution conflicts may arise in the case of capital mobility. Fiscal competition can thus also cause an increase in lobbying activities. To illustrate this point, assume, for example, that there are two groups of workers, skilled and unskilled, and that each group is represented by one individual.[24] The representative skilled worker is endowed with L^S units of labor, whereas the unskilled is endowed with L^U units, with $L^S > L^U$. Capital is equally distributed, such that both individuals are endowed with $\overline{S}$ units of capital. The influence of a capital tax on the allocation of capital is given by (1), with $S = 2\overline{S}$ and $L = L^S + L^U$. The influence of the capital tax on net incomes is then

---

23   Tax competition is modeled in Besley and Smart (2002) as an increase in the marginal costs of public funds or as yardstick competition.

24   This effect is also considered in Lorz (2001) in a model of local public input provision where immobile land is unequally distributed between households.

$dC_1^S/dt_1 = -\overline{S} + 0.5\ [L^S - L^U]\ F_{KL}\ dK_1/dt_1$ as well as $dC_1^U/dt_1 = -\overline{S} - 0.5\ [L^S - L^U]$ $F_{KL}dK_1/dt_1$.[25] In a closed economy, $dK_1/dt_1 = 0$, and the tax on capital does not redistribute between the skilled and the unskilled. In an open economy, however, tax-induced changes in the invested capital stock have a stronger effect on the income of the skilled than on the income of the unskilled ($dC_1^S/dt_1 < dC_1^U/dt_1$). Capital mobility then causes a redistribution conflict between skilled and unskilled workers, as both want a different tax rate on mobile capital. This redistribution conflict is absent in the closed economy.

Wilson and Wildasin (2001) formulate a model that combines lobbying by capital owners with lobbying by sector-specific labor. Their model endogenizes the formation of interest groups assuming fixed costs of organizing common interests. In such a setting, an interest group representing capital owners may only exist in a closed economy but not with capital mobility, whereas sector-specific labor may only organize in an open economy.

4   Some Empirical Impressions

Against the background of the theoretical results on fiscal competition, the question arises as to how fiscal policy has actually developed in recent decades and whether trends are visible that are in accordance with the theoretical results on fiscal competition.

Table 1 depicts tax revenues in the OECD between 1970 and 1999. The table does not show a race to the bottom in this period. Instead, total tax revenues (including social security contributions) increased from 28.8 percent of GDP in 1970 to 37.3 percent of GDP in 1999. If social security contributions are excluded from this figure ("pure" tax revenues in Table 1), the tax increase is less pronounced but still substantial – from 23.2 percent of GDP in 1970 to 27.7 percent in 1999.

4.1   Capital and Labor Taxes

As the development of tax revenues in Table 1 does not show a decline in aggregate tax levels in industrialized economies, the focus is now shifted to the composition of taxes. Figure 1 depicts average tax revenues in the EU as published by

---

[25]   The factor income of the skilled individual is $C_1^s = \overline{S}[1 + r] + w_1 L^s$. Differentiating yields the equation $dC_1^s/dt_1 = -\overline{S} + \overline{S}F_{KK}\ dK_1/dt_1 + L^s F_{LK}\ dK_1/dt_1$. With $K_1F_{KK} + [L^S + L^U]\ F_{LK} = 0$ and $K_1 = 2\overline{S}$, the equation for dC_1^s/dt_1 in the text follows. dC_1^U/dt_1 can be derived in the same way.

Table 1: Tax Revenues as a Share of GDP (OECD average)

	1970	1980	1990	1999
Total tax revenues	28.8	32.1	35.0	37.3
"Pure" tax revenues	23.3	24.7	26.8	27.7

Source: OECD (2000).

Eurostat (2000) – divided into revenues from taxes on capital, labor, and consumption. According to Figure 1, the revenues from labor taxes increased from 16.7 percent of GDP in 1970 to 23.6 percent in 1997, whereas capital tax revenues only increased from 6.5 percent to 7.8 percent of GDP. The increase in revenues from labor taxes was therefore more pronounced than the increase in revenues from capital taxes. As a result, the share of labor taxes relative to total tax revenues increased (from 48.5 percent to 55.1 percent).[26] However, as Figure 1 also shows, the main part of the increase in labor tax revenues occurred already between 1970 and 1980 (5.5 percentage points). After this period, labor tax revenues increased only slightly, by 1.4 percentage points.

As a large part of tax revenues can be attributed to social security contributions, the question arises as to what degree social security contributions cause the increase in total labor taxes. Table 2 therefore divides revenues from taxes on employed labor into "pure" taxes and social security contributions. As this table shows, the trend in social security contributions is roughly comparable to the trend in "pure" labor taxes. Both variables increased mainly in the 1970s, whereas from 1980 to 1997 "pure" labor taxes stayed constant and social security contributions increased only slightly. Of course, the absolute increase in labor taxes is far lower if social security contributions are excluded: "pure" labor taxes as a share of GDP increased by only 2.4 percentage points from 1970 to 1997.

The increase in tax revenues in Figure 1 may not show trends in tax rates accurately because tax revenues as a share of GDP also include changes in the respective tax base relative to GDP. Figure 2 therefore depicts estimates for implicit tax rates derived from national accounts.[27] These tax rates are calculated by dividing tax revenues by a measure for the corresponding tax base. Eurostat (2000) publishes such implicit tax rates on employed labor, consumption, and other factors.

---

[26]   Comparable to the OECD data in Table 1, total tax revenues as a share of GDP increased substantially in the EU-9 countries – from 34.3 percent of GDP in 1970 to 42.8 percent of GDP in 1997.

[27]   Starting with Mendoza et al. (1994), several authors and institutions have computed implicit tax rates from national accounts data. See Martinez-Mongay (2000) and Volkerink and de Haan (2001) for conceptual surveys and own estimates.

Figure 1: Tax Revenues in Europe (tax revenues as a share of GDP, weighted EU-9 average; countries: B, DK, D, F, IRL, I, NL, L, UK)

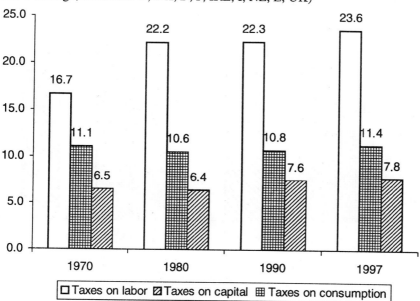

Source: Eurostat (2000); own calculations.

The tax rate on other factors is an aggregate measure that includes taxes on capital but also taxes on self-employed labor. As Figure 2 shows, the development of the implicit tax rate on labor differs from the development of the respective tax revenues. The implicit tax rate on employed labor continued to increase between 1980 and 1997, by 7.0 percentage points, whereas revenues from taxes on employed labor increased by only 1.4 percentage points (Table 2). The tax rate on other factors declined from 1980 onwards to reach only a slightly higher level in 1997 than in 1970.

Table 2: Taxes on Employed Labor as a Share of GDP (weighted EU-9 average; countries: B, DK, D, F, IRL, I, NL, L, UK)

	1970	1980	1990	1997
Total	14.7	19.8	20.0	21.2
"Pure" labor taxes	5.3	7.7	7.4	7.7
Social security contributions	9.4	12.1	12.6	13.5

Source: Eurostat (2000); own calculations.

Figure 2: Implicit Tax Rates in Europe (weighted EU-9 average; countries: B, DK, D, F, IRL, I, NL, L, UK)

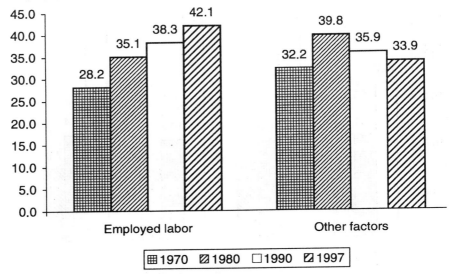

Source: Eurostat (2000); own calculations.

4.2   Corporate Taxes

The implicit tax rate on other factors may appear to be too broadly defined as a measure for taxes on mobile capital.[28] Figure 3 therefore shows trends in the tax rate on corporate income in Europe as calculated from two recent empirical studies. These studies derive the effective corporate tax rate from micro data using financial accounts of individual firms.[29] Taxes on corporate income make up a substantial part of capital income taxes, such that their development may be indicative of trends in total capital taxes.[30] The first series in Figure 3, based on Altshuler et al. (2000), shows effective tax burdens of subsidiaries of U.S. companies between 1980 and 1992. The second series, based on Gorter and de Mooij (2001),

---

[28]   See Devereux et al. (2001), who discuss and compare several indicators for the development of the tax rate for mobile capital.

[29]   Another way to estimate effective tax rates from micro data is to consider hypothetical investment projects and to calculate marginal or average tax burdens for these projects (see, e.g., Chennells and Griffith 1997).

[30]   The tax on capital income, however, is also influenced by the way corporate and personal income taxes are integrated (see Genser and Haufler 1999).

Figure 3: Effective Average Corporate Tax Rates (weighted EU-8 average; countries: B, DK, D, F, IRL, I, NL, UK)

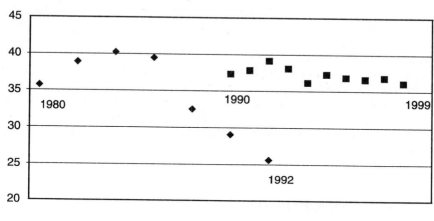

◆ Altshuler et al.   ■ Gorter and de Mooij

Source: Altshuler et al. (2000); Gorter and de Mooij (2001); Eurostat (2000); own calculations.

depicts effective tax rates in European companies between 1990 and 1999. As both series are based on different company samples and different time periods, their results are not directly comparable. In addition, both series show different trends in corporate taxation over time: according the data used by Altshuler et al. (2000), the average effective tax rate of U.S. companies investing in Europe declined by 10 percentage points between 1980 and 1992 from 36 to 26 percent; according to the data used by Gorter and de Mooij (2001) the average effective tax rate of European companies declined only by one percentage point from 37 percent in 1990 to 36 percent in 1999.

Two additional empirical studies contribute to this heterogeneous picture: Chennells and Griffith (1997) estimate average tax rates from accounting data of companies in 6 OECD countries between 1985 and 1994. According to their estimates the average corporate tax rate fell by 7.4 percentage points from a level of 40.0 percent in 1985 to 32.6 percent in 1994. Nicodeme (2001) calculates average effective corporate tax rates in manufacturing for 11 EU countries and even finds a rise in tax rates from 12.8 to 15.5 percent between the two periods 1990/1994 and 1995/1999.[31]

---

[31]   The estimated tax rates in Nicodeme (2001) are comparatively low because they are computed by using gross operating profits before depreciation. This may also explain some of the difference between the estimates of Nicodeme (2001) and of Gorter and de Mooij (2001) with respect to the development of tax rates in the 1990s.

To summarize, the tax data considered show an increase in the tax rate on labor in Europe that does not seem to have occurred in the case of the tax rate on capital. There is also some indication that average corporate tax rates in Europe have declined. Aggregate tax revenues, however, have not declined in recent decades; rather, they have increased substantially. The general empirical impression is therefore inconclusive. Of course, the trend in tax rates or tax revenues is not a direct indicator of the influence of locational competition on fiscal policy. It is also an indicator of other important factors such as demographic change, economic growth, or labor market conditions. However, it shows that – although some tax changes have taken place – the welfare state has not collapsed and that tax sources other than immobile labor have still contributed substantially to the financing of the welfare state.[32]

5   Concluding Remarks

Do national governments lose their maneuvering space in the era of locational competition? This paper has identified a couple of theoretical reasons why this may indeed be the case: locational competition increases the elasticity of the tax base – not only with respect to mobile but also to immobile production factors, it changes the redistribution effects of fiscal policy, it has consequences for the employment of immobile labor, and it alters the framework for public expenditure policy. The policy implications that follow from theoretical models on locational competition are less clear. The standard theory of tax and expenditure competition focuses on externalities in competition between welfare-maximizing governments. In this approach, fiscal competition can lead to inefficiencies with respect to the level and composition of taxes and public expenditures. Incorporating political economy aspects into the theory, however, gives a different picture of the welfare effects of fiscal competition: competition between governments then does not need to be bad for all citizens but instead may also have positive welfare implications. The potential positive and negative welfare effects of fiscal competition are not exclusive, but coexist at the same time. Further research that helps to assess the relative importance of these effects appears to be necessary.

---

[32]   Several recent regression studies deal with the consequences of trade integration and capital mobility on taxation and the level of public spending (see, e.g., Garrett 1995; Rodrick 1997; Iversen and Cusack 2000; Swank 2002; and Bretschger and Hettich 2002). The empirical picture provided by these studies is generally ambiguous, but, as Schulze and Ursprung (1999: 345) conclude in their extensive literature survey, the evidence "thus far does not lend support to any alarmist view" concerning the nation states' ability to conduct independent fiscal policies.

Appendix

The following equations describe the symmetric capital market equilibrium in the basic tax competition model with a given level of savings, S: $F_{K1} - t_1 = 1 + r$, $F_{K-1} - t_{-1} = 1 + r$ and $K_1 + [N-1] K_{-1} = NS$. Totally differentiating these equations yields $F_{KK} dK_1 - dt_1 = dr$, $F_{KK} dK_{-1} - dt_{-1} = dr$, and $dK_1 + [N-1] dK_{-1} = NdS$. Equation (1) in the text can be derived by setting $dS = dt_{-1} = 0$. The net factor income of the representative citizen in country 1 is $C_1 = S[1 + r] + w_1 L$. Differentiating yields then $dC_1/dt_1 = -S + [SF_{KK} + LF_{LK}] dK_1/dt_1$. With the property $KF_{KK} + LF_{LK} = 0$ of the constant returns to scale production function and with $K = S$, this equation simplifies to $dC_1/dt_1 = -S$.

With endogenous savings, equation $U'(Q - S) = 1 + r$ determines the relationship between the world interest rate and the level of savings. Totally differentiating yields $-U'' dS = dr$. Inserting this term for dr into the equations of the preceding paragraph leads to equation (3) in the text.

In the labor tax version of the model, the first-order conditions are $F_{K1} = F_{K-1}$, $F_{L1} - \tau_1 = w_1$, $F_{L-1} - \tau_{-1} = w_{-1}$, $Z'(L_1) = w_1$, $Z'(L_{-1}) = w_{-1}$, and $K_1 + [N-1] K_{-1} = NS$. Totally differentiating and setting $d\tau_{-1} = dS = 0$ yields then $F_{KK} dK_1 + F_{KL} dL_1 = F_{KK} dK_{-1} + F_{KL} dL_{-1}$, $F_{LK} dK_1 + [F_{LL} - Z''] dL_1 = d\tau_1$, $F_{LK} dK_{-1} + [F_{LL} - Z''] dL_{-1} = 0$, and $dK_1 + [N-1] dK_{-1} = 0$. From these equations and with $F_{KK} F_{LL} - [F_{KL}]^2 = 0$ and $SF_{KK} + LF_{KL} = 0$, equation (4) in the text can be derived. With $C_i = S[1 + r] + w_i L_i$ the influence of τ_i on private consumption can be derived as $dC_i/d\tau_i = -L_i + w_i dL_i/d\tau_i$.

The first-order conditions for the capital market equilibrium in the tax competition model with adjustment costs and rigid wages are $F_K(S - X, L_1) - t_1 = F_K(S + X, L_2) - t_2 - cX$, $F_L(S - X, L_1) = \overline{w}$, and $F_L(S + X, L_2) = \overline{w}$. Totally differentiating these first-order conditions and setting $dS = dt_2 = d\overline{w} = 0$ yields $-F_{KK} dX + F_{KL} dL_1 - dt_1 = F_{KK} dX + F_{KL} dL_2 - cdX$, $-F_{LK} dX + F_{LL} dL_1 = 0$, and $F_{LK} dX + F_{LL} dL_2 = 0$. With $F_{KK} F_{LL} - [F_{KL}]^2 = 0$, $KF_{KL} + LF_{LL} = 0$, $X = 0$, and $L_1 = L_2$ these conditions lead to equation (8) in the text. Aggregate net factor income in country 1 for $X \geq 0$ is given by $C_1 = [S - X][F_{K1} - t_1] + X [F_{K2} - t_2] - 0.5cX^2 + \overline{w} L_1$. Inserting the first-order condition for X yields $C_1 = S[F_{K1} - t_1] + 0.5cX^2 + \overline{w} L_1$. After differentiating, this yields $dC_1/dt_1 = -S - F_{KK} S dX/dt_1 + F_{KL} S dL_1/dt_1 + cX dX/dt_1 + \overline{w} dL_1/dt_1$. Inserting from (8), setting $X = 0$, and using the property $KF_{KK} + LF_{KL} = 0$ then yields $dC_1/dt_1 = -S + \overline{w} dL_1/dt_1$.

Bibliography

Altshuler, R., H. Grubert, and T.S. Newlon (2000). Has U.S. Investment Abroad Become More Sensitive to Tax Rates? In J.R. Hines (ed.), *International Taxation and Multinational Activity*. Chicago: University of Chicago Press.

Apolte, T. (2001). How Tame Will Leviathan Become in Institutional Competition? *Public Choice* 107: 359–381.

Beck, J.H. (1983). Tax Competition, Uniform Assessment and the Benefit Principle. *Journal of Urban Economics* 13: 127–146.

Besley, T., and M. Smart (2002). Does Tax Competition Raise Voter Welfare? CEPR Discussion Paper 3131. London.

Brennan, G., and J. M. Buchanan (1980). *The Power to Tax: Analytical Foundations of a Fiscal Constitution*. Cambridge: Cambridge University Press.

Bretschger, L., and F. Hettich (2002). Globalisation, Capital Mobility and Tax Competition: Theory and Evidence for OECD Countries. *European Journal of Political Economy* 18: 695–716.

Bucovetsky, S. (1991). Asymmetric Tax Competition. *Journal of Urban Economics* 30: 167–181.

Bucovetsky, S., and J.D. Wilson (1991). Tax Competition with Two Tax Instruments. *Regional Science and Urban Economics* 21: 333–350.

Chennells, L., and R. Griffith (1997). *Taxing Profits in a Changing World*. London: Institute for Fiscal Studies.

Devereux, M.P., R. Griffith, and A. Klemm (2001). Have Taxes on Mobile Capital Declined? Mimeo. Institute for Fiscal Studies, London.

Dixit, A. (1986). Comparative Statics for Oligopoly. *International Economic Review* 27: 107–122.

Edwards, J., and M. Keen (1996). Tax Competition and Leviathan. *European Economic Review* 40: 113–134.

Eurostat (2000). *Structures of the Taxation Systems in the European Union: 1970–1997*. Luxemburg.

Fuest, C. (2000). The Political Economy of Tax Competition as a Bargaining Game between Bureaucrats and Politicians. *Public Choice* 103: 357–382.

Fuest, C., and B. Huber (2001). Tax Competition and Tax Coordination in a Median Voter Model. *Public Choice* 107: 97–113.

Garrett, G. (1995). Capital Mobility, Trade, and the Domestic Politics of Economic Policy. *International Organization* 49: 657–687.

Genser, B., and A. Haufler (1999). Harmonization of Corporate Income Taxation in the EU. *Aussenwirtschaft* 54: 319–348.

Gerber, R.I., and D.P. Hewitt (1987). Decentralized Tax Competition for Business Capital and National Economic Efficiency. *Journal of Regional Science* 27: 451–460.

Giovannini, A. (1991). International Capital Mobility and Tax Avoidance. *BNL Quarterly Review* 177: 197–223.

Gordon, R.H. (1986). Taxation of Investment and Savings in a World Economy. *American Economic Review* 76: 1087–1102.

Gorter, J., and R. de Mooij (2001). *Capital Income Taxation in Europe: Trends and Trade-offs*. Den Haag: SDU.

Haufler, A. (1997). Factor Taxation, Income Distribution and Capital Market Integration. *Scandinavian Journal of Economics* 99: 425–446.

Haufler, A. (2001). *Taxation in a Global Economy*. Cambridge: Cambridge University Press.

Hayek, F.A. von (1978). Competition as a Discovery Procedure. In F.A. von Hayek, *New Studies in Philosophy, Politics, Economics, and the History of Ideas*. Chicago: University of Chicago Press.

Hoyt, W.H. (1991). Property Taxation, Nash Equilibrium, and Market Power. *Journal of Urban Economics* 30: 123–131.

Huang, Y. (1994). *Tax Competition with Involuntary Unemployment*. CIER Economic Monograph Series 34. Taipeh.

Huizinga, H., and S.B. Nielsen (1997). Capital Income and Profit Taxation with Foreign Ownership of Firms. *Journal of International Economics* 42: 149–165.

Iversen, T., and T.R. Cusack (2000). The Causes of Welfare State Expansion: Deindustrialization or Globalization? *World Politics* 52: 313–349.

Keen, M., and M. Marchand (1997). Fiscal Competition and the Pattern of Public Spending. *Journal of Public Economics* 66: 33–53.

Kemp, M.C. (1962). The Benefits and Costs of Private Investments from Abroad: Comment. *Economic Record* 38: 108–111.

Lopez, S., M. Marchand, and P. Pestieau (1998). A Simple Two-Country Model of Redistributive Capital Income Taxation. *Finanzarchiv* 55: 445–460.

Lorz, O. (1997). *Standortwettbewerb bei internationaler Kapitalmobilität – Eine modelltheoretische Untersuchung*. Kieler Studien 284. Tübingen: Mohr Siebeck.

Lorz, O. (1998). Capital Mobility, Tax Competition and Lobbying for Redistributive Capital Taxation. *European Journal of Political Economy* 14: 265–279.

Lorz, O. (2001). On the Effects of Capital Mobility on Local Infrastructure Policy and Rent-Seeking. *Regional Science and Urban Economics* 31: 319–337.

Martinez-Mongay, C. (2000). ECFIN's Tax Rates: Properties and Comparisons with Other Tax Indicators. ECFIN Economic Paper 146. Brussels: European Commission.

Matsumoto, M. (1998). A Note on Tax Competition and Public Input Provision. *Regional Science and Urban Economics* 28: 465–473.

Mendoza, E.G., A. Razin, and L. Tesar (1994). Effective Tax Rates in Macroeconomics: Cross-Country Estimates of Tax Rates on Factor Incomes and Consumption. *Journal of Monetary Economics* 34: 297–332.

Mintz, J., and H. Tulkens (1996). Optimality Properties of Alternative Systems of Taxation of Foreign Capital Income. *Journal of Public Economics* 60: 373–401.

Nicodeme, G. (2001). Computing Effective Corporate Tax Rates: Comparisons and Results. ECFIN Economic Paper 153. Brussels: European Commission.

Oates, W.E. (1972). *Fiscal Federalism*. New York: Harcourt Brace Jovanovich.

Oates, W.E., and R. Schwab (1988). Economic Competition among Jurisdictions: Efficiency Enhancing or Distortion Inducing? *Journal of Public Economics* 35: 333–354.

Oates, W.E., and R. Schwab (1991). The Allocative and Distributive Implications of Local Fiscal Competition. In D.A. Kenyon and J. Kincaid (eds.), *Competition among State and Local Governments*. Washington, D.C.: Urban Institute Press.

OECD (2000). *Revenue Statistics 1965–1999*. Paris: OECD.

Perroni, C., and K.A. Scharf (1999). Interjurisdictional Tax Competition: A Political-Economy Perspective. In A. Razin and E. Sadka (eds.), *The Economics of Globalization: Policy Perspectives from Public Economics*. Cambridge: Cambridge University Press.

Persson, T., and G. Tabellini (1992). The Politics of 1992: Fiscal Policy and European Integration. *Review of Economic Studies* 59: 689–701.

Rauscher, M. (1998) Leviathan and Competition among Jurisdictions: The Case of Benefit Taxation. *Journal of Urban Economics* 44: 59–67.

Rauscher, M. (2000). Interjurisdictional Competition and Public Sector Prodigality: The Triumph of the Market over the State? *Finanzarchiv* 57: 89–105.

Rodrik, D. (1997). *Has Globalisation Gone Too Far?* Washington, D.C.: Institute for International Economics.

Schulze, G., and H. Ursprung (1999). Globalisation of the Economy and the Nation State. *The World Economy* 22: 295–352.

Siebert, H. (2000). The Paradigm of Locational Competition. Kiel Discussion Papers 367. Institute for World Economics, Kiel.

Sinn, S. (1992). The Taming of Leviathan. *Constitutional Political Economy* 3: 177–196.

Swank, D. (2002). *Global Capital, Political Institutions and Policy Change in Developed Welfare States*. Cambridge: Cambridge University Press.

Tiebout, C.M. (1956). A Pure Theory of Local Expenditure. *Journal of Political Economy* 64: 416–424.

Volkerink, B., and J. de Haan (2001). *Tax Ratios: A Critical Survey*. OECD Tax Policy Studies 5. Paris: OECD.

Wellisch, D. (2000). *Theory of Public Finance in a Federal State*. Cambridge: Cambridge University Press.

Wildasin, D.E. (1989). Interjurisdictional Capital Mobility: Fiscal Externality and a Corrective Subsidy. *Journal of Urban Economics* 25: 193–212.

Wilson, J.D. (1986). A Theory of Interregional Tax Competition. *Journal of Urban Economics* 19: 296–315.

Wilson, J.D. (1991). Tax Competition with Interregional Differences in Factor Endowments. *Regional Science and Urban Economics* 21: 423–451.

Wilson, J.D. (1999). Theories of Tax Competition. *National Tax Journal* 52: 269–304.

Wilson, J.D., and D.E. Wildasin (2001). Tax Competition: Bane or Boon? Mimeo. Michigan State University, East Lansing, and University of Kentucky, Lexington.

Zodrow, G., and P. Mieszkowski (1986). Pigou, Tiebout, Property Taxation and the Underprovision of Local Public Goods. *Journal of Urban Economics* 19: 356–370.

Comment on Oliver Lorz

Horst Raff

The paper by Oliver Lorz interprets locational competition as tax competition for mobile capital. Tax competition and its effects on the provision of public goods have been examined in the large literature on local public finance, and the paper does a nice job of reviewing relevant aspects of this literature and evaluating them in the light of the empirical evidence. The starting point of the paper is a basic model with two goods (a private consumption good and a public good), one mobile factor (capital), and one fixed factor (labor) (see Wilson 1999 and Gordon and Hines 2002 for other recent surveys). Using this model and several extensions, the paper points out several consequences of capital mobility. First, tax competition leads to a lower tax on capital, and the tax burden is shifted to immobile labor. Second, this form of tax competition is inefficient if governments maximize social welfare. But it may actually raise welfare if policymakers are motivated by other concerns, such as maximizing tax revenue. The empirical evidence presented provides some support for the basic model.

In my discussion I want to raise four interrelated issues:

1. The predictions of the standard tax competition models presented in the paper are only weakly supported by the data. Tax revenue as a percentage of GDP has gone up in the OECD countries. So at first glance there appears to be no shortage of tax revenue to pay for public goods, at least not yet. Governments seem to have plenty of maneuvering space. This view is of course a bit extreme. There are studies that show a drop in corporate income tax rates, for instance, in Europe (e.g., Benassy-Quere et al. 2000). And, of course, high taxes do not necessarily deter business investment if these taxes finance public inputs such as infrastructure. But one gets the impression that the models discussed in the paper do not capture some important aspects of the problem.

2. The paper sets out to examine "locational competition" (the translation of Standortwettbewerb). But it defines locations in a rather narrow sense as places with a government and a supply of immobile labor. This is certainly a natural first step and one that has led to much fruitful research. But one wonders if there is not something more to "locations" than this. For instance, if we think about locations in geographic space, then distance and transportation or communication costs will play a role. How will tax competition be affected if we consider these types of costs?

3. The paper focuses on the liberalization of capital markets. But barriers to trade have also come down dramatically over the past decades. How does increased capital mobility interact with trade liberalization to determine the degree of tax competition? Do we need to account for the fact that labor mobility, too, has increased?

4. What role do multinational enterprises play in locational competition? The models presented in the paper with their perfect competition, perfect capital mobility, etc., do not fit well the type of economic environments in which multinationals operate.

To address these issues I will briefly discuss two alternative approaches to "locational competition":

Locational competition as competition between geographic locations

Suppose locations are separated in geographic space and there are trading costs. Further, assume that technology exhibits increasing returns to scale, consumer preferences exhibit love of variety, and market structure is monopolistically competitive. Combining this with factor mobility puts us into the framework of the "new economic geography," where economic activity is subject to agglomeration effects (see Fujita et al. 1999). If spatial agglomeration takes place, firms are no longer indifferent between locations: they prefer locations with more input suppliers and more customers. Governments in attractive ("core") locations may be able to charge higher tax rates than governments in the periphery. In this context, trade liberalization may strengthen agglomeration effects and lead to higher equilibrium taxes (see, e.g., Baldwin and Krugmann 2000 and Ludema and Wooton 2000).

Locational competition as competition to influence the location decisions of multinational enterprises

There is substantial empirical evidence that countries do engage in tough competition for foreign direct investment (FDI). To a significant extent this competition is based on incentives. According to UNCTAD (1996), the use of fiscal incentives to attract FDI, such as tax holidays, has increased in Europe, the United States, and Canada since the mid-1980s. Case studies of incentive-based competition in Europe suggest that multinational firms, after identifying possible locations for a project, shop around for the most attractive combination of location-specific fundamentals and incentives. Econometric studies find that multinational enterprises react to differences in tax rates (see, e.g., Hines 1996). Hence, in the case of FDI, one can clearly see how pertinent the issue of locational competition is.

The question is to what extent this competition offsets the potential benefits of FDI, such as greater production efficiency, knowledge transfer, etc. The answer will partly depend on the degree of product-market integration. If tariff barriers fall, countries lose one instrument with which they can influence FDI location decisions, forcing them to rely more on taxes and incentives and increasing competition with these instruments (Raff 2002). On the other hand, if some of the benefits that FDI can provide can also be obtained through trade, then a reduction in trade barriers may mean that there is less incentive for countries to compete for FDI and equilibrium taxes may rise (Haufler and Wooton 1999).

Bibliography

Baldwin, R.E., and P. Krugman (2000). Agglomeration, Integration and Tax Harmonization. Mimeo. Graduate Institute of International Studies, Geneva.

Benassy-Quere, A., L. Fontagne, and A. Lahreche-Revil (2000). Foreign Direct Investment and the Prospects for Tax Coordination in Europe. CEPII Document de travail No. 2000-06. Paris.

Fujita, M., P. Krugman, and A. Venables (1999). *The Spatial Economy: Cities, Regions, and International Trade*. Cambridge: MIT Press.

Gordon, R.H., and J.R. Hines (2002). International Taxation. NBER Working Paper 8854. Cambridge, Mass.

Haufler, A., and A. Wooton (1999). Country Size and Tax Competition for Foreign Direct Investment. *Journal of Public Economics* 71: 121–139.

Hines, J.R. (1996). Altered States: Taxes and the Location of Foreign Direct Investment in America. *American Economic Review* 86: 1076–1094.

Ludema, R.D., and I. Wooton (2000). Economic Geography and the Fiscal Effects of Regional Integration. *Journal of International Economics* 52: 331–357.

Raff, H. (2002). Preferential Trade Agreements and Tax Competition for Foreign Direct Investment. CESifo Working Paper 763. München.

UNCTAD (United Nations Conference on Trade and Development) (1996). *Incentives and Foreign Direct Investment*. New York: United Nations.

Wilson, J.D. (1999). Theories of Tax Competition. *National Tax Journal* 52: 269–304.

II.
Designing Global Governance

Ann Florini

From Protest to Participation: The Role of Civil Society in Global Governance

Tanks in the streets of Seattle. Molotov cocktails in Prague. Gunfire in Genoa. Such have been the headlines of recent years. Every time world leaders gather, a motley array of demonstrators rings their meetings in protest. But the news stories have rarely addressed the most important questions: Protest against what? What do the protestors want? Who are they? Can and should they be accommodated? If so, how?

This paper addresses those questions. First, it defines the concept of civil society, that amorphous realm of human associations that fills the space between families and the state, of which the protesters are a part. Then it focuses on the advocacy organizations that are the part of civil society most relevant to global governance, exploring who they are, why they have become so prominent, and why they are so concerned about globalization. Third, it examines what should be done – what demands are being made and how those demands should be addressed. The paper ends by exploring the broad question of global governance and civil society's role therein.

1   Civil Society

Civil society is a broad and much-contested term.[1] In American usage, it refers to the whole sweep of human associations beyond the scale of the family that are neither governmental nor (primarily) profit-seeking. Continental Europeans tend to include the for-profit sector as part of civil society. This paper follows the American definition, treating civil society as the "third sector" (beyond state and market).

---

[1]   For a useful review of the literature on defining civil society, see Najam (1996). See also Hann and Dunn (1996) and Hunt (1999).

Even excluding the business sector, civil society is an enormous arena. Included within its ambit is everything from parent-teacher associations to Amnesty International to terrorist networks. Although the terms tend to be used interchangeably, "civil society" and "non-governmental organizations" are not the same thing. Civil society includes NGOs, but also book clubs, neighborhood associations, and transnational chat groups. NGOs are legally recognized non-governmental entities that pursue public purposes. The advocacy organizations that make up most of the protest movement tend to be NGOs.

Civil society has existed in something approaching its current form since the rise of the nation-state system more than three centuries ago, often ignored or misunderstood, yet growing in significance all the while. The term "civil society" emerged during the Scottish Enlightenment, as thinkers struggled to come up with alternatives to religion as the basis for social morality. As scholar Adam Seligman describes, these philosophers turned to the concept of civil society as "a realm of solidarity held together by the force of moral sentiments and natural affections" strong enough to root individuals in a community of natural sympathy and collective action (Seligman 1992: 33, 57). Others, such as David Hume, failed to share their optimism that individual interests would be so readily subordinated to group goals. Over time, the focus of political philosophy shifted from "civil society" to "citizenship," and the term "civil society" faded away.

But while the term fell out of use, the reality continued to grow. As states grew stronger, they required an industrial base, a legal infrastructure, and a citizenry "with the skills necessary to staff the armies, pay the taxes, and turn the wheels of industry," in the words of Sidney Tarrow (1994: 66). The communications and transportation infrastructure created by the emerging states made it easier for geographically separated individuals and groups to recognize common interests and join together to carry out collective action independently of the state, and often in reaction against increasing state penetration.

Of course, in some cases the state became so dominant and coercive that no political space was left within which alternative societal groupings could emerge. Such was the case in the Soviet Union and, to a lesser extent, some of its satellites. When the Soviet bloc began to disintegrate in the late 1980s, the citizens and new governments of the former Warsaw Pact countries were forced to rethink how more democratic countries deal with the plethora of collective action problems that face all modern societies. Thanks in part to the urgings of Western, and particularly American, funding agencies, the creation of a vigorous civil society was assumed to be a large part of the answer, and the term "civil society" returned to the limelight.

2   The Rise of Activism

At the same time that the concept of civil society was re-emerging, the reality of civil society was taking new shape, for two reasons. The triumph of free-market ideology in the 1980s, along with the spread of new information technologies, spurred moves toward an increasingly integrated global economy whose emergence sparked societal responses, a subject to which we will return below.

Simultaneously, civil society groups in disparate parts of the world began to develop increasingly strong ties with their counterparts elsewhere. This was only partially in response to economic integration. The "anti-globalization" protest movement is only the most visible manifestation of an extraordinary surge in activism, a surge that encompasses many causes and most regions of the globe. There is now a substantial literature of case studies describing transnational civil society networks that have become prominent actors on issues ranging from anti-personnel landmines to human rights to nuclear arms control (see, for example, Florini 2000, Keck and Sikkink 1998, Smith et al. 1997).

A series of broad trends helps to explain the rise of civil society as a force in international politics. One such driver is the information revolution. Information technology has provided powerful new means for transnational civil society to get its message out and to collaborate across borders. The process began with the Western social movements of the 1960s, which were transformed by television. TV made mass social organization cheap. A few mentions on the evening news could do much of what previously required massive organizing (Tarrow 1994: 143). This had been somewhat true in the age of print, but visuals are so much more compelling that they fundamentally shifted the repertoire available to non-state collective action entrepreneurs. The effects were national because television at that time was a national medium.

Now, however, new technologies are free of such geographical constraints. As information technology becomes cheaper and more widely available, what are rapidly becoming such basic tools as email and Internet access are enabling civil society networks to incorporate a vastly greater range of people than ever before possible. The protest events are coordinated via email listserves and web sites, which also serve as means for reaching out to broader constituencies.

In addition, thanks to higher levels of education and material standards of living, more and more people from all parts of the world have entered the middle class, with the skills and leisure time to participate in civil society (see, for example, Yamamoto 1995). Once civil society gets a foothold within a country, it tends to mushroom. People who become accustomed to acting in local civil society are more likely to be drawn into broader networks. Movements and coalitions often recruit their members from existing organizations that serve a different purpose.

Churches were the springboard of both the early American women's movement and the more recent civil rights movement, for example. But we seem to be reaching a self-sustaining cascade, as so many people are involved in some form of civil society organization that vast numbers are available for recruitment. As Sidney Tarrow (1994: 147) points out, with so many organizations providing "reservoirs for recruitment into a wide spectrum of movements, we may be witnessing the foundation for a movement society."

Another factor accounting for the rise of transnational civil society is the growth of *national* civil society in most parts of the world. Because all people live in territorial states, "transnational" civil society consists of networks of individuals and groups that are located within individual states. Moreover, most of the people who become part of transnational networks first become involved in local or national groups that are addressing local or national concerns. Thus, the development of transnational civil society depends significantly on the status of domestic civil society around the globe. That status depends in great part on what kind of civil society governments are willing to (or can be forced to) accept. And governmental acceptance varies wildly from one country to another.[2] The United States has long made it fairly easy for organizations to establish themselves, and is one of the few countries that encourages contributions to a wide range of civil society organizations by making them tax-deductible. Many Asian governments, in contrast, strictly regulate which organizations can be legally registered or allowed to exist at all (Yamamoto 1995: 26–27). China, for example, has about 200,000 registered "mass organizations," but given the obstacles to gaining official recognition it seems likely that many more remain unregistered or slip out of existence. Under State Council Order No. 43, no group can legally exist if it duplicates any function ostensibly filled by a government-registered organization, whether or not the function is actually carried out (Forney 1998).

But attitudes and policies are changing. The most spectacular growth of civil society is, of course, in the states of the former Soviet Union, because there the sector started from a base of near zero. Even in better-established democracies, however, there is a greater acceptance of civil society organizing. Until quite recently, Japan made it very difficult for non-governmental organizations to incorporate (requiring, for example, that an organization have three hundred million yen (about $3 million) in "basic capital" permanently in the bank), and severely limiting the tax incentives for contributions. In March 1998, however, Japan promulgated a new law dispensing with the cumbersome and arbitrary approval process and the "basic capital" requirement. The law still puts some obligations on civil society organizations (requiring them, for example, to submit

---

2   For a country-by-country analysis of the status of civil society and the extent of governmental control, see Civicus (1997).

all accounting documents and annual reports to local government administrative bodies each year) but it is expected to bring about the addition of some 10,000 new non-profit organizations to the ranks of those already registered in Japan (Japan Center 1998).

All this activity takes money. That money generally comes from three sources: governments (which are the largest contributors, especially to non-profit service providers like hospitals, educational institutions, and various charities), voluntary contributions from individuals, corporations, and foundations, and fees charged for services rendered.[3] To a substantial degree, the global rise of the kinds of civil society groups that can contribute to global governance reflects the policies of Western governments and foundations, stemming from a Western world view that emphasizes the importance of civil society to good governance. The World Bank estimates that in the early 1970s, 1.5 percent of income for development NGOs came from outside donors; by the mid-1990s this figure reached nearly 30 percent. In some countries, including Bangladesh, Sri Lanka and Kenya, the dependency on donor funds has reached as high as 90 percent (Commins 1997: 141; Bebbington and Riddell 1997: 111).

The next few decades are likely to see even more money available to support civil society. Some scholars have projected that in the developed countries, the next fifty years will witness a huge transfer of wealth from one generation to the next, totaling well over $10 trillion for the United States alone. Since bequests often provide a means for channeling large amounts of money from private hands to civil society organizations, a fair chunk of this money may go to support civil society. The examples of Bill Gates, George Soros, and Ted Turner, whose donations are in the hundreds of millions, or billions, of dollars, may spur other members of the world's growing group of extremely wealthy individuals to follow suit.

Such dependence on outside funding raises the hackles of many people in both rich and poor countries who question where a civil society funded from abroad reflects local people's needs and desires. If money drives the agenda, civil society in non-Western parts of the world may not play the truly democratic role that it does in the West. The Western governments that are providing much of the funding are accountable only to their own electorates, not to the people whose lives are most directly affected.

But the reliance on Western funding is not necessarily bad, especially if some of it gets directed to building up local sources of philanthropy. Social capital, like any capital, takes time to accumulate, and a little seed capital can help a lot. Effective and sustained civil society organizations rarely arise spontaneously at the grass-roots level, even in the West. The successful new civil society organiza-

---

[3] In the United States and most of Europe, private giving accounts for less than 20 percent of nonprofit income, with more than 80 percent coming from a combination of government support and fees (Salamon 1996).

tions usually have links to established organizations that provide materials, ideas, and organizational structure. Given the nascent level of civil society organization in many parts of the world, it is perhaps unsurprising that Western dominance currently looms so large. There are benefits: NGOs frequently assert that an attachment to donors helps them learn effective methodologies and acquire technical training (Hulme and Edwards 1997: 11).

Finally, global integration and efforts to govern it are themselves creating targets against which civil society groups can mobilize. Just as national civil societies arose partly thanks to the infrastructure provided by nation-states and partly in reaction against the activities of states, so the development of transnational civil society is benefiting from the development of even relatively feeble inter-governmental bodies like the United Nations and its associated agencies. The series of United Nations conferences on global issues that began in the 1970s were meant primarily to draw governments together to consider how to deal with everything from housing to population to food to the environment. But as it turned out, the most important role of the conferences was to provide a focal point around which global civil society could coalesce. Non-governmental groups appeared in force at the 1972 UN Conference on the Human Environment, with accredited NGOs outnumbering governmental delegations two to one. Over the next 25 years, the UN hosted more than a dozen conferences on everything from food to population to the role of women.[4] Each stimulated a flurry of networking among the non-governmental groups working on the issues.

The most conspicuous targets of civil society activity are of course the inter-governmental organizations that have real economic clout: the World Trade Organization, the World Bank, and the International Monetary Fund. These enjoy the unceasing attentions of a smorgasbord of NGOs and assorted protestors. So it appears that, thanks to the meetings and activities of governments, inter-governmental organizations, and corporations, transnational civil society is in no danger of running out of targets. These focal points are part and parcel of the processes of

---

[4]   See Charnovitz (1997: 261–262) and UN Briefing Papers/The World Conferences: Developing Priorities for the 21st Century. URL: www.un.org/geninfo/by/intro.html. The conferences were: the World Population Conference (Bucharest, 1974); the World Food Conference (Rome, 1974); the Conference of the International Women's Year (Mexico City, 1975); the UN Conference on Human Settlements (Habitat I, Vancouver, 1976); the UN Conference on Population (Mexico City, 1984); the World Conference on Women (Nairobi, 1985); the World Summit for Children (New York, 1990); the UN Conference on Environment and Development (Rio de Janeiro, 1992); the World Conference on Human Rights (Vienna, 1993); the World Conference on Population and Development (Cairo, 1994); the World Summit for Social Development (Copenhagen, 1995); the Fourth World Conference on Women (Beijing, 1996); the Second UN Conference on Human Settlements (Habitat II, Istanbul, 1996); and the World Food Summit (1996).

globalization. Unless global integration comes to a halt, the targets of opportunity will proliferate.

In short, it seems likely that the explosion of transnational civil society is still in its infancy. Globalization will continue to create targets of opportunity. More and more people will be able and willing to participate. Information technology will continue to lower the costs of staying connected to distant regions. Money, while not plentiful, will be available. And governments will accommodate the growing pressures for civil society participation by providing the legal conditions under which civil society groups can exist, and perhaps even flourish.

3   The "Movement"

What do these broadly favorable trends portend for the loose agglomeration of activists known as the "anti-globalization" movement? What is the movement's future? To answer such questions, we first must look at what the movement is and why it arose.

Although commentators have often dismissed the protestors as ill-informed Northern do-gooders or wild-eyed anarchists, most are neither. Their ranks include a large and increasingly influential Southern contingent. While some from both North and South are more interested in street theater than in serious substance, many of the groups are well-informed and deeply concerned with the substance of economic integration. And the violent fringe is just that, a tiny minority widely resented by the much larger number of peaceful protestors.

Few are actually opposed to global integration per se. For all but a relative handful, the term "anti-globalization" is a misnomer at best. Most participants in the movement are more accurately referred to as "globalization's critics" – people who have specific objections to the consequences of certain types of economic integration, or to the political processes by which globalization is being governed, or both. Globalization's critics may have come together in a loose-knit "movement," but it is far from a single coherent group. Indeed, it is so broad that many of its participants, rejecting the "anti-globalization" label but unable to come up with an accurate replacement, simply call it "the movement."

The movement arose because many advocacy communities have found themselves drawn together around issues raised by globalization and global institutions. Many of the activists whose primary concerns are local and national have come to believe that the roots of their problems lie at the global level. Those concerned with national environmental protection or labor rights must pay attention to global trade rules that affect domestic regulations. Those concerned with national economic development can hardly ignore the implications of IFI conditionality or financial volatility.

The movement came together over the course of the 1990s in response to the rise of what George Soros has called "market fundamentalism," the school of thought that saw open, unfettered competition as the best way to run economies. The market fundamentalists tend to see economic integration as both economically efficient and politically beneficial, because the opening of national economies to foreign goods and investment enforces policy discipline, forcing countries to adopt "good" economic policies and clean up corruption to attract foreign investment.

The preference for openness formed the basis of the Washington Consensus – the set of policies that the IMF, the World Bank, and the U.S. Treasury Department wanted poor and transition countries to follow. The Washington Consensus rules called on countries to reduce or eliminate barriers to trade, financial flows, and foreign competition, and to reform governmental practices on the collection and expenditures of revenues. As labels often do, the term took on a life of its own, standing as shorthand for an ideology that favored getting national governments out of the way of market forces.[5] The attendant policy prescriptions were promulgated through a variety of mechanisms, such as IMF and World Bank conditionality, trade rules, bilateral investment agreements, and the terms of bilateral assistance.

Over the course of the 1990s, a vast array of civil society groups came together to protest many elements of the policy prescriptions and the mechanisms used to enforce them, arguing that both the economic and the political consequences left much to be desired. The resulting loose network included labor unions, environmentalists, development groups, and others who argued that the new trade and investment rules favored the interests of large corporations over those of ordinary people.

The protest movement is not a unified entity. The biggest divide falls between those who want to reform global economic integration and those who want to stop it. The latter are a small minority, further splintered into two categories. The nationalists (à la Patrick Buchanan) object in principle to the idea of open borders or any kind of supra-national authority. The rejectionists (à la Walden Bello) see no hope of reforming global institutions to serve the interests of ordinary people. The rejectionists also include the so-called Black Bloc anarchists, who oppose all kinds of authority and have proven themselves willing to use violence to make their point.

The much larger reformist camp is where globalization's insiders can hope to find common ground with the protestors. Its many strands include trade unions,

---

5   The term was coined by John Williamson (1990).

environmentalists, human rights groups, and development NGOs. Although most groups started with a concern for just one issue, in recent years they have formed an increasingly dense web of connections across issue areas and geographical regions. The International Forum on Globalization, which began in 1994 in response to NAFTA, now brings together 60 groups from 25 countries, including most of the most prominent individuals and organization. Its board of directors includes Maude Barlow of the Council of Canadians, Walden Bello from Focus on the Global South (Thailand), John Cavanagh of the Institute for Policy Studies (US), Martin Khor from Third World Network (Malaysia), Sara Larrain from Chile Sustainable, Vandana Shiva from the Foundation for Science, Technology, and Ecology (India), and Lori Wallach from Public Citizen's Global Trade Watch (US), among others.

Those connections have evolved in many ways, but two overlapping channels have been key. One is centered around the World Bank (and to a lesser extent the IMF), where three different transnational civil society networks – on poverty, environment, and structural adjustment – have coalesced around opposition to World Bank projects and procedures (Nelson 1996). The other grew up around trade agreements and the World Trade Organization.

The Bank network has been growing steadily for the past two decades. It began as a Northern-based network of environmentalists outraged by the environmental destructiveness of many Bank-funded projects like dams and roads. In the 1980s, those groups joined forces with representatives of poor-country communities involuntarily resettled from lands made uninhabitable by those projects (and often dumped in new places that offered no prospect of livability), along with proponents for indigenous peoples whose cultures and livelihoods were rapidly disappearing. Collectively they have pushed the Bank to adopt a more forthcoming disclosure policy, to follow its own environmental and human rights standards, and to establish a procedure to allow those who are affected by a Bank-funded project to complain directly to the Bank.

Despite some progress, and despite numerous efforts at dialogue, most groups in the Bank network see the need for much greater change. The Mobilization for Global Justice, organizer of what was to have been the large demonstration around the planned IMF-World Bank meetings in late September 2001, had issued a set of four demands. These were:

1. Open all World Bank and IMF meetings to the media and the public.
2. End all World Bank and IMF policies that hinder people's access to food, clean water, shelter, health care, education, and the right to organize. (Such "structural adjustment" policies include user fees, privatization, and economic austerity programs.)

3. Stop all World Bank support for socially and environmentally destructive projects such as oil, gas, and mining activities, and all support for projects such as dams that include forced relocation of people.

4. Cancel all impoverished country debt to the World Bank and IMF, using the institutions' own resources.

The list was drawn in part from a set of eight demands put forward by the Fifty Years Is Enough Network.[6] As the Mobilization for Global Justice was careful to stress, that list of eight was generated in consultation with members in Haiti, Nicaragua, Panama, Brazil, Cameroon, Senegal, South Africa, Tanzania, Kenya, Zimbabwe, Mauritius, the Philippines, Thailand, and India.

The IMF did not respond, but the World Bank did in late September with a point-by-point rebuttal.[7]

1. It claimed that the Bank had in fact already opened up significantly to the media and the public, referring in particular to its newly revised disclosure policy (a policy with which most NGOs who follow Bank disclosure policy remain deeply dissatisfied).

2. It pointed out that the Bank is the world's largest external funder for education, health, and HIV/AIDS, and argued that the Bank does not promote user fees for primary education or basic health care.

3. It argued that natural resource exploitation and extractive industries can help to reduce poverty and promote economic development, and essentially said it planned to continue with its current policies.

4. On debt relief, the Bank reiterated its support of debt relief through the Heavily Indebted Poor Countries (HIPC) initiative.

The Bank then added a demand of its own: that groups renounce and denounce violence, and that groups concerned about poor people in developing countries shift their energies to more constructive dialogues and partnerships with the Bank.

The Mobilization for Global Justice responded with a rebuttal of the rebuttal, providing a detailed critique on numerous points. On transparency, for example, it noted that the Board of Executive Directors of both the World Bank and the IMF continue to operate in almost total secrecy, and that draft documents are still not released to allow for public input before decisions become final. On user fees, it claimed that only as of September 2001 had the Bank changed its policy of aggressively promoting user fees for primary education and health care. On energy, it referred to the Bank's own studies to argue that the poor would be best

---

6   http://www.50years.org/s28/demands.htm.

7   http://www.worldbank.org/html/extdr/pb/pbfourdemands.htm.

served by clean and renewable sources of energy, but that most Bank energy lending continued to be for fossil fuel projects.

Such exchanges are a far cry from the earlier contemptuous dismissals that too often constituted all that there was in the way of dialogue. But the Mobilization for Global Justice (2001) made clear that it did not consider "dialogues and partnerships" to constitute sufficient mechanisms for achieving real reform:

> There are sometimes compelling reasons for organizations to meet with the IMF and World Bank, but there are equally compelling reasons to build opposition to the institutions' policies by lobbying their governments, engaging in grassroots public education, and organizing vivid demonstrations of the passion and numbers of people who oppose IMF and Bank policies. It is important to note that there are no rigid divisions among IMF/World Bank opponents; indeed those who compile studies frequently participate in mass marches. Working to improve the economic and political position of the Global South means seeking immediate policy changes and building public support for a fundamental shift in global power relations. (p. 15)

The document went on to argue that the Bank's efforts at dialogue had not proved satisfactory:

> Many groups that have tested the Bank's expressed desire for dialogue in recent years have found the Bank's response disingenuous. They have met with the Bank to address issues such as large-dam development (World Commission on Dams), structural adjustment (SAPRI), fossil fuels and other extractive industries, forestry, and poverty (PRSPs), as well as a number of safeguard policies and the Bank's information-disclosure policy. These groups have found the Bank fundamentally unresponsive to citizen input – even when the Bank has requested it – and to the initiatives' findings and recommendations. Civil-society participants in those initiatives have been frustrated, finding that the Bank seeks to manipulate its joint endeavors with civil society, use its consultations to validate and advance its own positions, and turn the initiatives into public-relations exercises. (p. 15)

The paper was signed by most of the major Northern NGO networks that have been active in the long-running campaign around the World Bank. These are the groups that constitute the Mobilization for Global Justice, which takes responsibility for organizing protests in Washington. (All the major protest events have local coordinators made up of local NGOs.) The signatories noted that their arguments echoed those of many groups in the Global South. And in general, it is true that what used to be a Northern-dominated coalition has become much better balanced and representative of a broader range of concerns and constituencies.

The network that has grown up around trade includes among its leading lights groups from several regions. Global Trade Watch (headed by Lori Wallach), part of the organization Public Citizen, based in Washington, and Third World Network (headed by Martin Khor) in Malaysia, are two of the best known.

The trade debate tends to face more divisive issues, particularly over environment and labor rights. But Northern and Southern groups also share many concerns. There are two chief objections. One concerns the tendency for trade rules to "trump" domestic policy making, even on health, safety, and environmental standards that meet domestic needs and often are not protectionist in intent. The other concerns the persistent North-South inequities in trade rules and rule making.

The civil society critics argue that it has stopped making sense to think of international trade as a distinct issue that can be dealt with separately from others. Yet that isolation is exactly what the current system for regulating trade requires. The WTO's mandate and procedures are meant to promote free trade, not to balance among competing concerns. And there are no equivalent international institutions standing up for those competing global values. The critics claim that previous rounds have sacrificed environmental and safety standards and lowered workers' wages (Dunne 1999).

There are many competing ideas within the movement about how to redress the imbalance between trade goals and other issues. One key mechanism through which civil society groups have attempted to ensure that non-trade considerations are taken into account is through the WTO's dispute settlement procedure. Although panel hearings are closed, NGOs have submitted amicus curiae ("friend of the court") briefs. The Appellate Board has ruled that it has the authority to accept such briefs. But that ruling is hotly disputed by a number of Southern governments, so hotly that panels and the Appellate Board have in practice paid little attention to the amicus curiae briefs they have accepted. As legal scholar Jeffrey L. Dunoff (2001) notes in his detailed review on the subject:

> …the resulting practice is actually a step backwards for those who urge greater NGO involvement. In practice, NGO submissions are frequently rejected. In those few instances when they are even considered, they typically are considered only when adopted by a party. In these cases, NGOs do not participate as independent actors, but rather as 'appendages' to the parties' submissions. In practice, they participate at the sufferance of the parties to the dispute. But, by effectively turning NGOs from independent actors into entities that simply echo government arguments, the panels eliminate the potential advantages of NGO participation.

Some Northern NGOs have demanded that environment, labor practices, and human rights considerations be included within the WTO itself, with trade sanctions employed in support. However, as the ties between Northern and Southern NGOs have strengthened, Northern groups have begun to take into account their counterparts' fears that such an expansion of WTO authority would further disadvantage the South.

North-South inequity remains a dominant theme of the movement's objections to the trade regime, objections that are shared by many developing country governments. The critics have forcefully contended that both the substance of the agreements and the processes by which rules are made are unfair. On agriculture, for example, developing countries have agreed to drop their domestic tariffs and support programs. Because the rich countries continue to subsidize agriculture heavily, domestic producers in developing countries have found themselves unable to compete with the resulting surges in agricultural imports.

The critics find the processes of trade rule making as objectionable as the substance. They note that, while all member governments are ostensibly entitled to equal voice, some voices in reality are able to speak much more loudly and frequently than others. Nearly thirty WTO members cannot afford to keep even a single representative at the WTO's Geneva headquarters, and most developing countries have too few representatives to cope with the often simultaneous meetings of more than 30 WTO committees, subcommittees, and working groups.

The inequities are widely acknowledged. Supachai Panitchpakdi, the director of the WTO, has argued that "if the future agenda of the World Trade Organization is to... command the support of the whole international community, then the WTO's members, both great and small, must be equal partners in its formulation and must be able collectively to claim ownership of it" (Panitchpakdi 2001: 29). Malaysia's Martin Khor, director of the Third World Network, has called attention to the "... need to reform the decision-making processes" of international financial institutions "so as to give developing countries their right to adequate participation" (Khor 2000: 102).

Although the World Bank, IMF, and WTO have served as focal points around which much of the movement has coalesced, they are not the only targets that have drawn attention. Other civil society groups have begun by focusing on other specific issues, although as they become active they tend to be drawn into more holistic approaches. One notable example is the Jubilee 2000 network that has campaigned indefatigably for debt relief. Bono, lead singer for the rock group U2, is the famous face, but the coalition has included the combined efforts of thousands of people in many countries to force the rich countries and the international financial institutions to pay serious attention to the debt issue. Jubilee 2000's campaigners, including Bono, continue to press for debt relief but have expanded their campaign to include broader issues of development assistance and the design of the global economy. Similarly, ATTAC (the Association for the Taxation of financial Transactions for the Aid of Citizens) began as a campaign to push for the Tobin tax to raise money for development assistance and to tame capital market volatility (see http://www.attac.org). ATTAC has become a central player in the protest movement.

4   Moving From Protest to Participation

At the national level, civil society is generally an essential component of democracy. Its associations embody the social trust that provides the essential basis for sustained collective action. At the national level, the interlacing network of civil society organizations that exist within a country well-endowed with social capital is the necessary complement to democratic government, providing the broad societal values that make sustained and effective democracy possible.

But there is an enormous difference between the national and global roles of such organizations and movements. National civil society functions in a context set by national governments. Political mechanisms exist to work out competing interests. Those mechanisms do not always work well, but the principle is clear.

There are no global counterparts to these political processes. Political activism, to be constructive, requires two things: individuals willing to act, and political structures through which their actions can be channeled. As is clear from the above, there appears to be no shortage of individuals willing to act. Channeling their activism to constructive ends, however, has proved more difficult.

Part of the problem, of course, is that no single substantive change would satisfy the entire movement. Different groups have different interests. They ally themselves where they find that their interests overlap, but what would satisfy the concerns of one group might leave another outraged. Having found a common enemy in some global institution or inter-governmental agreement does not mean that they would find a common friend in a revised institution or agreement.

Yet there is one set of issues on which all but the most diehard opponents of economic integration seem to agree. That is the set of issues dealing with the *processes* by which global rules are made and enforced. Globalization's critics consistently demand an end to secretive and exclusionary processes of decision making. The leaders of the mobilization planned for September 2001, for example, called for "institutional reform to make openness, full public accountability and the participation of affected populations in decision making standard procedures at the World Bank and the IMF." Pervading the movement is the complaint that corporations are getting far too much say in setting the rules for economic integration, and that other interests, including the public interest, are getting far too little.

To date, the protestors argue, the rules of the newly global economy are being made primarily by a relative handful of true believers. The resulting rules largely reflect the interests of a handful of rich-country governments, and in particular those of the United States. This is no great surprise to students of power politics. The G-7 dominate the global economy, and the United States, which by itself accounts for over a fifth of global GDP, is the 800-pound gorilla in economic negotiations.[8] Given that virtually all of the world's largest multinational corporations are based in G-7 countries, and that most foreign direct investment originates there, it is hardly surprising that those governments promote corporate freedom of action. But that, say the activists and many Southern governments, leaves most other interests, including those of the vast majority of national governments, relegated to the sidelines.

Not only is the decision-making process exclusionary, it is often unduly secretive. When the International Monetary Fund offers loans to a developing country, the consultations take place in confidence between the IMF and one or two ministries of the national government, usually the finance or planning ministry. There is little scope for public debate. When the World Trade Organization considers whether one country's environmental legislation constitutes an illegal barrier to another country's imports, it does so in closed hearings using confidential documents.

There is no shortage of proposals for fixing the lack of adequate involvement by Southern governments in global governance. It is widely recognized that developing countries need help with training and resources, although the assistance being offered by the rich falls far short of the need. But even if all developing countries could participate as full equals in all international institutions, the critics of globalization argue that the problem of finding democratic ways to govern globalization would not be solved, for two reasons.

First, the "representative" approach to global governance assumes that domestic procedures hold these decision makers accountable for their actions. Often, that assumption is false. The lack of democratic governance is most obvious in autocracies where elections, if held at all, are at best shams. But even free and fair elections are not enough to ensure accountability and adequate representation of the views and desires of diverse populations. Democracy flourishes only when citizens have channels of voice and influence over governments between and beyond elections. Those channels are provided by civil society. Yet despite the growth of the third sector, many of the people most affected by globalization – the

---

[8]   If calculated as a percentage of total world GDP, the United States economy weighs in at a whopping 28 percent. By PPP calculations, the United States is still a respectable 21 percent. The G-7 countries are Britain, Canada, France, Germany, Italy, Japan, and the United States. They began meeting as a group in 1975. Their combined gross domestic product in 1998 was $18.68 trillion, 65 percent of the total world GDP of $28.73 trillion or by PPP calculations about 45 percent (World Bank, *World Development Indicators*, 2000, Table 4.2, p. 186).

poor, indigenous peoples, the politically marginalized and disenfranchised – still have too little access to the ear of the powerful within their own governments.

Second, governments speak for *national* interests, not for the global public good. But some problems require a degree of global collective action that national governments have shown themselves little inclined to provide. On climate change, for example, the woeful pleas of the members of the Association of Small Island States, who are in danger of sinking beneath the rising seas, have attracted little attention from the U.S. government, which remains unwilling to impose reductions in greenhouse gas emissions. On issues such as infectious disease, governments continue to be vulnerable to the temptation to wait for someone else to solve the common problem.

Advocacy organizations may help provide a global public conscience, a means of assuring that officials in one part of the world must consider the interests of people elsewhere. Their insistence on the universality of basic human rights and the need for economic development to be environmentally sustainable can help hold governments and corporations to international standards that are high aspirations, rather than lowest common denominators. By and large, these organizations espouse broad goals that are hard to criticize: protecting the environment, raising the living standards of the poor, promoting democracy and governmental accountability, and reducing the threat of catastrophic war.

The question is not so much *whether* citizens' groups should be participating in global decision making, but *how*. As advocacy organizations acquire greater capabilities and cross-border connections, heated debate is raging over whether their newfound power is a good thing. Civil society *within* countries is widely lauded as the essential intermediary between the state and the citizen. In global governance, the story is quite different: there is neither a true world government nor a true global citizenry between which civil society groups can mediate. There is much disagreement over what roles the non-profit sector should have in global governance. Should advocacy and grassroots groups have the right to present their views directly in global negotiations, or should they be required to work through national governments? Should they be limited to expressing their opinions, or should they sit at the table as equals with governments, having a vote as well as a voice?

Probably the subject most amenable to consensus is the movement's demands for greater transparency in the institutions and processes of global governance. Information, after all, is the lifeblood of both democracies and markets. Without information, citizens have no basis upon which to evaluate their representatives or voice their opinions, and both elections and the very process of representation become a meaningless sham. Without information, the financial markets upon which modern economies depend become irrational exercises in guesswork, and governmental regulators cannot hope to carry out their responsibilities. The key to good governance and efficient economic integration alike is thus to make governments and markets transparent. And as the world becomes more tightly integrated, a compelling need is arising to ensure that people in one part of the globe have access to information about what is going on elsewhere, so that they can have voice in far-away matters that now affect them directly.

No international organization has faced more vociferous demands to open up than the World Bank. Beginning in the early 1980s, a wide range of NGOs began pressuring the Bank to be more forthcoming about its plans and policies, arguing that "if development bank project planning and design were open and transparent ... fewer disastrous projects would be approved and a greater opportunity to promote development alternatives would exist"(Udall 1998: 391).

These pressures for transparency have had an impact, in part because the argument has resonated so effectively with U.S. policymakers. Members of Congress proved willing to hold funding for the Bank hostage to the establishment of new Bank disclosure policies (Udall 1998: 403). Under the disclosure policy established over a decade ago, the Bank releases a project information document on every project. Also available are final staff appraisal reports, environmental impact statements, and other documents.

Since then, there has been much rhetoric from the Bank promoting a more participatory model of development. Bank President James Wolfensohn began emphasizing the importance of "inclusive decision-making" processes. Bank publications began stressing the importance of "empowerment" in reducing poverty. Because access to information is a necessary (though not sufficient) condition for such participatory development, expectations were high when the disclosure policy came up for revision in 2000. But the revision of the disclosure policy turned out to entail a considerable fight, one that usefully illustrates the ongoing political struggle over transparency throughout the world.

The Bank staff who drafted the revisions found themselves facing competing pressures. Although the Bank already releases enough information to allow for after-the-fact accountability, its disclosures do not enable citizens to participate in policy debates before decisions are made. On one side were civil society groups from all parts of the world, along with the governments of a few wealthy countries, who called for much more disclosure of Bank documents. This side argued that information disclosure is essential to foster informed public debate and constructive engagement between society and government, a crucial if often missing piece of the development puzzle. Moreover, the pervasive fears of Bank and Fund interference with national sovereignty can only be assuaged if the public, including the legislature and other representative institutions, are informed about what decisions are actually being made and by whom. Disclosure of what the Bank is doing and what agreements it is signing with governments is necessary if the Bank is to deliver on promises to include new voices in the deliberative process.

On the other side were many governments, particularly from the larger developing countries. (Smaller countries have already essentially been forced by the world's wealthiest nations to disclose documents that richer developing countries are still permitted to keep secret.) They argued that it should be up to them, not to the Bank, to determine what information ought to be released at what time and to whom. Information needs to be restricted to prevent market upheavals and to "protect the deliberative process." When pushed, off the record some said that what they most objected to was the possibility that their political opposition at home would use information from Bank documents in political fights against them.

In the end, anti-transparency forces largely won. The Bank's revised disclosure policy makes only minor improvements, and most significantly does not release project appraisals or country assistance strategies before the Bank's Board takes action on them. In other words, the policy continues to permit only after-the-fact accountability, not informed participation during the planning and decision-making processes.

The problem at the Bank and at other international organizations is the lack of governmental consensus on whether civil society is entitled to have voice on decision making. Many governments, especially from developing countries, object strongly to calls for greater citizen participation. In the context of the World Trade Organization, for example, they have argued that public input should take place only at the national level and that both negotiations and dispute settlement are properly handled exclusively by governments, who will decide for themselves what information to release to their citizens. In part, their objections stem from the North-South imbalance. Northern civil society groups, including trade associations, generally have the resources to engage the WTO. Many Southern governments fear that allowing greater civil society participation will further turn the odds against them.

But the WTO's relationship with the outside world has already begun to change. Growing public interest in its work has compelled the WTO to organize public meetings and consultations, as well as engage in a series of regional conferences and workshops designed to encourage interaction between the Secretariat and the public. The WTO Secretariat has also made some progress toward document availability. Its 1996 derestriction policy, informal but regularized meetings with the public, and the Internet now enable more people around the world to review its material. Nevertheless, citizens still lack access to information that would enable them to comment on policy as it is being considered.

Other intergovernmental organizations have done better. Indeed, efforts to remain opaque are swimming against a powerful tide of greater citizen participation in global institutions. The United Nations and many of its agencies routinely involve NGOs in their deliberations, with standard procedures in place for accreditation. In intergovernmental treaty negotiations on many issues, non-governmental organizations have become constructive players with full access to information. They are routinely incorporated into negotiations on environmental issues, receiving country position papers and draft treaties as a matter of course.

On issues of economic integration, however, policy insiders still tend to be dismissive, if not hostile, toward the demands of activists for greater inclusion. The bluntest example of what often remains a contemptuous attitude toward the protesters came from U.S. trade negotiator Robert Zoellick. In the aftermath of September 11, the protest movement was reeling, fractured over the question of what kinds of protests, if any, were desirable in the new environment, and what issues deserved highest priority. This would have been a golden opportunity for policy makers to reach out for a constructive dialogue with that vast majority of the protest movement that is reformist and committed to non-violence. Instead, Zoellick gave a speech in which he argued that

> it is inevitable that people will wonder if there are intellectual connections [between the terrorists and] others who have turned to violence to attack international finance, globalization, and the United States.... Here's a lesson I learned from history: Change breeds anxiety. Anxieties can be manipulated to force agendas based on fear, antagonisms, resentments, and hate. And then those who are the weakest, those with the least influence, are hurt the most by cold and hard people who overrun openness and liberty and the rule of law in the name of ill-defined causes.

In short, Zoellick portrayed those who disagreed with him as either manipulated and anxious people unable to think for themselves, or "cold and hard" people with intellectual connections to mass murder. He went on to raise a host of strawman arguments:

> Let me be clear where I stand: Erecting new barriers and closing old borders will not help the impoverished. It will not feed hundreds of millions struggling for subsistence. It will not liberate the persecuted. It will not improve the environment in developing nations or reverse the spread of AIDS. It will not help the railway orphans I visited in India. It will not aid the committed Indonesians I visited who are trying to build a functioning, tolerant democracy in the largest Muslim nation in the world. And it certainly will not placate terrorists.

Zoellick's extreme language is certainly not shared by all decision makers working on economic integration. Others have accepted at least some of the arguments made by globalization's critics. Former WTO director general Renato Ruggiero has called for "a new vision of global governance" that goes beyond capital movements and trade liberalization to include environmental, social, labor, human rights, and development concerns.[9] Former EU Trade Commissioner Sir Leon Brittan has called for the reconciliation of "the competing demands of economic growth, environmental protection, and social development."[10]

But Zoellick's adamant rejection of the protest movement's claims is widely enough shared that it is useful to try to understand the fears created by civil society's demands for broader inclusion in economic policy decisions. It is true that channeling that participation presents governments with daunting obstacles. Civil society groups are not necessarily democratically motivated, broadly representative, or willing to cooperate in good faith with other groups or the government. Political leaders today understandably have profound misgivings about working out policy questions with groups whose involvement will surely make the process more cumbersome and confrontational.

The objections to broader inclusion fall into two general categories. First, it is argued that civil society groups are special interests that undermine the ability of governments to pursue the public interest. According to this argument, civil society groups tend to organize themselves as special interests and pursue narrow, particularistic benefits. Worse still, the more concentrated the potential gains of a policy, the more tenacious and effective organized groups are likely to be in pressuring politicians. Pushing reform through the political system, therefore, requires that government officials be insulated from parochial, selfish interests. Bypassing citizen groups takes politics out of the process, and leads to deeper and more comprehensive reform.

One version of the anti-inclusion argument claims that the more stable and mature a democracy becomes, the more acute the sclerosis. The economist Mancur Olson (1982) famously argued that accessible institutions and democratic inclusiveness inevitably leads to national decline. As self-interested groups multiply and lobby to increase their share of the distributional pie, the outcome of interest group competition is political gridlock and policy incoherence.

But the evidence from rich and poor countries alike fails to support this prediction. If the hypothesis were true, the United States should be dead in the water, frozen into immobility by its vast array of competing interest groups, associations, think tanks and NGOs. The hypothesis also suggests that more authoritarian governments that strictly limit civil society activity should do the best in adopting good policies. Yet when it comes to pushing through structural market reforms, numerous studies show that democratic governments that allow the formation and

---

9   Opening Remarks to the High Level Symposium on Trade and Environment, Geneva, 15 March 1999.

10   Speech to the WTO High Level Symposium on Trade and Environment, Geneva, 15 March 1999. Available at www.wto.org/english/tratop_e/envir_elbenv.htm.

mobilization of autonomous groups perform at least as well as, if not better than, authoritarian ones.[11]

In fact, Olson's basic premise is wrong. Not all private, independent organizations are driven purely by narrowly defined self-interest. Whatever one may think of the array of advocacy groups that are now competing to insert themselves into the policy process, they are indisputably pursuing a much broader, and often self-less, set of goals.

Not only are independent groups not necessarily bad news for policy; recent research reveals that they can be good news for society. Specifically, the creation of "social capital" – relations within and among civic groups – has been found to make a significant contribution to economic growth (Putnam 2000). In short, vigorous civil society participation is not an evil that constrains economic dynamism. It is essential for sustained growth.

Second, it is claimed that civil society does not represent society – governments do. Civil society groups don't have to face elections. Their opponents argue that this is a serious problem in developing countries where, they claim, civil society organizations are often simply branch offices of Northern NGOs who represent the interest of the rich world's middle class. They conclude that, at least within democracies, the executive and legislature best serve the broad economic interests of all citizens. Now that a growing number of developing countries have formal elections and universal suffrage, civil society already enjoys basic political rights and has access to representative institutions, so there is no need to expand its direct participation into the actual policy-making process. As *The Economist* complained, "it seems odd for the [World] Bank to demand that third-world governments, often these days democratically elected, should design their reforms alongside civil groups that are unelected, unaccountable and very often unrepresentative."[12]

This argument ignores both the strong and growing Southern participation in the protest movement and the broad reality of how democracies actually work in practice. Electoral systems are only one of the mechanisms providing voice for citizens and accountability for officials. The existence of elected representatives alone by no means ensures adequate representation of all major groups in policy issues. The world's well-established democracies by and large have a well-devel-

---

[11]   See, for example, Remmer (1990) and Geddes (1994). Remmer finds that, controlling for the debt burden inherited from previous autocracies, Latin American democracies in the 1980s did just as well as autocratic regimes in terms of promoting growth, containing fiscal deficits, controlling inflation, and limiting debt growth. Looking at a broader set of countries over a longer span of time, Geddes (1994: 107) finds "little evidence that authoritarianism as such increases the likelihood of [market-oriented] transitions."

[12]   *The Economist*, "Angry and Effective." September 23–29, 2000, p. 87.

oped set of advocacy organizations that provide information and articulate demands that profoundly shape the decisions of elected officials.

Moreover, the objections to including civil society groups because they are "unrepresentative" ignores the reality that some very unrepresentative interests already have a meaningful voice in policy processes. The most consistently well-represented non-governmental voice in global economic policy making is the private sector. Movement participants have pointed with outrage to the case of the Quebec City trade negotiations, when citizens were denied access to the negotiating text that was nonetheless granted to hundreds of corporate leaders attending the negotiations. Encouraging broader civil society participation helps to balance the influence of business, so that the broader interests of society are represented.

Civil society organizations may not speak for everyone, but they do often speak for constituencies that are otherwise ignored. While some NGOs represent only themselves, others speak for a broader public interest. As the World Bank now acknowledges, "by offering a perspective which is unique from that of the government or the private sector, NGOs can help [public officials in] making decisions aimed at the 'overall optimal good.'"[13] The trick for policy makers is to learn to distinguish between the well-intentioned groups that strive to provide honest and useful information and those that do not. This is difficult, but it is far better than ignoring all input on the grounds that some may be flawed.

5   Conclusion

Civil society, that amorphous third sector beyond state and market, is becoming stronger virtually everywhere, often organized into non-governmental organizations (NGOs) that serve to channel, or create, demands for participation. Their emergence is not a fluke, and their strength is likely to continue to grow.

This is partly a normal and desirable consequence of democratization. Governments around the world are facing new pressures from their citizens to enact laws establishing legal conditions for NGOs and to ensure that governmental policies and practices are transparent to citizen scrutiny. But there is more to the story of the growth of "civil society." Technology is playing a significant role, making it easier and cheaper for groups to organize themselves and to acquire and disseminate information. Economic integration itself is providing a growing number of focal points around which such groups can coalesce. Civil society is still largely a national phenomenon, but increasingly groups are linking up across borders, learning from one another and finding strength in numbers. Private and official

---

[13]   World Bank, "Working With NGOs." Operations Policy Department, 1995, p. 22.

donor agencies have in the past few years poured vast sums into fledgling civil society organizations in developing and transition countries. Some donors are aiming to support CSOs as part of a democracy assistance strategy. Others who are funding economic development projects have been persuaded that increasing citizen participation in such projects renders them far more effective. The World Bank and IMF have jointly endorsed the participation of civil society in the formation of Poverty Reduction Strategies.

For all these reasons, the question is no longer whether there should be broader participation in economic decision making. Exclusion generates a powerful, and avoidable, backlash, and can prevent decision makers from having timely access to crucial information about the impacts and social acceptibility of various policies. The question is *how* to open the policy-making process to a wide range of voices and interests.

At the least, that "how" should include much more forthcoming disclosure policies by governments and inter-governmental organization. There is no valid reason to cloak high-level decisions in secrecy, just as democratic parliaments are not allowed to deliberate and vote in secret.

The protest movement's frustration go beyond the slow pace of advances on transparency. Civil society's right to voice is being increasingly accepted in rhetoric, but practice lags far behind. NGOs are allowed to air their views in WTO dispute settlement procedures – but those views are ignored unless they parallel those of goverments. The World Bank takes great pride in promoting multi-stake-holder dialogues with its critics – but pays little attention to what they say.

These practices should change. The risk of ignoring pressures for a more open and transparent policy-making process far outweighs the risk of engagement. Economic policy necessarily involves a political, democratic debate about risks and tradeoffs of various policies. Politics is an inherent part of the process, not a distraction from some perfect policy.

With the end of the Cold War, the spread of democratic ideology, and the back-lash against the Washington Consensus, a new model of policy-making has become inevitable. Leaders can either resist the clamoring voices and invite confrontation, or include the more reasonable and representative groups and invite their cooperation. Greater inclusion may make the policy process less efficient, but it will also make policy results more sustainable.

Bibliography

Bebbington, A., and R. Riddell (1997). Heavy Hands, Hidden Hands, Holding Hands? Donors, Intermediary NGOs and Civil Society Organizations. In D. Hulme and M. Edwards (eds.), *NGOs, States and Donors: Too Close for Comfort?* New York: St. Martin's Press.

Civicus (1997). *The New Civic Atlas: Profiles of Civil Society in 60 Countries.* Washington, D. C.: Civicus.

Charnovitz, S. (1997). Two Centuries of Participation: NGOs and International Governance. *Michigan Journal of International Law* 18(2): 183–286.

Commins, S. (1997). World Vision International and Donors: Too Close for Comfort? In D. Hulme and M. Edwards (eds.), *NGOs, States and Donors: Too Close for Comfort?* New York: St. Martin's Press.

Dunne, N. (1999). The Next Round. *International Economy* 13 (33): 20.

Dunoff, J.L. (2001). Civil Society at the WTO: The Illusion of Inclusion? *ILSA Journal of International and Comparative Law.*

Florini, A.M. (ed.) (2000). *The Third Force: The Rise of Transnational Civil Society.* Tokyo and Washington, D.C.: The Japan Center for International Exchange and the Carnegie Endowment for International Peace.

Forney, M. (1998). Voice of the People. *Far Eastern Economic Review,* 7 May: 11.

Geddes, B. (1994). Challenging the Conventional Wisdom. *Journal of Democracy* 5(4): 104–118.

Hann, C., and E. Dunn (1996). *Civil Society: Challenging Western Models.* New York: Routledge.

Hunt, L.D. (1999). Civil Society and the Idea of a Commercial Republic. In M.G. Schecter (ed.), *The Revival of Civil Society.* New York: St. Martin's Press.

Japan Center for International Echange (1998). New NPO Law Fosters Enabling Environment. *Civil Society Monitor* 4 (April): 1.

Keck, M., and K. Sikkink (1998). *Activists Beyond Borders.* Ithaca, NY: Cornell University Press.

Khor, M. (2000). *Globalization and the South: Some Critical Issues.* Penang, Malaysia: Third World Network.

Mobilization for Global Justice (2001). Civil Society Demands and World Bank Distortions: A Civil Society Rebuttal to the World Bank's Response to Four Demands from the Mobilization for Global Justice.

Najam, A. (1996). Understanding the Third Sector: Revisiting the Prince, the Merchant, and the Citizen. *Nonprofit Management and Leadership* 7(2): 203–219.

Nelson, P. (1996). Internationalizing Economic and Environmental Policy: Transnational NGO Networks and the World Bank's Expanding Influence. *Millennium: Journal of International Studies* 25(3): 605–633.

Olson, M. (1982). *The Rise and Decline of Nations: Economic Growth, Stagnation, and Social Rigities.* New Haven, Conn.: Yale University Press.

Panitchpakdi, S. (2001). Balancing Competing Interests: The Future Role of the WTO. In G. Sampson (ed.), *The Role of the World Trade Organization in Global Governance*. New York: United Nations University Press.

Putnam, R. (2000). *Bowling Alone: The Collapse and Revival of American Community*. New York: Simon & Schuster.

Remmer, K. (1990). Democracy and Economic Crisis: The Latin American Experience. *World Politics* 42(3).

Salamon, L., et al. (1996). *The Emerging Sector: A Statistical Supplement*. Baltimore: Johns Hopkins Institute for Policy Studies.

Seligman, A. (1992). *The Idea of Civil Society*. New York: Macmillan.

Smith, J., C. Chatfield, and R. Pagnucco (eds.) (1997). *Transnational Social Movements and Global Politics: Solidarity Beyond States*. Syracuse, NY: Syracuse University Press.

Tarrow, S. (1994). *Power in Movement: Social Movements, Collective Action, and Politics*. Cambridge: Cambridge University Press.

Udall, L. (1998). The World Bank and Public Accountability: Has Anything Changed? In J.A. Fox and L.D. Brown (eds.), *The Struggle for Accountability: The World Bank, NGOs, and Grassroots Movements*. Cambridge, MA: MIT Press.

Williamson, J. (1990). *Latin American Adjustment: How Much Has Happened*. Washington, D.C.: Institute for International Economics.

Yamamoto, T. (1995). *Emerging Civil Society in the Asia Pacific Community*. Tokyo: Japan Center for International Exchange.

Comment on Ann Florini

Thilo Bode

Although it is possible to agree with large parts of Professor Florini's paper, her analysis of the reasons why civil society's participation in global governance has become so important needs a closer look. Some rather different conclusions regarding the role, strategy, and future of the civil society movement in global politics can be made.

It is not so much information technology, education, and an expanded middle class that is behind the rise of an international civil society as the fact that an increased number of political challenges must be addressed at a global level and that global institutions and/or their national representatives are failing to solve pressing global issues centered on the environment, social and economic development, and human rights. Information technology, especially the comparably cheap Internet, has facilitated the organization of international groups. The rise of civil society at a national level has been less of a driving force for the international movement, whose rise is clearly connected to the large number of issues needing to be addressed at the global level.

The modern "anti-globalization movement" was born in 1998 when a coalition of many small groups based in the Northern and Southern hemispheres campaigned successfully against the OECD-sponsored process to establish a "Multinational Agreement on Investment" (MAI). The OECD did not reach out to civil society to discuss concerns regarding the social and environmental standards of multinational investments; it was severely hit by a mostly Internet-based protest and finally dropped the project. Suddenly, many groups protesting for years against single issues such as World Bank projects, IMF policy, or human rights abuse discovered the power of joining forces. Now of historic significance, the internationally organized protest against the agenda of the first WTO ministerial conference in Seattle followed at the end of 1998. The disruption of this conference gave the movement international prominence.

It is true that an overwhelming majority of the international civil movement, despite its diverse character and differing goals and interests (between Northern and Southern groups, for instance), cannot be thought of as being against economic globalization as such. Rather, this majority criticizes the way globalization is taking place and its lack of transparency and democratic control. One element that strongly unifies the whole movement, besides its commonly shared mistrust of international corporations, is its criticism of the global governance system's lack of democracy.

The global governance system is increasingly expected to make decisions to solve global problems. But at the same time, it does not possess political decision-making processes comparable to those at the national level; democratic control, as would be found in a global parliament, for example, does not exist. Even if delegates only from democratically elected governments of countries came together and made certain decisions, no one could be held accountable for their decisions.

The lack of a direct chain of accountability is what creates the lack of democracy. Countries have delivered national sovereignty rights to international bodies, treaties and conventions but they have not provided for necessary democratic control. Democracy means the delegation of power as well as the control of power.

The EU Council of Ministers is an example of such a lack of democracy. Its decisions severely lack democratic legitimacy, not least because the European Parliament has restricted rights only. If the European Union were to apply for membership in the European Union it would be rejected for having an insufficiently democratic constitution.

In the debate about the role of NGOs in democratic processes, democratic legitimacy and democratic representation are often confused. NGOs are not elected and are not representative, but they certainly have democratic legitimacy. This legitimacy is based on basic political rights: the right of assembly, freedom of opinion, and the right to form coalitions. It is absolutely clear that at the end of a pluralistic decision-making process, only elected powers, meaning a government and its parliament, can make final decisions.

More than ever, NGOs are an indispensable element in a pluralistic society and are needed to frame and influence the political decision-making process. They are a necessary counterweight to organized commercial interests that influence this process in a much less transparent way (such as the Global Climate Coalition, an industrial association, did during negotiations on the Climate Convention).

The legitimacy of international NGOs is also derived from their performance record. Governments have rarely initiated any of the international conventions or treaties agreed upon in the past decade. Almost all of them have been initiated by civil society and supported by the science community. From the International Court of Justice to the Climate Convention, from the Montreal Protocol to the Jubilee 2000 debt relief agreements for highly indebted poor countries (HIPC Initiative), the driving force was civil society.

This impressive performance record, however, also reflects the severe inability of the international governance system to solve fundamental problems. The more prominent role of international civil society in the global governance system is therefore not exclusively a positive phenomenon.

As Professor Florini rightly points out, the participation rights of international civil society organizations in the decision-making process of international institutions dealing with economic integration (WTO and IMF, in particular) are weak, and the decisions these organizations make lack transparency. This makes them an easy target for criticism. It has to be pointed out, however, that in other areas the influence of international civil society is very productive and well organized, for instance, at the level of the United Nations and U.N. conventions and treaties. Article 71 of the U.N. Charter covers the involvement of NGOs. There are about 1,400 NGOs registered with the Economic and Social Council (ECOSOC). Depending on their status, NGOs have the right to call for conference papers, participate in sessions, make submissions, and speak.

It goes without saying that increasing both transparency and the involvement of civil society are necessary developments for those organizations and institutions dealing with economic integration. It will only be a matter of time until these organizations open up; otherwise, they will face increasing public pressure.

To conclude, the future role of NGOs depends on whether international politics deal with global problems in a more effective and democratic way. Sadly, this is not a current trend, which is why NGO pressure must increase. But even if decision-making processes become more inclusive and decisions more transparent, it will not be enough. Such processes organize the discussion better and eventually lead to more widely accepted decisions. But they do not address the root of the problem, namely, the lack of formal democracy in the global governance system.

There will be no movement from protest to participation in the sense that protest will decrease and participation increase. NGOs will continue to do both because they have no negotiating power. They are forced to mobilize public opinion to push their agendas. This is the inherent dialectic of NGO strategy.

There are some divisive issues within the international civil society movement which may influence its impact on the whole. Among these is the important question of the degree to which social and environmental standards will be linked to the international trade regime. Whereas Northern groups emphasize this link, Southern groups often fear, like their governments, that this link can be subject to hidden protectionist moves.

The real challenge, however, is to make international politics more democratic by establishing more democratic control. This has to be done on two sides by strengthening the role of national parliaments in framing international decisions and by providing for the more direct democratic control of international bodies/treaties.

The activities of international NGOs are necessary but they constitute only a second-best solution compared to truly democratic processes at the global level. Such processes need to be established over time.

What Are the Necessary Ingredients for the World Trading Order?

Sylvia Ostry

1 Introduction

The title assigned to this paper is a question: what are the necessary ingredients for the world trading order? The answer could be very short: leadership. That's always the answer, of course, and it's hardly very enlightening. But the world trading system is in dire need of reform and the reformers – if they exist – are nowhere to be seen, neither in Geneva nor in national capitals. And the stakes are high, no less than the sustainability of the rules-based multilateral system.

This paper will begin with a brief sketch of the background to the formidable challenges to the institution that houses the trading system, the WTO. These arise from the unintended consequences of the Uruguay Round and are compounded by Doha. I will then turn to the issue of reform and sketch some suggestions to improve both the WTO's internal functioning and its external relations with stakeholders.

2 The Political Economy of Trade Policy Making

The Uruguay Round was the eighth negotiation under the auspices of the GATT (General Agreement on Tariffs and Trade), created in 1948 as part of the postwar international economic architecture. The primary mission of GATT was to reduce or eliminate the border barriers which had been erected in the 1930s and contributed to the Great Depression and its disastrous consequences. The GATT reflected its origins in the postwar world in that it provided rules to buffer or interface between the *international* objective of sustained liberalization and the objectives of *domestic policy*, primarily the Keynesian Consensus of full employment and the creation of the welfare state. This accord was reached with little difficulty since few countries were involved; they were almost all developed countries; and they could operate as a "club" whose members broadly shared basic norms and values with respect to trade (Keohane and Nye 2000).

Before the Uruguay Round, the GATT club worked very well. Tariffs and non-tariff barriers were significantly reduced and trade grew faster than output as each fed the other. Most rounds were essentially managed by the United States and the European Community. The developing countries were largely ignored as players. Agriculture was virtually excluded from negotiations so the transatlantic alliance, helped by the Cold War's constraint on trade frictions, was the effective manager of the international trading system.

The Uruguay Round was a watershed in the evolution of that system. For the first time agriculture was at the center of the negotiations and the European effort to block the launch of the negotiations to avoid coming to grips with their heavily subsidized and protected Common Agricultural Policy went on for half a decade. This foot-dragging also spawned a new single-interest coalition – the Australian-led Cairns Group, which included Southern countries from Latin America and Asia determined to ensure that liberalization of agricultural trade would not be relegated to the periphery by the Americans and the Europeans as it always had in the past.

But the role of a group of developing countries, tagged the G10 hardliners and led by Brazil and India, was in many ways even more important in the Uruguay Round's transformation of the system. The G10 were bitterly opposed to the inclusion of the so-called "new issues" – trade in services, intellectual property, and investment – central to the American negotiating agenda.

Although the "new issues" are *not* identical – obviously negotiations on telecommunications or financial services differ from intellectual property rights – they do have one common or generic characteristic. Thus, they involve not the border barriers of the original GATT but domestic regulatory and legal systems embedded in the institutional infrastructure of the economy. The degree of intrusiveness into domestic sovereignty bears little resemblance to the shallow integration of the GATT with its focus on border barriers and its buffers to safeguard domestic policy space. The WTO thus shifted from the GATT model of *negative* regulation – what governments must not do – to *positive* regulation – or what governments must do.

The inclusion of the new issues in the Uruguay Round was an American initiative and this policy agenda was largely driven by American MNEs (multinational enterprises) who were market leaders in the services and high tech sectors. These corporations made it clear to the government that without a fundamental rebalancing of the GATT they would not continue to support a multilateral policy but would prefer a bilateral or regional track. But they didn't just talk the talk, they also walked the walk, organizing business coalitions in support of services and intellectual property in Europe and Japan as well as some smaller OECD countries. The activism paid off and it's fair to say that American MNEs played a key – perhaps even *the* key – role in establishing the new global trading system. I'll return to this shortly.

By the onset of the 1990s a major change in economic policy was underway. The debt crisis of the 1980s, and thus the role of the IMF and the World Bank, plus the fall of the Berlin Wall – a confluence of two unrelated events – ushered in a major transformation in the economic policy paradigm of developing countries. Economic reforms – deregulation, privatization, liberalization – were seen as essential elements for launching and sustaining growth. Economic regulatory reform is at the heart of the concept of trade in services. Even without the thrust from the Uruguay Round, many developing countries began to see the reform of key service sectors such as telecommunications as essential building blocks in the soft infrastructure underpinning growth and the GATT as a means to furthering domestic reform.

Thus, well before the end of the Round the hardline coalition had disappeared and coalitions of developing countries concentrated on the liberalization of agriculture and textiles and clothing and were among the strongest supporters of the negotiations they so adamantly opposed in the 1980s. What I have called a North-South Grand Bargain was completed and was quite different from old-time GATT reciprocity – I'll open my market if you'll open yours. It was essentially an implicit deal: the opening of OECD markets to agriculture and labor-intensive manufactured goods, especially textiles and clothing, for the inclusion into the trading system of trade in services, intellectual property, and (albeit to a lesser extent than originally demanded) investment. Also – as virtually a last minute piece of the deal – the creation of a new institution, the WTO, with the strongest dispute settlement mechanism in the history of international law. Since the WTO consisted of a "single undertaking" (in WTO legal-ese) the deal was pretty much take it or leave it for the Southern countries. So they took it but, it's safe to say, without a full comprehension of the profoundly transformative implication of this new trading system (an incomprehension shared by the Northern negotiators as well I might add).

The Northern piece of the bargain consisted of some limited progress in agriculture, with a commitment to go further in new negotiations in 2000; limited progress in textiles and clothing with most of the restrictions to be eliminated later rather than sooner; a rather significant reduction in tariffs in goods in exchange for deeper cuts by developing countries. The essence of the South side of the deal – the inclusion of the new issues – requires major upgrading and change in the institutional infrastructure of many or most Southern countries. These changes will take time and cost money. Implementation thus involves considerable investment often with uncertain medium-term results.

It is also important to note that the Uruguay Round Grand Bargain did not only include *economic* but also *social* regulation. In the OECD countries, but not the South, social regulation (environment, food safety, labor, etc.) started in the late

1960s, driven in large part by environmental and consumer NGOs, and has been accelerating since then. Since the establishment of the WTO the most high-profile and contentious disputes have concerned social regulatory issues (food safety and the environment) which are very sensitive in the OECD countries and this has emboldened the NGOs in their attack on the WTO's lack of transparency.

There were two significant unintended consequences to this Grand Bargain (or Bum Deal). One is a serious North-South divide in the WTO. While the South is hardly homogeneous, there is a broad consensus that the club model is no longer operational; that the asymmetry of the Uruguay Round must be ameliorated and must never be repeated; and thus Southern countries must play a far more proactive role in all WTO activities. This was evident at Doha, of which more below. Many of the countries are far better organized and informed, in part because of the rise of democracy and the growing awareness of trade policy issues in the general public, political institutions, and the business community. But also because of the role of a number of NGOs created in developing countries during the 1990s to provide information ranging from technical research to policy strategy papers. And since the mid-1990s the Internet has accelerated the linkages of South NGOs with a number of Northern partners in both Europe and the United States. These NGOs together act, in effect, as a "virtual secretariat."

The other, and equally important, unintended consequence of the Uruguay Round has been the rise in profile of the MNEs, in part due to their role in the Round. Indeed, for the more paranoid the Round was simply a conspiratorial collusion between American corporations and the U.S. government. In any case, the global current of deepening integration, accelerated by the Uruguay Round, has evoked a counter-current focused both on the MNEs and the WTO. Let me deal first with the MNEs.

The active role of the corporations in the Uruguay Round certainly raised their profile and made them a magnet for anti-trade advocates and made the WTO a magnet for what came to be called anti-corporate globalization. This was evident to anyone who watched on TV the battle of Seattle or the demonstrations at meetings in Washington or Prague or Genoa or Quebec City. But the most significant recent example concerns the pharmaceutical industry and the Aids crisis in Africa. As a result of a well-orchestrated campaign led by Oxfam and Médecins sans Frontières, pharmaceutical companies withdrew a lawsuit against South Africa; the United States abandoned a dispute against Brazil; and the Doha declaration included a remarkable political statement concerning the TRIPS agreement and health emergencies. And we can certainly expect a coordinated campaign over "enronitis." As one expert has wryly noted, a new service industry has emerged – the avoidance industry – comprised of financial wizards, lawyers, and creative accountants. The full impact of the avoidance industry, whose objective is avoidance of disclosure of accurate information, has yet to be revealed and should provide grist for the mill of the anti-corporate globalization movement. A summary description of that movement is worth a brief digression.

The rise in the profile of the MNEs in the Uruguay Round helped to make the WTO a magnet for anti-corporate globalization. Before expounding on the concerted attack on the WTO, I want to make clear that there is no homogeneous set of institutions called NGOs. Even if we separate out the development groups in poor countries from the advocacy NGOs, whose main objective is to shape policy, one has to divide the latter into several categories. For example, I've already noted the new virtual secretariat for Southern countries, and there has been a remarkable proliferation of groups centered on establishing business codes of conduct, and there are groups rich in technical and legal expertise who usually consult "inside" the system, and all of these are rather different from what I've termed the *Mobilization Networks*, for whom a major objective is to rally support for dissent at a specific event – a WTO ministerial meeting, the Summit of the Americas, a meeting of the World Bank and International Monetary Fund, the G8 Summit and so on.

The main objectives of the mobilization networks are to heighten public awareness of the target international institution's role in globalization and, by doing so, to change its agenda and mode of operation – or, in the case of the more extreme members, to shut it down. While these networks are loosely knit coalitions of very disparate groups, an analysis of the networks at Seattle (in 1999), Washington, Bangkok and Prague (in 2000) and Quebec City, Genoa and Doha (in 2001) show that there is a core group – let's call it dissent.com – of mainly North American and European NGOs but also including some from developing countries. These NGOs are headed by a new breed of policy entrepreneurs who have very effectively utilized the Internet to create what could be termed a new service industry – the business of dissent. It's important to stress that the dissent industry is largely a product of the Internet revolution which provides advocacy NGOs with economies of scale and also of scope by linking widely disparate groups with one common theme: anti-corporate globalization and pro-democracy. The main charge is that the WTO is dominated by the interests of the MNEs and that is rules and procedures are secretive and undemocratic.

Of course individual members of these networks pursue many other advocacy routes including lobbying as a means (greatly aided by the media) of influencing national governments. But the strategy of the networks to focus on demonstrations at specific events was designed to influence public opinion and through that route initiate change in the policy processes of the international institutions. So has the dissent industry been successful? In the case of the WTO, I would argue that while it's early to tell, there *has* been an impact on the agenda. The emphasis on development as the core of the new Doha round (or rather "development agenda") and the political statement on health emergencies in poor countries, are probably in part due to a shift in emphasis by NGOs to issues with strong moral resonance. And, it is worth emphasizing, their consistent and insistent refrain of lack of transparency has, for some, struck at the heart of the institution's legitimacy.

But the shift in NGO strategy was essential for other reasons. While there was destruction of property in Seattle and other meetings there was nothing comparable to Genoa where one protester was killed. A number of mainline NGOs stayed away because they were fearful of being associated with the violence planned by the anarchist Black Bloc and neo-fascists although no one could have foreseen what occurred, including the extraordinary brutality of the police. There is probably an inevitable tendency for all demonstrations to attract extremists – a free ride is hard to decline. Escalating violence generates the need for more police security which likewise generates more violence and attracts more extremists. And, of course, Genoa was hardly the end of the story.

The terrorist attack of September 11, while unrelated to the anti-globalization movement per se, greatly added to the pressure for dissent.com to adopt a new strategy and changes are underway. In the United States, attempts of the left to morph into a peace movement – centered on attacking the war against terrorism and American support of Israel – is hardly attracting mainline NGOs or the labor unions. The recent (April, 2002) Bank–Fund meetings in Washington attracted few demonstrators and those who marched and chanted were ignored by the media. But the impact of the NGO campaign on global health as exemplified by the Doha declaration may also be a signal of a new shift in strategy from dissent to dialogue. A recent report released by Oxfam International entitled *Rigged Rules and Double Standards* (2002) asserts that international trade can benefit the poor if the rich countries would reduce their protectionist barriers, especially in agriculture and labor-intensive products, and then elaborates on a range of policy proposals. The report has been attacked by some NGOs who still prefer dissent to dialogue but welcomed as a basis for discussion by some governments and international institutions. It is obviously too early to tell whether these examples – in effect centered on alleviating third-world poverty and disease – will serve to unify or re-create the anti-globalization movement. But it's also premature to declare that the movement died after September 11, as exemplified by a *Wall Street Journal* editorial headline "Adieu Seattle."[1] Whatever the outcome, the NGOs' demand for more transparency in the WTO will certainly not go away.

In sum, the Uruguay Round and its unintended consequences transformed the multilateral trading system and the political economy of policy making. The Round, in effect, initiated one small step in the creation of a global single market – a step for which a majority of its members were totally unprepared. The intru-

---

[1]   See also Rushford (2002: 7): "What began with a sizzle in Seattle has now fizzled. Maybe the actual day that the anti-globalist movement fizzled was September 11, 2001...".

siveness of the new system touched the exposed raw nerve of sovereignty. And yet, to undertake the formidable role of housing and sustaining the system, the negotiations produced a minimalist, member-driven institution with extremely weak legislative and executive powers and an extremely strong, judicialized dispute settlement system. This is an asymmetry which must be rectified. Clearly, the system is in dire need of reform. Yet at the Ministerial Meeting in Doha reform was not mentioned. And Doha initiated another potential transformation of the WTO into a "development institution." Let me briefly review the Doha outcome before turning to some suggestions for strengthening the WTO.

It's worth stressing that it's more than symbolic that the outcome of Doha was termed a "development agenda" and not a round. While it's true that the Doha Declaration was a masterpiece of creative ambiguity and the devil remains in the details of negotiation, the major objective of the meeting was to avoid a repeat of the Seattle debacle which ended with a walkout of virtually all Southern countries. Thus the great success of Doha was that it didn't fail and this involved convincing developing countries, especially the poorest in Africa, that trade was good for development. Both the United States and the European Community visited Africa to woo Ministers and the Declaration repeatedly refers to technical assistance and capacity building now called, only half in jest, the new conditionality. Pushed by the successful NGO campaign about AIDS in Africa, the Americans were willing to antagonize Big Pharma. The Europeans were most skilful in securing a waiver for their preferential arrangement with the ACP (African, Caribbean and Pacific) countries by wily deal making with the Latin American banana exporters. So Doha was unique in its focus on the South and on development.

Doha, of course, included many other agenda items. Market access for industrial products; agriculture and services; rules such as countervail against subsidies and anti-dumping; as well as the so-called Singapore issues of competition policy, investment, government procurement, and trade facilitation. And for the first time in the history of the trading system environment was specifically added to the agenda. Most of these items have a North-South dimension and negotiations will be complex and difficult. Indeed the ambiguous drafting – for example in agriculture and the Singapore issues – leaves considerable uncertainty about how the negotiations will proceed and whether the target date of 2005 is feasible or even realistic.

But that uncertainty rests on more than the usual difficulties of complex negotiations: after all, the outcome of the Uruguay Round in 1994 could certainly not have been forecast at the launch in Punta del Este in 1986. I would argue that adding another layer, i.e. development, to the already weak and strained infrastructure of the WTO, significantly adds to the need for strengthening the WTO. A very positive sign of the new Doha focus was the March 11, 2002 Pledging Conference which established a Global Trust Fund and more than doubled the WTO budget for technical assistance. But there remains considerable disagreement over how to effectively deploy the funds and concern about the WTO's lack of institutional capability in this field. While seminars and workshops – the customary form of WTO technical assistance – may provide technical information about the WTO it will not build trade policy-making capacity in individual countries which is a far more complex task requiring involvement of indigenous institutions. This capacity building would have to be customized by country and trade policy would have to be integrated into the overall development strategy so that countries could exploit the opportunities of open markets. The WTO certainly recognizes that that approach lies well outside its range of expertise. Indeed, the main responsibility rests with the World Bank, regional development banks and other institutions such as UNCTAD. Thus the WTO confronts an enormous challenge of coordination: international coherence writ large! This will require not only some additional resources (trade expertise will not suffice) but, since the ideas of "mainstreaming trade into development" and "aid for trade" (Hoekman 2002: 23–26) are both complex and contentious, an ongoing policy dialogue will be essential. It's doubtful that the Committee on Trade and Development could serve that purpose since dialogue would be chilled by linkage to negotiations – a generic difficulty in the WTO as will shortly be discussed.

Of course the outcome for Doha has recently been further clouded by the looming tit-for-tat steel safeguard battle launched by the United States and, even more by the astonishing Farm Bill which increases agricultural subsidies by $190 billion or 80 percent over the next decade and will hurt the poorer countries most of all. Both these actions, but especially the latter, illustrate what H.L. Mencken described as the essential character of Congressional trade policy: if a congressman had cannibals in his district, he would promise them missionaries for breakfast. This was changed by legislation in the 1930s when Congress, chastened by the Smoot–Hawley tariffs, yielded its constitutional authority for trade policy to the Executive branch. But it now appears that we're back to the 1930s. The continuing "clawback" by Congress of trade policy from the Executive reflects not only the end of the Cold War, with its spillover from high policy to low policy, but also the growing divisions in both parties over trade issues and the lack of interest of the American business community. After playing a major role in the Uruguay Round and in lobbying for Chinese membership in the WTO, American MNEs were conspicuous by their absence in both Seattle and Doha and in supporting fast-track trade bills in Congress. This apathy has profound implications because there is no effective counterbalance to the well-heeled protectionist lobbies. Of course the saying that trade policy is the most domestic of all policies is true everywhere and not only in Washington.

Indeed the significant rise in anti-dumping investigations in 2001 (348 compared with 251 in 2000 and an annual average of 232 in the 1990s (Mayer et al.

2001)) is especially worrying. Anti-dumping, the protectionist weapon of choice for the rich countries, is now widespread with India ranking second after the United States and China (the main target country) aiming to join the anti-dumping superpowers. It was once assumed that if developing countries began to use the trade remedy laws that would prove to be an incentive for reform. Nothing could be further from the truth as the debate over fast track in the U.S. Senate reveals. A number of Senators have insisted on a special exception for anti-dumping which would, in effect, remove the Executive authority to negotiate. While this is unlikely at present, the effort reflects the deeply entrenched opposition to reform of trade remedies in the U.S. Congress ("Fast Track": A4).[2] Since reform of anti-dumping was a centerpiece of the Southern countries at Doha (as was elimination of agricultural subsidies), the recent rise in protectionism will certainly worsen the prospects for a successful outcome.

But if Doha is in jeopardy, perhaps that could concentrate the minds of some negotiators on the need for reform. Even if that is wishful thinking, it can't do any harm to review some of the issues in the concluding section.

3   WTO: Suggestions for Reform

While the subject of WTO reform has recently evoked some interest in the academic community, as I've said, the same is not true in national capitals or in Geneva. After Seattle there was some desultory discussion on internal and external transparency, WTO-speak for internal reform to make the governance of the institution more open and inclusive, and external reform including more access to information and more opportunity for stakeholder participation. After a few meetings of the General Council which revealed strong opposition from many member countries – especially Southern – to even discussing the issues, the subject was dropped. After Doha, the General Council (after *four years* of deliberation) agreed on a set of procedures for de-restriction of documents and discussed some proposals for Ministerial preparatory processes and meetings which, if adopted, could impose a "straight jacket" on the consultation process and might "drive the real negotiations underground and ultimately lead to a less transparent procedure" (WTO Memorandum 2002; comment in Bridges 2002: 3).

As noted earlier, the WTO's executive (management) and legislative functions are extremely weak (especially but not only when compared with it's judicial pro-

---

[2]   The deal struck in Doha supposedly included negotiations on trade remedy laws because it was crucial "to preserve the illusion that we have room to manoeuvre in our discussions with M trading partners," according to a U.S. trade official. Some illusion, some deal!

cedures). This asymmetry in architectural design is grossly inappropriate to the broad and complex mandate imposed by the Uruguay Round and amplified by Doha. While there's no possibility of major institutional redesign in the foreseeable future, some modest incremental reform should not be ruled out. In this regard three priorities should be considered. The first two concern internal functions and the third deals with external transparency.

3.1   How Can the WTO Be Managed?

Although both Bretton Woods institutions included weighted voting, to ensure that the economic power of the United States and the United Kingdom (the founding fathers) would be reflected in both policy and management, this was not the case in the ITO (International Trade Organization). This apparent anomaly stemmed from the American view that since in the trade regime other countries had to implement the outcome of negotiations it was better to adopt a consensus approach which (in the small club of 23 members) would not be difficult to achieve. But, to ensure effective management – avoid paralysis by consensus – the ITO Charter included an Executive Board. The Executive Board was to consist of eighteen members, with broad geographic representation and should include "members of chief economic importance, in the determination of which particular regard shall be paid to their shares in international trade" (ITO 1948: Article 78).[3] There was provision for rotation of the 10 members who were not classified as "of chief economic importance" every three years. And the Executive Board was to be responsible "for the execution of the policies of the Organization" (ITO 1948: Article 81).

When the ITO died and the GATT became the home of the multilateral trading system, the ITO Charter was defunct. The WTO, its successor – with over 140 members at present and likely to reach over 170 in the near future – did not provide for an Executive Board. Indeed, if anything, the WTO rules provide less room for flexibility that did the GATT.

Article IX-1 of the WTO Agreement provides that "the practice of decision-making by consensus followed under the GATT 1947" (WTO 1994: 11). This consensus (the word didn't appear in the ITO Charter or the GATT) has been "elevated from its previous status as an unwritten practice to being enshrined as a rule" (Steger 2000: 153). And, as one WTO legal expert has noted, new rules were added which, *inter alia*, make decision-making and amendments of the Agreement "considerably more complex than the previous GATT provisions" (Steger 2000:

---

3   For an analysis of the American position against weighted voting see McIntyre (1954).

151).[4] More flexibility for the Club of 23 than the diverse and often conflictual Coterie of 144, soon to climb to 170!

As the negotiations on Doha proceed the examples of paralysis of decision making concerning even the most trivial matters are growing apace. Some informal discussion on how, for example, to separate out housekeeping operations from substantive issues, has been launched but is unlikely to yield results anytime soon, though if paralysis and bickering get bad enough perhaps reason may eventually prevail. Mike Moore, Director-General of the WTO raised the issue for discussion in his speech to the Public Symposium on the Doha Development Agenda in Geneva at the end of April 2002: "how are we going to respect the "consensus principle" in about five years time when the organization will account for more than 170 member governments? ... Shouldn't we soon start to discuss the need for some sort of managerial structure capable of taking care of day-to-day business of the WTO?" (WTO Press Release, April 29, 2002). It's worth noting that these questions are answered by a proposal made in a Joint Statement on the Multilateral Trading System in February 2001 by three former heads of GATT/WTO: Arthur Dunkel, Peter Sutherland, and Renato Ruggiero (*WTO News* 2001: 7).

These former Directors General propose establishing "a management board which could take routine decisions not affecting members' rights" (not unlike an executive board but with a more politically correct title). Their proposal was intended to be included in the Doha agenda.

It was not. They also made a second proposal that a "senior level policy consultancy group" be established to debate current trade issues in a "wider policy context". This reads like a reformulated version of a *policy forum* – CG18 (Consultative Group of Eighteen) – established in the GATT in 1975. A policy forum is *essential* if the WTO liberalization momentum is to be sustained. Let me briefly sketch out the history and function of the CG18 to explain why this is so.

3.2   Policy Forum: CG18 Redux

A policy forum would provide the locus for discussion and debate of basic issues – such as the definition of domestic policy space to be safeguarded in the international system. The GATT implicitly defined a domestic policy space in a number of ways: an escape clause; an article (Article XX) that spelled out exceptions to GATT rules for public policy objectives; a national security exemption; a balance of payments exception, etc. (Jackson 1997: 203–216). But these mechanisms designed to protect domestic sovereignty reflect the shared views of the Club in 1948 and obviously have to be reconsidered and redefined. This will, of course, hardly

---

[4]   See also Bronckers (1999).

be easy: there is no longer a consensus, Keynesian, Washington or whatever. The only way of grappling with this most fundamental issue is through debate informed by policy-analytic research. There are a number of other examples of policy-related concerns such as the relationship between trade, growth, and poverty or the effectiveness of capacity building in mainstreaming trade in development or the linkages between the trading rules and environmental rules, to cite a few. Then policy options could be proposed and if a consensus is achieved, the proposal would be sent to the General Council, the governing arm of the institution. There was, indeed, such a forum in the GATT, called the CG 18 (Consultative Group of 18: was the number an echo of the ITO?) but an attempt to establish a successor at the end of the Uruguay Round failed.

The CG18 was established in July 1975 not by trade ministries but as a result of a recommendation of the Committee of Twenty Finance Ministers after the breakdown of Bretton Woods. (The Committee of Twenty also established the IMF's Interim Committee.) Its purpose was to provide a forum for senior officials from *capitals* to discuss policy issues and not to, in any way, challenge the authority of the GATT Council. Because of the creation of the Interim Committee, the Committee of Twenty felt the need for a similar body in the GATT to facilitate international coordination between the two institutions. The composition of the membership was based on a combination of economic weight and regional representation but there was provision for other countries to attend as alternates and observers or by invitation. Each meeting was followed by a comprehensive report to the GATT Council.

Because it was a forum for *senior officials from national capitals*, it provided an opportunity to improve coordination of policies at the home base. This is now far more important because of the expansion of subjects under the WTO. (Indeed there is no " Minister of Trade" today but a number of Ministries with concerns covered by the WTO.) After the Tokyo Round the CG18 was the only forum in the GATT where agriculture was discussed and, in the long lead-up to the Uruguay Round, trade in services. The CG18 was the only forum for a full, wide-ranging, often contentious debate on the basic issues of the Uruguay Round. There was an opportunity to analyze and explain issues without a commitment to specific negotiating positions. Negotiating committees *inhibit* discussion because rules are at stake. Words matter and might be used, for example, in a dispute settlement ruling as was a report by the Committee on Trade and Environment with a predictable chilling effect on constructive dialogue. Thus the *absence* of direct linkage to rules is essential to the diffusion of knowledge which rests on a degree of informality, flexibility, and adaptability.

While establishing the policy forum would be a great step forward, it is unlikely to function effectively without an increase in the WTO's research capability. Analytical papers on key issues are needed to launch serious discussions in Geneva and to improve the diffusion of knowledge in national capitals. In order to keep up to date and reasonably small in size, the WTO could not possibly generate all its policy analysis in-house. The WTO secretariat would have to establish a research network linked to other institutions. This *knowledge networking* should include academic, environmental, business, labor, and intergovernmental organizations such as the OECD, UNCTAD, Bretton Woods, and environmental institutions. This becomes even more essential since Doha because, as should be underlined once more, the capacity building for developing countries will require complex and extensive coordination with the World Bank and other institutions. Moreover, establishing a research or knowledge network can enhance the ability of the WTO Director-General to play a more effective role leading and guiding the policy debate. This will be politically contentious but is essential. Just imagine what would have happened in the 1980s debt crisis if the head of the IMF had had the authority of the head of the GATT! There would have been a series of meetings to discuss meetings and so on while Latin America went down the drain.

In the terminology of the international regime literature the policy forum would become a broad meta-regime founded on mutually agreed basic principles and fostered by a combination of strategic assets: a knowledge infrastructure in the form of a research capability; a meeting infrastructure for knowledge diffusion, debate, peer group pressure; strategic planning and monitoring of policy performance. But no "hard power" to make rules.

A key difficulty in establishing the forum would be to determine the membership. One formula already exists in the former CG18 which was never officially terminated. But it would probably be necessary to include the policy forum as part of a North-South trade-off. And that would require the big powers to agree that institutional reform was essential to the sustainability of the system. Au fond, the raison d'être of the forum would be to inform, energize, and facilitate the rule-making capability of the WTO. Perhaps members should be reminded that there is another route to change, i.e. litigation. Faced with that alternative might clarify some minds.

While reform of the dispute settlement system is also a matter of high priority, a number of recent proposals have generated a healthy debate. So I prefer to skip that subject and conclude with my third proposal for improving external transparency.

3.3   External Transparency

As noted earlier, the demand for greater transparency at the WTO has continued unabated since its establishment and is gaining broad support. The WTO has responded by providing information, speedily and effectively on its website, through informal secretariat briefings and has engaged civil society groups in annual symposia and, in the case of the Committee on Trade and Environment, in discussion. But even these efforts have been opposed by a number of Southern Countries.

Curiously, the issue of transparency and the participation at the national level has only recently been raised. The "Open Letter on Institutional Reforms in the WTO" sent by a group of NGOs to members in October 2001 (just before Doha) includes the "development of guidelines for national consultation with relevant stakeholders" among a number of other proposals.[5] Since reform issues were not on the table in Doha, there was no response. A similar silence greeted U.S. efforts, after the Seattle débacle, to discuss national policy processes in the WTO (of which more below).

Yet the WTO may be an outlier in its rejection of the relevance of this issue. It's useful to "benchmark" other institutions in the rapidly evolving international policy environment because in a globalizing world "policy spillover" has become increasingly significant. A review of developments in the OECD, and in international environmental and human rights law will serve to illustrate this point.

OECD: Transparency, Trade, Environment and Development

In 1993, the OECD Joint Working Party on Trade and Environment proposed that Transparency and Consultation be established as a principle of policy making in this domain. (That this innovation in governance involved environmental policies was hardly a coincidence – see below.) The proposal was adopted by Ministers as was the initiative to undertake case studies of member governments' consultative mechanisms and practices. These case studies were published in 1999 and 2000 (OECD 1999; OECD 2000a; OECD 2000b; OECD 2000c). They revealed a wide diversity among the countries reflecting, inter alia, culture, history, and legal systems, but also underscored the importance of "capacity" – analytic and financial resources – as a factor in determining the nature of the process.

In July 2001, the OECD directorate responsible for research in public management (PUMA) published a Policy Brief outlining a number of principles for good governance. The title of the brief was *Engaging Citizens in Policy-Making: Information, Consultation and Public Participation*. The lead paragraph provides the rationale for the initiative:

> Strengthening relations with citizens is a sound investment in better policy-making and a core element of good governance. It allows governments to tap new sources of policy-relevant ideas, information and resources when making decisions. Equally important, it contributes to building public trust in government, raising the quality of democracy and strengthening civic capacity. Such

---

5   See Open Letter on Institutional Reform (2001). The NGOs were WWF International, IATP, Action Aid, FOE International, and CIEL.

efforts help strengthen representative democracy in which parliaments play a central role. (OECD 2001: 1)

The reference to building public trust and enhancing the credibility of governments is of key significance in catalyzing the OECD initiative and of particular relevance in the trade policy domain. The anti-globalization movement reflects a more pervasive secular change underway since the mid-1970s in all OECD countries: a clear, marked decline in confidence in government and all political institutions (Ostry 2001a). (While in the United States, the events of September 11 radically reversed this trend, it is not clear how this will affect, if at all, international economic policy.) There are less data on this phenomenon in non-OECD countries, but anecdotal evidence suggests that an alienation from the élite is growing in many Southern countries and in Central and Eastern Europe. This is likely to increase if the trade negotiations are seriously impaired by the American farm bill since agriculture is so dominant in these countries.

There are many different views on the reasons for this worrisome phenomenon and no doubt different factors are operative in different countries. But one response – and not only by the OECD – has been to foster "ownership" of the policy process by increasing information, consultation, and active participation by a wider range of stakeholders. As the case studies and other OECD research demonstrated, while information access has increased over the past decade, there are large difference in consultation and "active participation and efforts to engage citizens in policy-making – are rare – and confined to a very few OECD countries" (OECD 2001: 3). What follows in the Brief are a number of policy suggestions and a set of ten guiding principles for OECD governments to engage citizens in policy-making (OECD 2001: 5) While these principles are not binding on OECD governments – being a form of "soft law" – their adoption by Ministers is not without significance.

The Aarhus Convention

When we move from the OECD's soft law to the Aarhus Convention we're moving from soft to hard law. The UNECE (United Nations Economic Commission for Europe) Convention on Access to Information, Public Participation in Decision-Making and Access to Justice in Environmental Matters was adopted on June 25, 1998, in the Danish city of Aarhus at the Fourth Ministerial Conference of the "Environment for Europe" process. It entered into force on October 30, 2001 with 40 signatories including members of the Economic Commission for Europe as well as states with consultative status with the E.C.E. (mainly central and eastern European countries) and the European Community.

Aarhus is built on Principle 10 of the Rio Conference on Environment and Development (UNCED) which underlined the importance of a participatory process in formulating and implementing environmental policy at the national level (Ebbesson 1997: 51–53). The idea of transparency and participation is deeply rooted in the environmental movement and policy domain both domestically and internationally because, as a number of international environmental law experts have pointed out, non-state actors frequently have more and better information than governments. These actors include private firms and various and diverse NGOs all of which have stakes (albeit often competing) in outcomes either as objects or beneficiaries of regulation (Raustiala 1997: 537–586).

But Aarhus is quite radical both in its content and, perhaps in its implications for international law. The Convention is built on 3 pillars – access to information; participation; access to domestic courts – and spells out in detail what each of these rights includes. It recognizes that forms of participation must be adapted to different legal and institutional systems and are dynamic in concept, i.e. should and will evolve over time. The intention of Aarhus, however, is to identify basic or preliminary elements that would entail a participatory process. The Convention also includes the need for follow-up monitoring of implementation measures, which should be transparent. And to ensure transparency, the public is granted access to judicial review procedures when their rights to information and participation have been breached.

Whether or not the Aarhus Treaty will be endorsed by other countries, the implications for international law could be significant since there will no doubt be an effort by the proponents of transparency and participation to extend the Aarhus principles to customary international environmental law (see below). But while Aarhus concentrates on legal and administrative procedures, i.e. on procedural rights, it also includes a reference to human rights in the preamble and in some other provisions (Ebbesson 1997: 69–72). Many NGOs are pushing for a rights-based approach in the environmental domain and Aarhus may have opened up a small window of opportunity. But that aside, the human rights channel to greater transparency and participation looks very plausible, Aarhus or not.

Human Rights and Participatory Democracy

The push for including human rights in the WTO is linked to the ongoing – and often heated – debate on customary international law. In international law, the status of a rule is determined by its source. Thus international conventions such as Aarhus (hard law) presents rules and enforcement agreed by and applicable only to members while customary law relates to obligations established from "a general and consistent practice of states followed by them out of a sense of legal obligation" and binds all states (Howse and Mutua 2000: 7–10).

There is considerable disagreement as to whether and which human rights have status as custom and the proposal that human rights should prevail over international trade law, i.e. override those WTO rules which are alleged to violate basic human rights has generated a storm of controversy (Ostry 2001b: 11–13). The battle seems set to continue. Yet, as several experts have noted, recent rulings of the Appellate Board cite the Vienna Convention on the Law of Treaties which allows for the emergence of new laws in the future (Howse and Mutua 2000: 9–11). Thus, some legal experts have argued that the Preamble of the WTO Agreement, which refers to sustainable development and the need for the poorest countries to develop and grow, states values that could be interpreted as basic human rights (Petersmann 2001: 24–28).[6]

The legal (as opposed to the legislative) route to inserting human rights into the WTO was given a leg up by another decision of a dispute settlement panel concerning American trade law Section 301. Included in the Panel's decision was the statement that "it would be entirely wrong to consider that the position of individuals is of no relevance to the GATT/WTO legal matrix. Many of the benefits to members which are meant to flow as a result of the acceptance of various disciplines under the GATT/WTO depend on the activity of individual economic operators in the national and global market places" and thus "the multilateral trading system is, per force, composed not only of the States but also, indeed mostly, of individual economic operators."[7]

This astonishing conclusion of the Panel has certainly attracted the attention of WTO watchers in the legal community – though, evidently, not of member governments as one prominent legal expert noted:

> I would venture to guess that if this particular proposition were put to a vote in the General Council of the WTO, it would be rejected by governments who want to preserve the WTO as a cozy club of trade bureaucrats. In accordance with the WTO procedures, however, it was automatically adopted by the WTO Dispute Settlement Body. Thus, this cutting-edge decision will influence future WTO panellists and the *invisible college of international law* [emphasis added] in the years ahead. (Charnovitz 2001: 108)

Among the individual rights of interest to the invisible college is certainly the right of public participation in policy making as, for example, specified in the Aarhus Convention. Indeed an entire school of international law based on "interactional theory" points that "law is persuasive when it is perceived as legitimate by most actors" and legitimacy rests on inclusive processes (which) reinforce the commitments of participants in the system to the substantive outcomes achieved

---

6   The ruling of the Appellate Body in an environment trade dispute cited the Preamble in adopting an "updated" interpretation of the term "exhaustible natural resources" to include endangered species because of the evolution of international environmental law in recent years.

7   See Sections 301–310 of the Trade Act of 1974, Report of the Panel, 22 December 1999, WT/DS/152/R, paragraph 7.72 and 7.76.

by implicating participants in their generation (Brunnée and Toope 2000/2001: 53).[8] This sounds very much like the OECD approach, that norms generated through inclusive processes of decision making enhance governmental legitimacy and enjoy a greater degree of compliance. This is part of the spreading climate of ideas – we could call it "norm spillover." The WTO is unlikely to be immune. The "invisible college" will not be silent or inactive.

I would predict that if the *legal* route to inserting human rights law is chosen, the results will be profoundly traumatic for the WTO. Such a pervasive and open-ended transformation of the present system, determined by a panel or an appellate board, would be rejected by most if not all members and generate a furious back-lash against the "crown jewel" of the WTO – the dispute settlement mechanism. The issue of the WTO and human rights is an issue for debate – in a new policy forum. If there is to be any change in WTO rules it must be legislated not litigated.

WTO: "Legislate" don't Litigate

I insert the word "legislate" in quotation marks because my proposal need not in-volve a change in the formal rules of the WTO – a most difficult and lengthy prop-osition as everyone would agree. Rather, I would propose an informal, voluntary initiative to incorporate discussion of the national trade policy-making processes into the WTO under the broad rubric of transparency, a pillar of the GATT/WTO system from its origins. As I have argued above, there is a growing consensus among not only legal and policy-analytic communities but also in a number of in-ter-governmental institutions that participatory processes improve policy out-comes and enhance the legitimacy of policy and compliance with norms and laws. Let's briefly review the state of play in the relationship between the WTO and the trade policy stakeholders including the NGOs.

At the April 1994 Ministerial Meeting in Marrakesh which concluded the Uru-guay Round, Article V: 2 of the Agreement stated: "The General Council may make appropriate arrangements for consultation and co-operation with non-gov-ernmental organisations concerned with matters related to those of the WTO" (WTO 1994: 9).

In order to clarify the precise *legal* meaning of this broad directive the General Council on July 18, 1996 spelled out a set of guidelines covering transparency in-cluding release of documents, *ad hoc* informal contracts with NGOs, etc. Guideline 6 is most pertinent in the context of this present discussion:

> Members have pointed to the special character of the WTO, which is both a le-gally binding inter-governmental treaty of rights and obligations among its Mem-bers and a forum for negotiation. As a result of extensive discussions, there is

---

[8]   See also Koh (1997).

currently a broadly held view that it would not be possible for NGOs to be directly involved in the work of the WTO or its meetings. Closer consultation and co-operation with NGOs can also be met constructively through *appropriate processes at the national level where lies primary responsibility for taking into account the different elements of public interest which are brought to bear on trade policy-making* [emphasis added]. (Marceau and Pederson 1999: 45)

Nothing happened with respect to the admonition to focus on the national level until after the Seattle debacle. At a meeting of the General Council in July 2000 which included a discussion on external transparency (under the agenda item "other business") the Chairman suggested that members might make written contributions on the subject after making informal consultations in the autumn. This suggestion was criticized by several members as was the Chairman's decision to propose discussion under the heading of "Other Business." The Chairman explained that since there was strong opposition to place this issue on a formal agenda he had decided to raise it under "Other Business" but since some delegations did want to discuss external transparency "he believed it would be difficult to continuously postpone even an informal discussion" (WTO General Council 2000a: 60). After further discussion among the supporters and opponents of informal discussions, the meeting was adjourned.

On October 13, 2000 the United States made a submission to the General Council's Informal Consultations on External Transparency. After noting that the 1996 Guidelines suggested the consultations should take place at the national level and a brief review of U.S. Processes in this respect, the American delegation proposed that since all members "could benefit from an exchange of information on national experiences and approaches ... members be invited to provide information on this respective approaches to providing their public with information and opportunity for input on developments in the trading system" (WTO General Council 2000b: 3). On November 9, 2000 an Informal General Council meeting was convened to discuss external transparency. Nothing much happened. End of the story.[9]

The same countries (mostly developing) opposed to increasing transparency at the WTO level were also opposed to discussing the policy process at the national level. There has been criticism about the more powerful well-financed Northern NGOs demanding two bites of the apple. Fair enough – the issue merits discussion. But how realistic, in light of the current state of affairs in the multilateral trading system, to suggest *no* bite at the apple? For those countries who reject even an informal discussion of their domestic policy processes it's useful to spell out the benefits of such a project.

---

[9]   World Trade Organization General Council. Informal Consultations on External Transparency (2000, November 9). Sent to author in response to request for information to prepare this Chapter.

First and foremost it is very important to emphasize that a discussion about the national policy processes would be simply that – a means for informing other countries about one's own practices and learning about theirs. There is clearly no one-size-fits-all model but rather considerable diversity related to history, culture, legal institutions, level of development and so on. A pilot project I have undertaken in cooperation with the Washington-based Inter-American Dialogue and the Inter-American Development Bank revealed very significant differences among the 8 countries surveyed: Argentina, Brazil, Canada, Chile, Columbia, Mexico, United States, and Uruguay (Inter-American Development Bank 2002). Of these only Canada and the United States have established institutional arrangements involving both legislative bodies and a wide range of interested parties or stakeholders including business, farmers, unions, NGOs, and academics. This is not surprising since the OECD studies showed that participatory processes were rare in member countries. And a 1996 study by the Swiss Coalition of Development Organizations showed that of 30 countries surveyed (both developed and developing) only 3 had formal mechanisms for consultation (Canada, United States, and Switzerland) (Bellemann and Gerster 1996: 31–74).

Nonetheless, given this North-South dichotomy (and there are significant differences between Canada and the United States because of differences in basic governance, i.e. a parliamentary versus a presidential system) the Latin countries were by no means homogeneous and, further, in some an evolutionary process was underway partly in response to changes in trade policy such as Mercosur or the recent U.S. farm bill. The policy process should be evolutionary, reflecting systemic changes (such as the transformation from GATT to the WTO) and changes in the policy environment. A participatory consulting process allows governments to inform stakeholders on a continuing basis and while they may not always like what they hear (trade policy in the best of times involves change and change produces winners and losers) they will be less likely to reject the entire regime.

Moreover, by sharing information on national processes stakeholders in many countries without adequate technical or financial resources – like small and medium enterprises (SMEs) – gain useful information on market opportunities or other issues of interest. In a related point, it should be noted that lack of technical and financial resources for many stakeholders and also for some government ministries and parliaments was a major factor affecting the nature of the process in a number of Latin American countries.

While there are undoubtedly benefits accruing from a more participatory policy process there are also costs, which is certainly one reason many countries are wary of the project. There are costs for governments in terms of time, expertise, and financial resources and there are significant differences in resources among the stakeholders. Since business lobbies are better equipped than other groups, an insider-outsider mentality can develop and the media are always happy to highlight the battles. Or some stakeholders, simply by being engaged in the process, develop unrealistic expectations about outcome and are frustrated when all their demands are, inevitably, not delivered. For the wily "statesman" secrecy is considered essential, especially as the negotiations move to closure and the idea of a participatory process is an oxymoron – unless it provides an opportunity for co-option. All these issues arose in the Western Hemisphere country studies and the discussion repeatedly made clear that there were no magic bullets; the policy process was complex and messy; processes should be in a condition of continuing evolution. And the bottom line in all this deserves stressing: that it is the role of *government* to make policy; transparency and participation are *not* a replacement for *governmental responsibility.*

In the WTO context, weighing costs and benefits thus rests on the judgement of each member country. The arguments presented here suggest that there are likely to be significant systemic costs from doing nothing and these should be considered by members when rejecting any WTO initiative. The erosion of the multilateral system will impact the weaker more than the stronger because the alternative to a rules-based system is one based on power.

Having presented my case for a WTO external transparency initiative, let me conclude with a sketch of how it could be launched.

Transparency and the TPRM

Transparency was one of the founding principles of the postwar trading system.[10] Article 38 of the Havana Charter for the International Trade Organization became Article 10 of the GATT, which survived the death of the ITO. The article was entitled "Publication and Administration of Trade Regulations – Advance Notice of Restrictive Regulations" and was borrowed from the 1946 U.S. Administrative Procedures Act (APA). Transparency was greatly expanded in the WTO with the inclusion of services, and TRIPS and the word finally appears in the TRIPS agreement as a heading in Article 63.

In the United States the evolution of administrative law expanded the participatory role of stakeholders partly in response to the increase in regulation beginning in the 1970s and to the growing literature on the dangers of "regulatory capture" (Raustiala 1997: 577).[11] Many economists and legal scholars argued that the best antidote to the capture of regulatory agencies by those they regulate was to broaden the spectrum of interests whose voices should be heard before rules are laid down. This development is for the most part not reflected in the WTO which focuses, with limited exceptions, on the rights and responsibilities of *governments,*

---

[10]   The discussion on transparency is taken from Ostry (1998).

[11]   See also Raustiala's references to George Stigler, Richard Posmer, and Ralph Nader.

not *stakeholders* (Marceau and Pedersen 1999: 37–40).[12] So WTO external transparency begins at home – with one major exception, the Trade Policy Review Mechanism (TPRM).

The TPRM was based on a recommendation of the FOGS (Functioning of the GATT System) negotiating group in the Uruguay Round. It was designed to enhance the effectiveness of the domestic policy-making process through informed public understanding, i.e. transparency (Ostry 1997: 201–203). Section B spells it out:

> Domestic Transparency
>
> Members recognize the inherent value of domestic transparency of government decision-making on trade policy matters for both Members' economies and the multilateral trading system, and agree to encourage and promote greater transparency within their own systems, acknowledging that the implementation of domestic transparency must be on a voluntary basis and take account of each Member's legal and political systems. (WTO 1994: 434)

In order to underline that the TPRM is voluntary and flexible in subject matter, the declaration of Objectives in Section A that "it is not intended to serve as a basis for the enforcement of specific obligations under the Agreements or for dispute settlement procedures, or to impose new policy commitments on Members" (WTO 1994: 434).

The TPRM's origins and objectives clearly embrace the policy-making process and thus seems the logical venue for launching this project – on a voluntary basis and as a pilot to be assessed after an agreed period. The WTO Secretariat is already seriously overburdened so it might be necessary for the volunteers to ante up some funding. If the pilot took off and a number of developing countries became involved, the issue of more permanent funding would have to be faced since there would be capacity-building and technical assistance requirements. But these latter costs should clearly come under the arrangements agreed at Doha on capacity building. Enhancing capacity to improve and sustain a more transparent trade policy process sounds like a good investment. It's hardly a new idea. In the 1970s, during the Tokyo Round, an American official remarked to an academic researcher that the advisory committees established under the 1974 Trade Act were working extremely well because "when you let a dog piss all over a fire hydrant he thinks he owns it" (Winham 1986: 316). That's a rather less felicitous version of today's concept of ownership.

---

[12]   The exceptions cited include the Subsidies and Countervail Agreement, Dumping Safeguards, TRIPs and GATS all of which provide for some procedural participatory rights.

4   Conclusions

As argued here, the multilateral rules-based trading system is under severe strain and there are worrying signs of increasing protectionism. Even under the best of circumstances the WTO, a minimalist, legalistic, member-driven institution, lacks the necessary infrastructure to carry out its ever-expanding mandate. The alternatives to multilateralism are quite clear – increasing bilateralism (especially by the United States which wants to "catch up" with the European Union) and regionalism (the newest development being a China-Asean agreement excluding the United States and Japan). A growing fragmentation in a world of ever-deepening integration represents more than a threat to trade. The Cold War involved a spillover from "high" to "low" policy. The opposite may well be the case in the future.

Thus the need for reform of the WTO seems obvious. Except to its member governments, that is. The modest proposals suggested here would require no fundamental renegotiation of rules – just a little foresight. But as Machiavelli so wisely noted: All reform of a system is "doubtful of success. For the initiators have the enmity of all who would profit by the preservation of the old system and merely lukewarm defenders in those who would gain from the new one." Let's hope some of the Princes prove him wrong.

Bibliography

Bellemann, C., and R. Gerster (1996). Accountability in the World Trade Organization. *Journal of World Trade* 30(6): 31–74.

Bridges Weekly Trade News Digest (2002). WTO Updates Info Dissemination, Discusses Internal Transparency. Volume 6, No. 18. International Centre for Trade and Sustainable Development. ⟨www.ictsd.org/weekly/02-05-15/story1.htm⟩ Accessed 25/02/03.

Bronckers, M.C.E. (1999). Better Rules for a New Millennium: A Warning Against Undemocratic Developments in the WTO. *Journal of International Economic Law* 2(4): 547–566.

Brunnée, J., and S.J. Toope (2000/2001). International Law and Constructivism: Elements of an Interactional Theory of International Law. *Columbia Journal of Transnational Law* 39(1): 19–74.

Charnovitz, S. (2001). The WTO and the Rights of the Individual. *Intereconomics* 36(2): 98–108.

Ebbesson, J. (1997). The Notion of Public Participation in International Environmental Law. In J. Brunnée and E. Hey (eds.), *Yearbook of International Environmental Law*. Volume 8. Oxford: Oxford University Press.

Hoekman, B. (2002). Strengthening the Global Trade Architecture for Development: The Post Doha Agenda. In World Trade Organization, *World Trade Review: Economics, Law, International Institutions.* Volume 1, No. 1. Cambridge: Cambridge University Press.

Howse, R., and M. Mutua (2000). Protecting Human Rights in a Global Economy: Challenges for the World Trade Organization. Occasional Paper prepared for the International Centre for Human Rights and Democratic Development. Montreal.

Inter-American Development Bank (2002). The Trade Policy-Making Process: Level One of the Two Level Game. Country Studies in the Western Hemisphere. IDB-Intal Occasional Paper 13. Buenos Aires.

ITO (International Trade Organization) (1948). *Havana Charter for an International Trade Organization.* March 24, 1948. Washington, D.C.: U.S. Govt. Printing Office.

Jackson, J.H. (1997). *The World Trading System: Law and Policy of International Economic Relations.* Cambridge, Mass.: MIT Press.

Keohane, R.O., and J.S. Nye, Jr. (2000). The Club Model of Multilateral Cooperation and Problems of Democratic Legitimacy. Paper prepared for the American Political Science Convention, August 31–September 3, 2000. Washington, D.C.

Koh, H.H. (1997). Why Do Nations Obey International Law? *The Yale Law Journal* 106(8): 2599–2659.

Marceau, G., and P.N. Pederson (1999). Is the WTO Open and Transparent? A Discussion of the Relationship of the WTO with Non-Governmental Organizations and Civil Society's Claim for More Transparency and Public Participation. *Journal of World Trade* 33(1): 5–49.

Mayer, Brown, Rowe & Maw (2001). *Global Trade Protection Report.* London.

McIntyre, E. (1954). Weighted Voting in International Organizations. *International Organization* 8(4): 484–497.

OECD (Organization for Economic Cooperation and Development) (1999). National Case Studies. COM/TD/ENV(99) 26/FINAL. Paris.

OECD (Organization for Economic Cooperation and Development) (2000a). NGO Consultation Summary Record. Paris.

OECD (Organization for Economic Cooperation and Development) (2000b). *Transparency and Consultation on Trade and Environment.* Volume 1. Paris.

OECD (Organization for Economic Cooperation and Development) (2000c). *Transparency and Consultation on Trade and Environment in Five International Organizations.* Paris.

OECD (Organization for Economic Cooperation and Development) (2001). Engaging Citizens in Policy Making: Information, Consultation and Public Participation. Public Management (PUMA) Policy Brief No. 10. Paris.

Open Letter on Institutional Reform (2001). WTO Activist Listserv, Administered by the Institute for Agriculture and Trade Policy, Geneva. Received: 10/09/2001.

Ostry, S. (1997). *The Post-Cold War Trading System: Who's on First?* Chicago: University of Chicago Press.

Ostry, S. (1998). China and the WTO: The Transparency Issue. *UCLA Journal of International Law and Foreign Affairs* 3 (Spring/Summer): 1–22.

Ostry, S. (2001a). Global Integration: Currents and Counter-Currents. Walter Gordon Lecture, Massey College, University of Toronto. Access at: http://www.utoronto.ca/cis/ostry.html.

Ostry, S. (2001b). Dissent.Com: How NGO's Are Re-Making the WTO. *Policy Options* 22(5): 6–15.

Oxfam International (2002). *Rigged Rules and Double Standards: Trade, Globalisation, and the Fight Against Poverty*. Geneva.

Petersmann, E.-U. (2001). Human Rights and International Economic Law in the 21st Century: The Need to Clarify Their Interrelationships. *Journal of International Economic Law* 4(1): 3–39.

Raustiala, K. (1997). The 'Participatory Revolution' in International Environmental Law. *Harvard Environmental Law Review* 21(2): 537–586.

Rushford, G. (2002). *The Rushford Report: The Politics of International Trade and Finance*. Vienna, Virginia: Greg Rushford.

Steger, D.P. (2000). The World Trade Organization: A New Constitution for the Trading System. In M. Bronckers and R. Quick (eds.), *New Directions in International Economic Law: Essays in Honour of John H. Jackson*. The Hague: Kluwer Law International.

Wall Street Journal (2002). Fast-Track Bill Is Hurt by Anger over Zoelick Trade Deal in 2001. (May 16, 2002).

Winham, G.R. (1986). *International Trade and the Tokyo Round Negotiation*. Princeton, N.J: Princeton University Press.

WTO (World Trade Organization) (1994). Marrakesh Agreement Establishing the World Trade Organization (LT/UR/A2). *The Results of the Uruguay Round of Multilateral Trade Negotiations: The Legal Texts*. Cambridge: Cambridge University Press.

WTO (World Trade Organization) (1999). Trade Act of 1974, Report of the Panel (WT/DS/152/R). December 22.

WTO (World Trade Organization, General Council) (2000a). Minutes of Meeting (WT/GC/M/57). July 17 and 19, Geneva.

WTO (World Trade Organization, General Council) (2000b). Informal Consultations on External Transparency (WT/GC/W/413/Rev.1). October 13.

WTO (World Trade Organization, Office of the Director General) (2002). Implementation of the Decision of the General Council on May 14, 2002 on the Procedures for the Circulation and Derestriction of WTO Documents (WT/L/452). Memorandum.

WTO News (2001). Joint Statement on the Multilateral Trading System (February 1, 2001).

Comment on Sylvia Ostry

Meinhard Hilf

The constitutionalization of the WTO might be a tentative answer to the proposals of Mrs. Ostry. She presented a rich report which contains too much to comment on. Of particular importance are the insights into the rather intransparent life of the U.S. Congress, where senators and representatives seem to do everything to satisfy their constituencies. I simply do not believe that they would get "a missionary for breakfast" if someone asked for it. Each constitutional system of the WTO members determines its own constitutional framework within which the developments under the WTO are addressed. And it seems that there is no other constitutional system which gives so much attention to international developments as is given by the democratic process under the U.S. constitution.[1]

From a German perspective, I would like to put my comment into a frame which I take from Article 23, paragraph 1, of the German Grundgesetz (constitution). Article 23 requires Germany to participate in the development of the European Union, provided that this Union is committed to "Democratic Rule of Law," social and federal principles, and the principle of subsidiarity, and that the Union ensures the protection of basic rights comparable in substance to those afforded by the Grundgesetz. This article demands a degree of constitutional homogeneity which is reflected in Articles 6 and 7 of the Treaty of the European Union (EUT). I would like to suggest that this requirement has to be followed whenever Germany is taking part in an international system that has important repercussions on the exercise of public powers. The WTO clearly is such a system. Therefore I propose discussing the basic elements of the requirement as the "necessary ingredients for the World Trading Order." Without similar or even the same constitutional restraints, no international regime can attract, in public, sufficient credibility and legitimacy, which are necessary ingredients for the functioning of the World Trading Order.

---

[1] Cf. the comparative analysis of national procedures relating to the ratification of the results of the Uruguay Round by Jackson and Sykes (1997).

Democratic Foundation

As to the democratic foundation of the WTO, a general decline in most democratic systems is observable, leading to a "democratic deficit." A revealing demonstration for this decline is the lack of attention given by national parliaments during the procedures of ratification of the WTO agreements. Thus, it seems inevitable that national parliaments will have to get more access to ongoing international negotiations such as the negotiation rounds under the WTO. This could be accomplished by an ad hoc involvement of national parliamentary committees. Another widely discussed suggestion – to which I subscribe – is to create a Consultative Parliamentary Assembly which would be composed of a number of national parliamentarians. Such an assembly could meet at least twice a year at the seat of the WTO to discuss all relevant problems and items of the agenda with repercussions on national economic and legal systems. Of course, such an assembly would not be legitimated to take any binding decisions. The advantage could, however, be that national parliaments will be much better informed and will have the possibility to produce ideas and suggestions to be dealt with within this assembly. Thus, a mutually beneficial link between the WTO and the national democratic systems could be established.

Transparency, Participation, and Responsiveness

Transparency, participation, and responsiveness are constitutional requirements which are closely linked to the principles of democratic and good governance. Mrs. Ostry cites interesting references from the OECD relating to internal and external transparency. Here, a reference is necessary to the corresponding memoranda of the WTO Secretariat.[2]

Mrs. Ostry characterizes nongovernmental organizations and multinational enterprises as a kind of "black box" in the decision-making processes of the WTO. According to Mrs. Ostry, it is important for every member government to organize its own negotiations without being submerged by proposals of the "dissent-industry." It will always be very difficult to regulate and contain NGOs and MNEs. Nevertheless, an effort should be made to acknowledge and invite the participation of these privately organized bodies and to make available public scrutiny of their involvement in national and international decision-making processes. As to the WTO's Dispute Settlement Body, it has been regarded with great skepticism that NGOs strive for having access to this delicate approach of finally settling disputes

---

[2]   Note by the Secretariat, Transparency, WT/WGTI/W/109, 27 March 2002; page 1 et seq.; General Council, Minutes of Meeting, WT/GC/M/57, 14 September 2000, paras. 132 et seq. and paras. 282 et seq.

between members. However, it is important to strike a balance between the necessary engagement of citizens and the observance of institutional procedures frequently involving government-to-government negotiations. Governmental responsibilities must be maintained and guaranteed. This applies to the WTO decision-making process too, though there may be some modifications.

In all, the principles of transparency, participation, and responsiveness define the individual as the final focus of the WTO, but, even when recognizing this modern development in the field of public international law, any improvement in this direction will not replace government's final responsibility for the functioning of the WTO system.

Rule of Law

Considerations about better guaranteeing the rule of law have been explicitly omitted in Mrs. Ostry's report. However, according to her impression, negotiators incomprehensively finalized many texts such that there were unintended consequences. I would like to extend this statement particularly to the agreement on sanitary and phytosanitary (SPS) measures, in which obviously no one was aware that the *codex alimentarius* was to become a quasi-binding instrument.[3]

The rule of law is addressed most prominently in the Dispute Settlement Understanding (DSU), which provides binding conclusions and recommendations that cannot be escaped by members. The dispute settlement system of the WTO comes very close to being an obligatory system of international adjudication. In fact, in the absence of a negative consensus, any recommendation made by the Appellate Body will have binding effect. Certainly, the Appellate Body must not add or diminish the rights and obligations members have agreed on in the various agreements. This position which is reflected in Article 3:2 and Article 19:2 DSU did not prevent the Appellate Body from changing the entire GATT case law from a merely power- or rule-oriented approach to a principle-oriented approach (Hilf 2001). Close scrutiny of the Appellate Body reports will show that in the WTO legal system many general principles of law have been taken from various sources such as public international law, the various WTO agreements, or even the national legal orders of the WTO members. Thus, it has been possible to deduct some 50 principles – the last being the principle of proportionality, which is one of the most important principles developed especially under European Community law (Hilf and Puth 2002).

On the basis of this approach which is not uncontroversial amongst WTO members one may perceive a shift from a WTO being based on treaties to a WTO

---

3   EC-HORMONES, Appellate Body Report, WT/DS26,48/AB/R, adopted 13 February 1998, paras. 157 et seq.; see also Pauwelyn (1999).

bringing together a new legal order under public international law. Such a shift entails a more objective interpretation of the various agreements which distances itself from references to the negotiating history.

Finally, I would like to consider some of the more important suggestions for reforming the dispute settlement process to be necessary ingredients for the future World Trade Order. Especially, a standing body of panelists should be established. The role of the WTO Secretariat should be defined more precisely and the agreements should allow for provisional measures in order to make the dispute settlement process more effective. Introducing the idea of direct applicability of WTO law would certainly presuppose an intensive linking of the dispute settlement process to the various national dispute settlement systems. For the time being, there are no such links, so that any direct applicability considered on the national level might lead to surprising and irresponsible results (Hilf 1997).

Any future reform of the WTO system probably should also reconsider the possibility of levying sanctions, as I have the impression that we do not need them to make the system more effective. Sanctions are trade-destroying instruments which, by the way, have never been considered within the European Communities.

Solidarity

The rule of law, as it might be understood in modern constitutionalism, should be very closely linked to the idea of procedural fairness and social justice. This idea meets with the principle of solidarity, especially with the interest of developing and least developed countries as it has been underlined in the Doha declaration. This focus on development will certainly be reflected in the future task of reforming the organizational structure of the WTO.

Subsidiarity

The principle of subsidiarity should be recognized as one of the basic principles of the WTO. In numerous decisions under the WTO system, especially in many conclusions under the Dispute Settlement System, emphasis has been put on the importance of preserving the sovereignty of members. Any system of law above the traditional state would certainly be bound to fail if it did not include a sufficient degree of deference to national democratic processes. National policies designed to protect citizens are most important for the functioning of the WTO legal system. The Doha Declaration on public health has highlighted the importance of a local definition of public health and the necessities of fighting plagues.

Effectiveness

Finally, effectiveness seems to be the most important principle and at the same time a challenge for any system of government. No such system has a *raison d'être* if it does not effectively fulfill its functions. This idea is expressed by the notion of leadership to which Mrs. Ostry rightly refers. The asymmetry between the weak legislative process and the very strong judicial system is highlighted by Mrs. Ostry. The prospects for an effective rebalancing are not very promising.

Nevertheless, the WTO Secretariat has the potential capacities to stimulate the ongoing negotiations amongst WTO members. I do agree with Mrs. Ostry on a sort of "CG18"-concept. If it were used with the necessary sensitivity, it could have an important influence on the ongoing negotiations amongst all members. In this context one could certainly take into account experiences and results stemming from regional processes of integration.[4] Under all circumstances, it will be necessary to come to a more effective policy-making process. At the same time, results from the dispute settlement process will transform the WTO into a reliable, stable, and predictable legal order, as provided for in Article 3:2 DSU. WTO law, in the first instance, should be the result of the political process which should always be determining the final shape of the system. This process will not be successful if it does not correspond to the above-mentioned six constitutional principles. Thus, a future approach furthering these principles could be seen as a process of "constitutionalization" of the WTO.

Bibliography

Hilf, M. (1997). The Role of National Courts in International Trade Relations. *Michigan Journal of International Law* 18(2): 321–356.

Hilf, M. (2001). Power, Rules and Principles, Which Orientation for WTO/GATT Law. *Journal of International Economic Law* 4(1): 111–130.

Hilf, M., and S. Puth (2002). The Principle of Proportionality on Its Way into WTO/GATT Law. In A. von Bogdandy et al. (eds.), *European Integration and International Co-ordination*. Studies in Transnational Economic Law in Honour of C.-D. Ehlermann. The Hague: Kluwer Law International.

Jackson, J.H., and A.O. Sykes (eds.) (1997). *Implementing the Uruguay Round*. Oxford: Clarendon.

Pauwelyn, J. (1999). The WTO Agreement on Sanitary and Phytosanitary (SPS) Measures as Applied in the First Three SPS Disputes. *Journal of International Economic Law* 2(4): 641–664.

---

[4]   Mrs. Ostry (p. 145) seems to be reluctant to share this opinion, fearing a possible fragmentation of international economic law, but regionalism is likewise a "school of integration" which makes members experience first limitations of their national sovereignty.

Barry Eichengreen

Predicting and Preventing Financial Crises: Where Do We Stand? What Have We Learned?

1 Introduction

Relative to crisis prevention, crisis management receives disproportionate amounts of attention. Comparing the number of the LexusNexus hits on the combination of International Monetary Fund and Argentina with references to the Financial Stability Forum or to Financial Section Assessment Program (FSAP) of the IMF and World Bank suffices to establish the fact.[1] But in economics as in medicine, prevention, together with early detection of developing abnormalities, is the better part of the cure. Regular checkups and the economic equivalent of blood tests can minimize the need for painful therapy down the road. And a balanced diet and healthy lifestyle can be the key to a long and prosperous life. It is important not to lose sight of these facts amidst the controversy surrounding large-scale official rescues and the IMF's proposal for a sovereign debt restructuring mechanism.

This paper is a modest attempt to redress the balance. Its two principal sections assess where we stand on crisis prediction and crisis prevention. It turns out that similar analytical issues and policy problems arise in the two contexts. This is then followed by a discussion of the contagion problem, which poses special difficulties for prediction and prevention. A final section concludes.

2 Crisis Prediction

Economic forecasting is like weather forecasting except that our knowledge of the underlying science is less complete. Outcomes are produced by structural

Remark: I thank Pipat Luengnaruemitchai for careful research assistance.

[1]   Between July 2001 and March 2002 inclusive, this data base contains 870 articles mentioning both the IMF and Argentina but just 52 mentioning the Financial Stability Forum and 29 mentioning the FSAP.

relationships that interact in nonlinear and state-contingent ways. Despite the progress that has been made in both chaos theory and computing power, our ability to forecast and simulate complex nonlinear processes remains limited. Complex systems often have multiple equilibria, selection between which is sensitive to small perturbations.[2] And in financial markets, unlike meteorology, there is the fact that the behavior of the components can be affected by the forecast.

It is not surprising, then, that many economists adopt the same skeptical attitude toward the prediction of crises as toward economic forecasting generally.[3] Academic authors, while having pioneered the development of the relevant models, are generally dubious of the reliability of predictive exercises. They question the stability of reduced-form relationships. Having been taught to respect the Lucas critique, they worry that even if investigators succeed in identifying reliable early warning indicators, markets and governments will react by attacking the currency or the banking system as soon as adverse movements in those indicators begin to be detected, or else governments will move more quickly to take corrective action that prevents those indicators from moving, either way robbing the early-warning system of its predictive power. Economists working in government, multilateral organizations, and private financial institutions, in contrast, see such forecasting as a necessary evil.[4] Their clients want forecasts, and they have no choice but to provide them.

The first notable attempt to predict crises was Kaminsky et al. (1998) (KLR).[5] KLR analyzed a 20 country sample over the period 1970–1995. They selected thresholds for individual macroeconomic and financial indicators that minimized the noise-to-signal ratio – that is, the ratio of months in which an indicator signaled a crisis that did not occur to months in which that indicator did not signal a crisis that in fact occurred; when that threshold was breeched, a crisis was signaled. Their optimal threshold was indicator specific but not country specific.[6]

---

[2]   There is of course a large literature on the circumstances under which multiple equilibria can arise in crisis models (see Morris and Shin 2000).

[3]   The profession has been even more skeptical of exchange rate forecasting than of forecasting in general since the influential work of Meese and Rogoff (1983). Forecasting large changes in the exchange rates (i.e., currency crises) is of course essentially a special case of exchange rate forecasting.

[4]   This is the same evolution that has affected macroeconomic forecasting, with academics growing more skeptical of its merits but practitioners continuing to apply the standard techniques, except that the tendency for such forecasting to fall from academic fashion has been even faster if anything in the case of crisis prediction.

[5]   There were earlier attempts, of course, to analyze the empirical correlates of crises; I like to think that Eichengreen et al. (1996a) was first. But we expressly resisted the temptation to use our model for predictive purposes.

[6]   Thus, it was constrained to be equal across countries.

Kaminsky (1998) constructed a composite indicator as the signal-to-noise-ratio-weighted sum of the individual indicators and calculated how often within the sample different values of this index were followed by a crisis within 24 months.[7]

Berg and Pattillo (1999a) provided an early evaluation of how well this approach predicted out of sample. They found that only eight of KLR's 15 macroeconomic and financial indicators were informative in the sense that a crisis in the next 24 months was more likely when the indicator emitted a signal than when it did not. When the weighted average of individual crises signals a crisis with at least 25 percent probability, 41 percent of crises are called correctly; when the cut-off probability is 50 percent, only 9 percent are correctly called.[8] False alarms are 63 percent of total alarms in the first case, 44 percent in the second.[9]

While these results are better than the naive estimates obtained by always predicting "no crisis," they are not exactly confidence inspiring. Out-of-sample forecasts for the Asian crisis are even more depressing: for the four crisis countries with the necessary data (Indonesia, Malaysia, South Korea, and Thailand), the estimated probability of a crisis was above 50 percent only four percent of the time in the 24 months immediately preceding the event.[10]

One can imagine various objections and qualifications to these pessimistic conclusions. It can be argued that these early exercises did not use optimal techniques. Probit models using the KLR indicators, as in Berg and Pattillo (1999a), do a bit better within sample – by construction, since they minimize a transform of the residual sum of squares – but the improvement in their out-of-sample predictive power is negligible.

Alternatively, it can be argued that these attempts to predict crises are largely unsuccessful because they neglect important financial information, such as the level and composition of external debt, which is conveniently available only on an annual basis. Frankel and Rose (1996) estimated a probit model of currency

---

[7]   The method was further elaborated by Goldstein et al. (2000).

[8]   For this analysis, Berg and Pattillo use a slightly different sample of countries (emerging markets only) and calculate thresholds using data only through 1995, so that the Asian crisis can be treated as out of sample. Obviously, the 50 percent threshold does better at predicting tranquil periods than the 25 percent threshold.

[9]   Osband and van Rijckeghem (2000) attempt to finesse the problem by turning the methodology on its head, using essentially the same approach to estimate safe periods in which currency crashes are unlikely to occur. Using a sample of emerging markets in the period 1985–1998, their model emits a false signal of safety only one percent of the time. The price, predictably, is a very high ratio of false alarms to total alarms (76 percent).

[10]   This improves to 32 percent of the time when the cutoff is lowered to 25 percent. Again, this is better than a naive forecast, but it is not heartening.

crashes for 100 developing countries in the period 1971–1992 using annual data and add a number of measures of external debt. Reestimating this model through 1996, Berg and Pattillo (1999b) show that the correlation between predicted and actual rates of currency depreciation in 1997 is only 33 percent. If the metric for success is short-term out-of-sample forecasting power, in other words, then time aggregation may be too high a price to pay for incorporating data on external debt.

Others will argue that these models neglect important information on financial structure and institutions, for example on the extent of corporate and banking-sector financial leverage and the strength of shareholder rights. Mulder et al. (2002) provide some evidence that measures of these characteristics of national financial systems enhance the fit of standard leading-indicator models. As yet, however, it is too early to tell whether they bear a stable relationship to crises and help to predict out of sample.

Still others will suggest that these models fail to incorporate information on the political determinants of governments' willingness and ability to counter speculative pressures. Leblang (2001a, 2001b) shows that attacks are more likely under left governments and in periods of political flux (when there is both the expectation and the realization of a significant change of government). Leblang (2001c) shows that governments are *less* likely to successfully defend against an attack in the period leading up to an election. (There are also some anomalies, including that right governments are *less* likely to defend against attacks and divided governments, if anything, are *more* likely to do so.) These results are still too recent to have been incorporated into the multilaterals' leading indicator models or to have had their predictive power evaluated. Nor has the key insight from recent theoretical models of speculative attacks, that it is the *interaction* of weak governments with weak fundamentals that sets the stage for successful speculative attacks, been tested directly.

Some partisans of prediction may suspect that a model tailored to the circumstances of the 1990s would do better, but Berg and Pattillo show that the Sachs–Tornell–Velasco (1996) model of the 1994–1995 "tequila crisis" has no predictive power for the subsequent "Asian flu."[11]

Others will argue that financial market participants have stronger incentives to develop reliable forecasting models. In fact, however, the leading private-sector models are not noticeably better at out-of-sample forecasting.[12]

---

[11]   Tornell (1999) shows that a similar structural model fits the data for the Asian crisis, but that is not the same thing as showing that the model when fitted to data for 1995 generates useful predictions for 1997–1998.

[12]   See IMF (2001). Private-sector models are generally designed to predict medium-sized (i.e., five percent) changes in exchange rates month to month, these "smaller" movements being of interest to market participants; hence, it is not surprising that they have no comparative advantage in predicting the large changes that constitute crises.

Finally, it could be that currency crises are harder to predict than banking crises. Banking crises, it might be argued, are rooted in slowly evolving fundamentals such as falling economic growth and adverse external shocks that raise nonperforming loans and in episodes of credit expansion that heighten balance-sheet vulnerabilities. But the work of Hardy and Pazarbasioglu (1999) provides little support for the notion that this translates into reliable prediction. Their probit model picks up little more than half of the cases of banking system distress within sample, and only about one-third of precrisis periods (the year immediately preceding an episode of banking system distress). The indicator approach actually does less well at predicting banking crises than currency crises (Goldstein et al. 2000).[13]

It is impossible to avoid concluding that the performance of leading indicator models leaves much to be desired. This pessimistic view is borne out by the most recent round of crises. To be sure, the KLR model and Berg and Pattillo's probit-based alternative (a more parsimonious respecification of KLR augmented with measures of the current account and reserve adequacy) emitted strong warning signs in the lead-up to Turkey's February 2001 crisis.[14] But the KLR model failed to predict the January 2002 crisis in Argentina: IMF (2002) reports that it failed to call a crisis after August 2000, while Berg and Pattillo's respecification sounded a weak warning in the lead-up to this event but counterfactually signaled a decline in its probability in the final months of 2001.

We can understand why by considering the variables on which these models focus – real overvaluation, the current account deficit, reserve adequacy, export growth, and short-term debt relative to reserves – in the run-up to these crises and seven others that occurred in the last three years.[15] Figures 1–9 show the evolution of the key variables in the IMF's respecification of the KLR model. The percentage change in the nominal exchange rate clearly moves around the time of crises – this is logical though not inevitable given that the rate of depreciation is one of the components of the conventional crisis indicator. What is notable, however, is that there is little sign of accelerating depreciation in the 12 or 24 months

---

[13] This is even more worrisome insofar as the commonly used banking crisis dates are themselves lagging indicators of serious banking-sector problems.

[14] On the IMF's probit-based reformulation of the KLR model, see Borensztein et al. (2000).

[15] These are the principal crises that show up according to the KLM criterion that the weighted average of exchange rate changes and reserve changes exceeded the mean by at least three standard deviations (other than some small or low-income countries for which data are missing). The Colombian case just misses the cutoff (it is only two standard deviations above the mean), but it is nice to have nine cases for a symmetrical diagram. Goldman Sachs and Credit Suisse First Boston publish crisis lists that overlap heavily with the cases considered here.

Figure 1: Percentage Change in the Nominal Exchange Rate

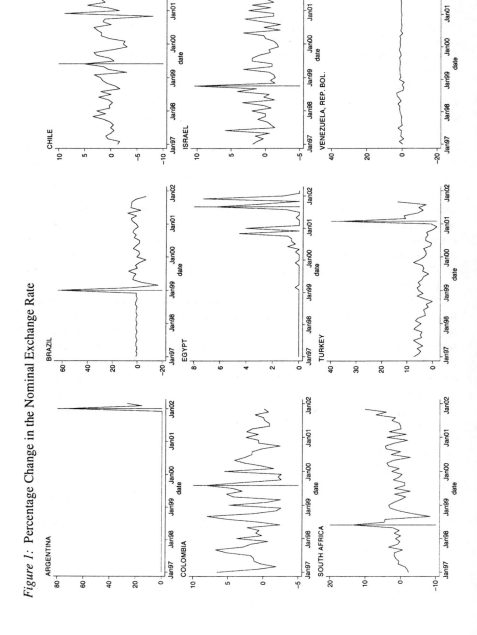

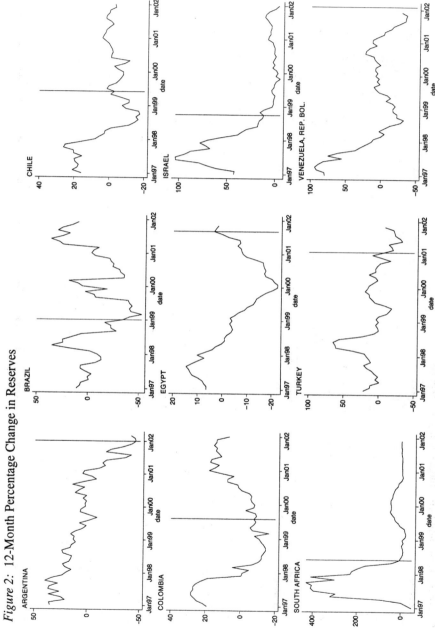

Figure 2: 12-Month Percentage Change in Reserves

Figure 3: 12-Month Percentage Change in Exports

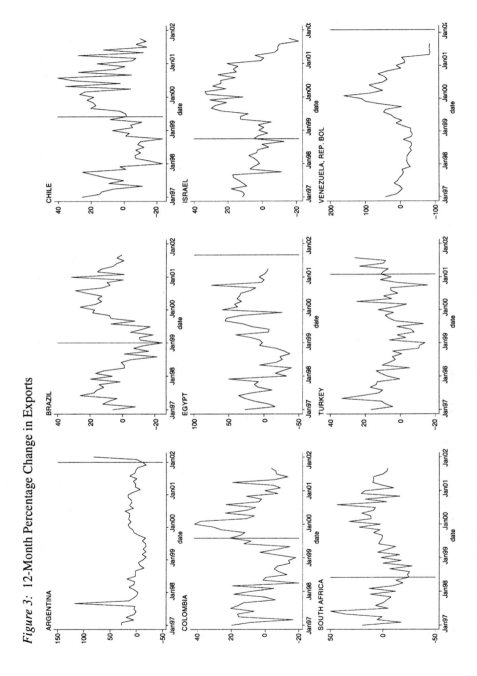

Figure 4: Real Exchange Rate (Jan 1997 = 100)

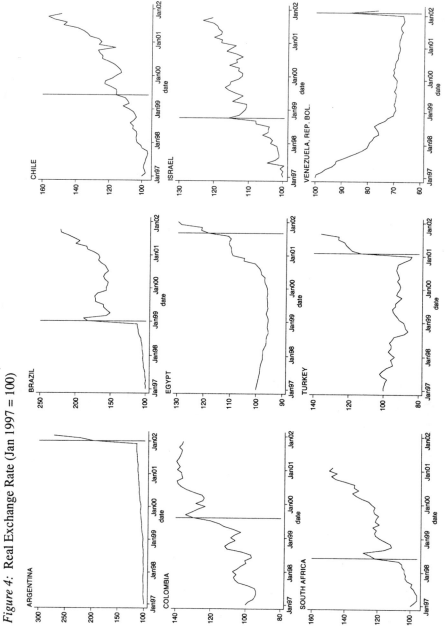

Figure 5: Real Exchange Rate Deviation from Linear Trend

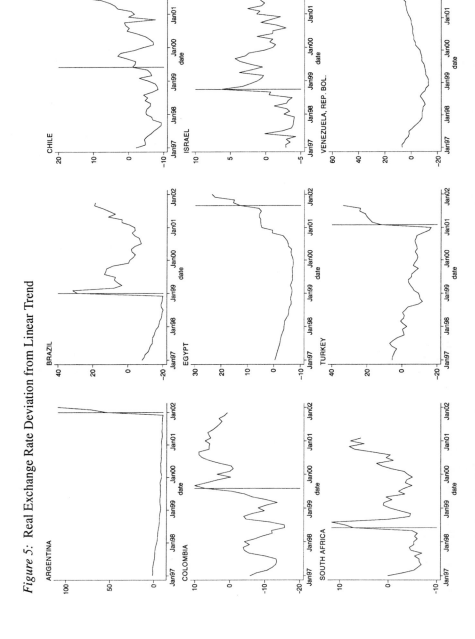

Figure 6: M2/Reserves Ratio

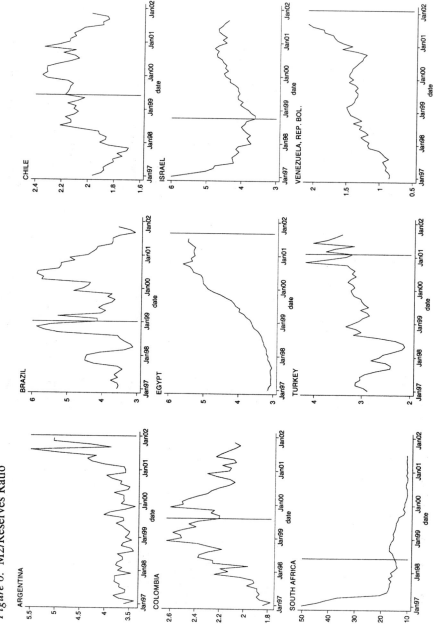

Figure 7: Rate of Growth of M2/Reserves

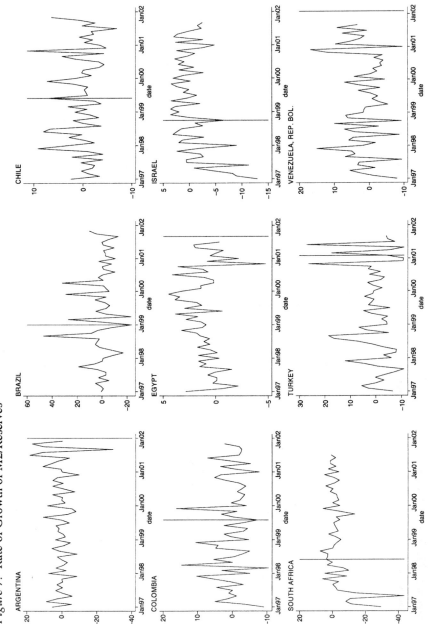

Figure 8: Deseasonalized Current Account/GDP (Percentage)

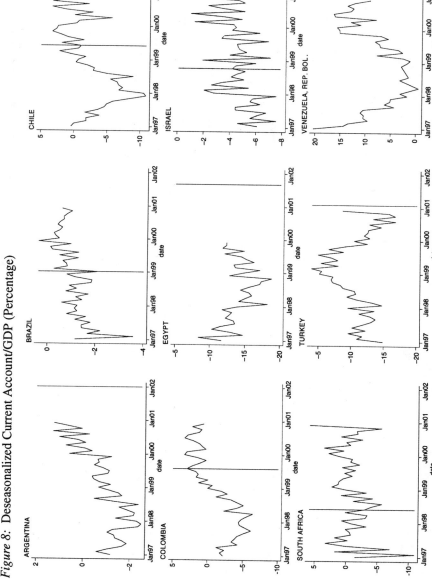

Figure 9: Short-Term Debt (BIS)/Reserves (Ratio)

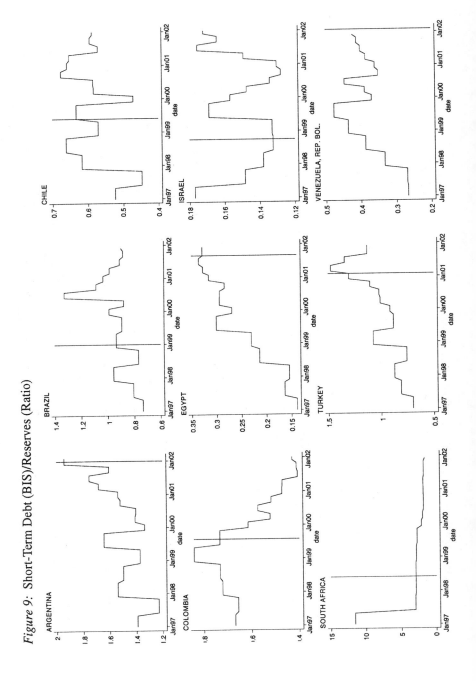

leading up to the crisis.[16] The other component of the conventional crisis indicator, the percentage change in reserves, is more informative, but not uniformly so. In some cases, like Turkey, it does not fall at all; in others like South Africa, the only observable change is that reserves stop rising.

What is true of the balance of payments as a whole is true of exports in particular: their growth decelerates in the 12 months leading up to the crisis in some cases (Brazil, Chile, Colombia, Israel), but not in others (Argentina, Turkey). Given the fact that exports are not a reliable leading indicator, it is not surprising that the real exchange rate does little better (of the cases considered, real rate movements are clearly evident in the period leading up to the crisis only in Venezuela). Detrending helps: there is some sign of real appreciation relative to trend in Argentina, Brazil, Turkey, and perhaps Egypt, although the small size of the deviation is an indication of how sensitive such indicators are to detrending method.

M2 over reserves, the conventional "credit boom" indicator, does relatively well (except in Israel and South Africa), but its rate of growth is noisier and less informative. The current account appears to have little predictive content, since both current account deficits and crises can occur for a variety of different reasons. Short-term debt relative to reserves is more informative but moves in the wrong direction in some cases (such as South Africa).

What should we conclude? Crisis prediction will always be imperfect for many of the same reasons that economic forecasting will always be imperfect. Crises are heterogeneous; they occur for different reasons in different times and places. Parsimonious models will capture only some of the circumstances under which crises occur; they will miss some crises unless the threshold for issuing a warning is set so low as to generate a large number of false positives. And a methodology that generates a large number of false positives ("11 out of the last 7 recessions") is not particularly useful for forecasting purposes. It is not even helpful for generating a watch list for officials, since if the threshold for emitting a warning is set at high levels, the resulting watch list will be misleadingly short, while if that threshold is set at low levels, that list will be too long for practical use.

In addition, crises are contingent. Rather than being inevitable and preordained, they generally afflict countries that have entered a danger zone where the government lacks the political and economic capacity to fend off financial pressure in the event of an intensification of the latter. If investor sentiment turns against the country, for whatever reason, the government of a country with a heavy financial burden or a weak economy may be unable to sustain the harsh policies of austerity needed to deflect mounting speculative pressures. If, on the other hand, market sentiment remains favorable, the same economic and financial fundamentals will be sustainable, and no crisis will result. This is a classic situa-

---

[16]   This variable is not a particularly useful leading indicator, in other words.

tion of multiple equilibria.[17] It does not mean that crises strike randomly or that all countries are equally vulnerable. But it does suggest that deterministic models are unavoidably poor predictors of intrinsically contingent events.

3   Crisis Prevention

The official approach to crisis prevention focuses on the benefits of greater transparency on the part of borrowers, lenders, and international financial institutions, so that crisis risks can be identified in advance and markets begin to take corrective action before things get out of hand. It focuses on the importance of strengthening banks and financial markets, which have been a particular source of vulnerability in recent crisis episodes, through the adoption of internationally recognized financial standards and systematic reviews of banking and financial-market vulnerabilities. It focuses on the need to rationalize exchange rate arrangements, reflecting the fact that pegged exchange rates have played a role in virtually every recent crisis.

The communiqué of the International Monetary and Financial Committee of the IMF following the Spring 2002 meetings of the IMF is the most up-to-date summary of the official thinking at the time of writing.[18] It highlights the need for firm surveillance of country policies and argues that surveillance can be further enhanced by taking the following steps.

- Refining the assessment of potential problems of debt sustainability and private sector balance-sheet exposure.
- Better understanding how the policies of the large advanced-industrial economies affect the rest of the world.
- More candidly assessing the merits of exchange rates and exchange rate arrangements.
- Expanding financial sector surveillance to include the offshore financial centers.
- Better coordination between the IMF, the World Bank, and other institutions.
- Further integration of multilateral, regional, and country surveillance.
- More systematic and extensive coverage of international capital markets.
- More attention to structural and institutional issues.

---

[17]   An application of this idea that multiple equilibria arise when fundamentals enter an intermediate range where they are neither so strong as to rule out crises nor so weak as to guarantee them is Eichengreen and Jeanne (2000).

[18]   I focus here on the role of multilateral surveillance because other authors (e.g., Mishkin 2001) have written extensively on country-specific crisis prevention measures.

In fact, behind this seemingly uncontroversial list lie important unresolved issues for the official community's crisis prevention efforts.

Debt Sustainability and Private Sector Exposure. The first item, refining the assessment of problems of public and private-sector debt sustainability, alludes to one of the more problematic aspects of the surveillance agenda, namely, the difficulty of measuring the off-balance sheet exposures of financial and nonfinancial firms. Enron's CEO has claimed in congressional testimony, perhaps disingenuously, that this ability eluded even that corporation's own management. Some have taken the Enron debacle as a critique of U.S. accounting practices and an argument for converging on European accounting standards. But the critique is more fundamental: no accounting standard may be capable of detecting vulnerabilities when firms can create special-purpose vehicles that not even sophisticated financial analysts can see through. We have come a long way since 1997, when President Suharto reportedly called the heads of Indonesia's 24 largest companies into his office and asked each of them to write down his firm's indebtedness on a slip of paper so that he might gain a sense of the overall exposure of the corporate sector and the country. Data on corporate debt exposures are now systematically gathered by the national authorities and regularly reported to the international financial institutions. The question is how much they are worth, and whether they will be worth even less with the spread of Enron-like financial instruments and vehicles to emerging markets.

These observations suggest three extensions of efforts in this area. Countries that permit accounting firms to also act as consultants and financial advisors should rethink these regulations. Governments should similarly rethink the elimination of restrictions on the range of activities in which financial institutions can engage (like Glass–Steagall in the United States).[19] Here I am aware of swimming against the tide, but recent experience raises questions about the compatibility of, say, security underwriting and investment advising.

In addition, subordinated debt as a mechanism giving a subset of market participants high-powered incentives to invest in the capacity to monitor the financial condition of the issuing entity may have a role to play in the nonfinancial as well as the financial sector. (Indeed, another lesson of the Enron debacle is the difficulty of drawing the line between financial and nonfinancial firms.) How much can be accomplished by giving corporations additional incentives to issue subordinated debt remains to be seen; one can imagine that a firm like Enron might

---

[19]   This is something that would require international cooperation, insofar as limiting the lines of business in which financial institutions can engage would limit their ability to exploit economies of scale and scope and cause them to lose business to the foreign competitors were the latter not simultaneously subjected to similar regulatory restrictions.

attempt to manipulate the price of its "sub debt," weakening the signal to market participants and regulators. Such problems are likely to be especially pervasive in emerging markets, where markets in debt instruments are relatively shallow and illiquid, facilitating attempts to manipulate secondary-market prices. But if the lesson of Enron is that neither the average investor nor the average regulator can be relied on to be able to assemble and process the relevant information, then it makes sense to move further in the direction of creating a set of stakeholders with special incentives to invest in that capacity.

The reference to debt sustainability in the first item on the IMFC's list suggests that there are unresolved issues in assessing the financial condition of countries, and not just corporations. Attempts to develop a framework for determining sustainable levels of debt have a long history.[20] These generally make assumptions about the interest rate and the growth rate and ask, given initial levels of debt, whether a given path of budget deficits is consistent with the debt/income ratio stabilizing at acceptable levels.[21] Recent experience suggests that such models can be dangerously misleading. If debt is public, the ability of the government to mobilize taxes may be the binding constraint.[22] If the debt is foreign, then the ability of the country to earn foreign exchange may bind first. If the debt is denominated in foreign currency, then an unforeseen change in the exchange rate may make a previously sustainable debt unsustainable.

Some of these observations point to the need for more sophisticated models. Others, like the fact that changes in the exchange rate can make previously sustainable debts unsustainable and render a shock to the foreign exchange market self-fulfilling (Krugman 2001, Cespedes et al. 2002), cast doubt on the premise that debt sustainability can be meaningfully assessed ex ante. The most subversive critique is probably that debt sustainability depends on political as well as economic factors. A given debt burden will be harder to sustain when there is less political support for the policies of austerity required for its maintenance. A given shock to the exchange rate, the growth rate, or the interest rate will be more likely to move the debt into the range where it is unsustainable when political support for those policies, and the painful belt tightening they require, is less. Thus, those who attempt to forecast debt sustainability must be able to forecast political as well as economic conditions. If this is what the IMFC means when it says that the

---

[20]   See, for example, Cohen (1991). Actually, these calculations go back even further, at least to the literature on the sustainability of German reparations after World War I.

[21]   This is the logic that implicitly or explicitly underlies the Maastricht Treaty's reference value of 60 percent for European public debts (Buiter et al. 1993).

[22]   Thus, one may want to consider the ratio of debt service to taxes rather than debt to GNP.

multilaterals must refine the way they analyze debt sustainability, then it does not engender much confidence that the results will be operational.

Impact of Large Country Policies. The tendency for globalization to increase the cross-country coherence of business cycle fluctuations (as noted by IMF 2002) motivates the IMFC's emphasis on large country policies.[23] Research has documented that OECD slowdowns and interest rate increases play a significant role in heightening the financial vulnerability of emerging markets (Eichengreen and Rose 2001). Unilateral trade policy actions by the large economies are clearly not helpful for emerging markets whose financial viability and growth prospects depend on their ability to export. Here my own country has much to answer for.

There are also mysteries. Traditionally, the volume of net capital flows to emerging markets is sensitive to interest rates in the advanced industrial countries (Calvo et al. 1992). The failure of flows to respond when U.S. interest rates were cut to low levels in 2000–2001 thus raises questions about whether this mechanism operates as powerfully as before, or whether it is increasingly overwhelmed by other determinants of international capital flows.[24]

Even accepting the premise, there is still the issue of what to do about it. This question echoes in the call for the large countries to take more seriously the impact of their policies on the rest of the world. It can be heard as a suggestion to revisit the international policy coordination exercises that occupied many academics and staff members of the multilaterals in the 1980s.[25] But the U.S. Treasury has not reacted sympathetically to IMF warnings of the size of the U.S. current account deficit and the high level of the dollar and over the impact of their elimination on other countries. History gives reasons to doubt whether the large countries are prepared to compromise their national policy objectives in order to ameliorate global strains. The lesson that emerges from discussions of and experience with policy coordination may be that the most important thing that the large economies can do to enhance financial stability in the rest of the world is to avoid actions that amplify the volatility of their own economies. The best thing they can do, in other words, is to more effectively tend their own gardens. This applies even to the least controversial application of the point, that the governments of the large countries should not succumb to protectionist pressures. They should resist

---

[23] The evidence is controversial. Bergman et al. (1998) argue that business cycles have grown more synchronized, while Backus and Kehoe (1992) argue the opposite. IMF (2002) comes down cautiously on the side of the first set of authors.

[24] There is also the mystery that systematic analysis has never really supported the existence of the strong linkage between the level of U.S. interest rates and emerging market spreads posited in the popular press (Eichengreen and Mody 1998).

[25] For evidence of this tendency, see Meyer et al. (2002).

in the interest of the developing countries, but first and foremost they should resist in their own interest.

Exchange Rate Regimes. The need to more candidly assess the merits of exchange rate arrangements is another one of those things that is easier to preach than to practice. The conventional wisdom is that soft pegs are fragile and that countries need to eliminate the exchange rate problem by eliminating the exchange rate or else move to greater flexibility.[26] Related to this is the argument that more freely floating exchange rates encourage hedging of foreign exposures by banks and firms, which limits their susceptibility to financial distress when the currency moves.[27]

None of this is easily reconciled with the belief in Europe, Asia, and Latin America that floating rates are problematic and that countries should continue to operate regimes of limited flexibility. Nor has anything ameliorated the dilemma for the IMF that if it labels an exchange rate regime as unsustainable it risks provoking a crisis.[28] This was apparent in the case of Argentina, where the IMF first refused to label the one-to-one dollar peg as unsustainable and then responded to the controversy over dollarization by observing that the choice of exchange rate regime is a national decision.[29]

I have long been skeptical of the prospects for exporting European Monetary System-like arrangements to other parts of the world (Bayoumi and Eichengreen 1999). Contrary to the conclusions of Government of France–Government of Japan (2000), I do not believe that the preconditions for a sustainable system of

---

[26]   The notion that the peg could be hardened by moving to a currency board has been discredited by the Argentine crisis. One wonders whether the notion that countries attracted by this solution should move further in this direction, by unilaterally dollarizing or euroizing, will similarly be challenged by some future crisis.

[27]   Thus, while large changes in exchange rates can occur when currencies are floating as well as when a peg collapses, the output costs are likely to be smaller in the first case (Mishkin 2001). An influential early statement of the connection between floating rates and hedging by the private sector is Goldstein (1998). There is some evidence for it (Martinez and Werner 2001) but also some evidence against (Arteta 2002).

[28]   The Council on Foreign Relations Task Force on Strengthening the International Financial Architecture (CFR 1999) suggested that the IMF should commit not to providing emergency finance to countries with "overvalued" exchange rates except in exceptional circumstances, but this last proviso provided a pretext for exceptions. The Meltzer Commission (International Financial Institution Advisory Commission 2000) urged the Fund to more actively warn governments about the risks of pegged rates in Article IV consultations, but it did not move beyond that point.

[29]   As the country's crisis deepened in the first half of 2002, and the choice contemplated by the domestic authorities became whether to float or to repeg (as opposed to dollarizing), the IMF did come out strongly in favor of continued floating.

collective pegs or bands are present in other regions, including Asia.[30] Compared to Europe, Asia trades more with and relies more on finance from outside the region. Its economies are more heterogeneous, raising questions about the suitability of any common basket peg for the entire grouping. Its nations are more jealous of their sovereignty and less willing to engage in meaningful regional surveillance (Manzano 2001). This in turn raises questions about the willingness of strong currency countries to support their weak currency counterparts.[31]

I am equally skeptical of the advisability of continuing to peg while claiming to float, which is a popular way of characterizing the de facto behavior of countries that display "fear of floating." Avoiding an explicit commitment to a target zone may avoid giving speculators a target to aim at, to be sure, but it also fails to produce "bias in the band" – that is, it fails to deliver stabilizing speculation. To put the point another way, saying one thing while doing another is unlikely to enhance credibility.

In practice, we see a growing number of countries floating more freely and anchoring their floats by inflation targeting. Brazil and Mexico are floating more freely, while in East Asia a number of the former crisis countries – Korea, Thailand, Indonesia, and the Philippines among them – are floating more and intervening less.[32] Recent work on inflation targeting suggests that countries can begin using that framework to anchor their currencies well before inflation rates have come down to the single digits or budget deficits have been eliminated (Mishkin and Schmidt-Hebbel 2001). The volatility of a floating rate can be limited by the adoption of an inflation target even before the central bank is fully independent or the full targeting apparatus has been adopted (Goldstein 2002). The IMF has climbed onto the inflation-targeting bandwagon, by urging countries like Turkey to move in this direction. That it has identified a viable alternative is likely to strengthen its hand when it urges countries to float more freely.

Integration of Multilateral, Regional, and Country Surveillance. The IMF has never had exclusive responsibility for multilateral surveillance. The OECD and the BIS have long engaged in surveillance and information sharing, although the fact that only the Fund has significant amounts of money to dispense has led governments to pay special heed to its surveillance exercises. What is distinctive about the current environment is the attention also being given to regional surveil-

---

[30] Unless those pegs are supported by a region-wide system of capital controls, which I do not regard as likely.

[31] All this, and more, can similarly be said of Latin America (Eichengreen and Taylor 2002).

[32] Eichengreen (2002a) finds a significant rise in the standard deviation of the change in the exchange rate relative to the standard deviation of reserves in all these countries since 1998.

lance. European countries are more concerned with the European Commission's assessments of their compliance with the Growth and Stability Pact (GSP) and with the Broad Economic Policy Guidelines that define multi-year deficit targets for EU members than they are with the IMF's Article IV reports or its comments on their policies in the *World Economic Outlook*.[33] Since 1998 the Association of Southeast Asian Nations has operated a regional surveillance process with the goal of facilitating cooperation in the formulation of monetary, fiscal, and financial policies through information exchange, peer review, and recommendations for action at the regional and national levels.[34] That process was recently strengthened by the establishment of local surveillance units in some ASEAN countries.[35] Even the Mercosur countries had plans for mutual surveillance before the crisis in Argentina put paid to their ambitions.

The IMF does not participate in these regional surveillance exercises. In some cases the motivation for developing them has been precisely to free the participants from the oversight of the Fund.[36] This is in contrast to Asia-Pacific Economic Cooperation (APEC) and the Group of Twenty, two trans-regional groupings with which the IMF is systematically involved.[37] Thus, it is not clear what officials have in mind when they say that regional and multilateral surveillance should be better integrated. Presumably they do not mean that an IMF rep-

---

[33]   Thus, in 2001, when the Fund observed that strict application of the GSP risked accentuating the economic cycle, EU countries essentially ignored its warning.

[34]   The ASEAN Surveillance process requires members to provide the ASEAN Surveillance Coordinating Unit (SCU) based in the ASEAN Secretariat in Jakarta with the same data supplied to the IMF in conjunction with its Article IV consultations and program negotiations.

[35]   The Chiang Mai statement of finance ministers of the ASEAN+3 countries (ASEAN plus China, Japan, and South Korea) announced a commitment to establish a "network of contact persons" to facilitate regional surveillance and the goal of creating a "well-coordinated economic and financial monitoring system in East Asia." The official statement of finance ministers at the Fifth ASEAN Finance Ministers Meeting in Kuala Lumpur in April 2001 stated that discussions were under way with the +3 countries on how to enhance and extend the ASEAN Surveillance Procedure, and in Honolulu in May 2001 these countries formed a study group on "enhancing the effectiveness of our economic reviews and policy dialogues." (Henning 2002: 16).

[36]   Thus, the Chiang Mai Initiative, which provides the impetus for the development of regional surveillance at the level of ASEAN+3, was an outgrowth of Japan's earlier proposal for an Asian monetary fund, which had itself been tabled with this motivation.

[37]   The Fund is a member of the Group of Twenty (which thus has 21 members). Along with a representative of the BIS, it attends the Manila Framework Group (a 14-country subset of APEC members – Australia, Brunei, Canada, China, Hong Kong, Indonesia, Japan, Korea, Malaysia, New Zealand, the Philippines, Singapore, Thailand, and the United States – that convenes meetings of deputy ministers of finance and deputy central bank governors) and in fact provides the technical secretariat.

resentative should be present in the European Commission when the latter determines whether an EU member state is in violation of the GSP. Nor do they mean that the Commission should mechanically accept IMF forecasts.[38]

If Europe is any guide, then the combination of strong regional institutions with strong regional surveillance may allow regions to "graduate" from multilateral surveillance, freeing themselves from the IMF's scrutiny. If an EU member state requires emergency assistance, this will almost surely be provided by its partners in the euro area, not by the IMF; this is all the more reason why EU members will increasingly disregard IMF surveillance.

The question is for how many other regions the same is likely to be true. My own view is that Europe is sui generis; its singular history has created a tolerance and, in some cases, even an appetite for political integration. This permits it to build transnational institutions like the ECB with substantial economic and monetary power. In Asia, in contrast, there is no desire for political integration and hence no willingness to construct strong institutions with the power to override national prerogatives (Katzenstein 1996). The ASEAN Surveillance Coordinating Unit lacks even the limited power of the GSP to compel policy adjustments by regional partners. This means that the strong currency countries will be reluctant to provide very extensive financial assistance to their weak regional partners. The Chiang Mai Initiative allows a country to draw more than ten percent of the swap credits provided by its regional partners only if it has negotiated an IMF program and is in compliance with the IMF's conditions. I see this agreement as reflecting not just U.S. pressure for the coordination of regional and multilateral arrangements but as the self-interested response of a group of countries not yet able to exercise firm surveillance of themselves. Once the Chiang Mai Initiative is tested, its members thus will have to figure out how to coordinate its surveillance and financial assistance with those of the IMF. It is Asia, then, that is likely to lead the way, through a process of trial and error, in determining how to practically coordinate regional and multilateral surveillance.

Surveillance and Regulation of Financial Markets. Reflecting its awareness of the importance of financial intelligence, the IMF has established a Capital Markets Department. It has created a Capital Markets Consultative Group (CMCG) that assembles market participants and IMF staff to discuss issues of systemic importance.[39] The Institute of International Finance proposes in addition the creation of a Private Sector Advisory Group to bring together creditors and the IMF

---

[38]   Given that EU countries represented on the IMFC would presumably oppose such a step.

[39]   Specifically, principles of crisis prevention and crisis management.

to facilitate discussions of country-specific problems.[40] How much this would add to the flow of information between the markets and the IMF and whether it would have a significant stabilizing influence is unclear. The Fund can use its already existing links with institutional investors, through the CMCG or bilaterally, to solicit their views. It can state its position on financial assistance by making public statements, issuing press releases, and attending meetings with investors convened by the economics or finance minister of the crisis country. Going a step further is not obviously desirable; establishing a Private Sector Advisory Group may only encourage the perception that the Fund is privileging some investors over others.[41]

While the IMF certainly can work to further refine its procedures for gathering financial intelligence, the more analytically demanding task is to give better advice on the supervision and regulation of financial institutions and markets. One important question is whether to advise countries to place the supervisory function in the central bank or to outsource it to an independent supervisory agency, along the lines of British and German practice. Arguments for housing the supervisory agency in the central bank are that supervisory information is valuable for the conduct of monetary policy and that the monetary authority should act as lender of last resort in times of crisis, an activity that must be informed by facts that only a supervisory authority can possess (Goodhart and Schoenmaker 1995, Haubrich 1996). The main argument against doing so is that this creates the potential for conflict with the monetary policy function, there being some evidence that central banks responsible for prudential supervision are more susceptible to inflationary pressures. My own view is that monetary policy is a relatively blunt instrument in many developing countries; the fine tuning facilitated by detailed information on what is going on in the banking system matters less than getting the basics right.[42] In any case, the monetary authority has a more limited ability to act as a lender of last resort in developing countries insofar as bank liabilities are heavily denominated in foreign currency.

These arguments suggest that the IMF should be pushing harder for the independence of supervisory agencies in the countries that need its advice the most.

---

[40]   Institute of International Finance (2002). In the event of an outright default, the PSAG would give way to a country-specific creditor committee that coordinated the creditors in restructuring negotiations.

[41]   In addition, providing the markets with more information about the Fund's intentions in a particular case prior to the eruption of a full-fledged crisis may erode the constructive ambiguity that limits moral hazard.

[42]   Working in the other direction is the fact that in countries with underdeveloped financial systems, the central bank may have to rely on interest rate ceilings and quantitative credit limits as instruments of monetary policy, in which case effective implementation may require supervisory authority.

Historically, countries that have separated supervision from monetary policy have encouraged their banks to hold high levels of capital to compensate for any additional lags in the response of the lender of last resort. This is another obvious implication for emerging markets.

This reference to capital requirements brings us to the revised Basel Capital Accord (Basel II). To a large extent the debate over its implications for emerging markets has focused on how the new risk-weighting procedures are likely to affect the cost and cyclicality of capital flows.[43] But from the point of view of crisis prevention, the revision is a mixed blessing. By keying risk weights to credit ratings, it will increase the procyclicality of capital flows, thereby amplifying an already existing problem. By steepening the gradient between risk weights and ratings, on the other hand, it will encourage the markets to be more discriminating when lending to risky credits, which should be helpful from the point of view of financial stability.

Also relevant is whether Basel II will address vulnerabilities in emerging-market banking systems. Few banks in emerging markets have the expertise and in-house models needed to adopt the internal-ratings-based approach to determining required capital that is the most dramatic innovation of Basel II.[44] They will continue to use the standardized approach, which under the revision will link risk weights to commercial ratings rather than to OECD–non-OECD status.[45] Moreover, because few corporations in emerging markets are rated by commercial agencies, banks will have to continue using the Accord's simple rule of thumb for corporate lending.[46] In other words, the associated capital charges will not encourage banks to effectively discriminate between corporate credits according to risk. This is troubling insofar as privatization and commercialization will

---

[43]   See, for example, Reisen (2001), Powell (2002), and Eichengreen (2002b).

[44]   Powell (2002) also notes that, insofar as only a few relatively sophisticated banks will adopt the IRB approach, which implies an even steeper gradient between capital requirements and risk than the standardized approach, there will be an incentive for those more sophisticated banks to shed high-risk credits and for less sophisticated banks to assume them, which is not obviously consistent with the quest for banking-system stability.

[45]   In addition to the ratings of commercial agencies, the new proposal would allow the use of export credit agency ratings. In practice, however, very few such ratings are available.

[46]   The risk weight for all unweighted corporate credits would be 100 percent. Powell (2002) reports that in Argentina just 150 out of some 80,000 corporate borrowers have external ratings. In addition, there is the issue that the proposal as it currently stands applies a lower capital charge to lending to corporations without ratings (100 percent) than to those with ratings below BB– (150 percent), which is a further disincentive for companies to seek ratings. One hopes that this anomaly will be eliminated before the revision is finalized.

almost certainly continue to heighten the prevalence of corporate relative to sovereign lending in emerging markets.

Powell (2002) suggests substituting information from public credit registries. Public registries operate in some 40 emerging markets; in many cases they receive reports of all bank loans extended to borrowers in the country.[47] In most cases they assign grades to those loans that could be mapped into ratings.[48] Some readers will hesitate to assign the responsibility of determining the rating to a government-owned or operated entity that is likely to be subject to political pressure. This, however, is little different from assigning bank regulation to a government agency. It simply points up the need to give the public agency in question political independence and dedicated budgetary resources (which could be obtained by levying a very small charge on each loan).

The bottom line is that the effort to develop better international financial standards, of which the Basel Accord for bank capital is the leading case in point, has devoted disproportionate attention to the circumstances of large banks in high-income countries. To be sure, large banks are particularly important for systemic stability. Large banks tend to be internationally active. There is some sign that the compression of spreads on bank-to-bank lending in the 1990s helped set the stage for subsequent problems.[49] For all these reasons, the emphasis on large, internationally active banks is not without reason. But the result of all the attention paid to the risks and opportunities they pose for gauging capital adequacy is that the problems of banks in emerging markets have not received comparable attention. The IMF and World Bank's Financial Sector Assessment Program addresses problems with individual banking systems on a case-by-case basis, but it is not informed by the kind of detailed international standards from which reviews of large countries in high-income countries benefit.

Institutional Reform. Finally, the IMFC urges the multilaterals to focus more on structural issues and institutional design. Financial institutions and markets should be designed to minimize mixed motives and conflicts of interest. Fiscal institutions should be designed to minimize free riding by special interests and subnational authorities. Political institutions should be designed to facilitate quick and coherent reactions to financial problems.

But the notion that the IMF and World Bank should pay more attention to structural issues is not easily reconciled with the desire to simplify and streamline their conditionality. The IMF Executive Board has agreed that structural conditions should be included in programs only when these are essential to the restora-

---

[47]   On credit registries, see Miller (2000).

[48]   Using procedures on which the multilaterals could usefully advise.

[49]   The evidence on this is somewhat mixed. See Eichengreen and Mody (2000).

tion of financial stability; this implies less emphasis on structural problems than in the past. Prescriptive advice on the design of political and economic institutions does not sit easily with the need for developing countries to display ownership of their reforms. Societies are less likely to feel invested in institutional reforms when these are imposed on them from outside. Nor is a greater emphasis on institutional design in IMF and World Bank programs and global standard-setting efforts obviously consistent with the value of local knowledge (Rodrik 2000, Stiglitz 2002). The imposition of institutional prescriptions from outside, in other words, is not obviously consistent with experimentation, discovery, and adaptation at the local level.

The multilaterals themselves are not immune to this call for institutional reform. Most discussions of this question, which focus on the creation of the IMF's Capital Markets Department or the Bank and IMF's Financial Sector Assessment Program, do not really address the fundamental issue. In contrast, statements by the British Chancellor of the Exchequer (Brown 2002) suggest introducing the presumption that the conclusions of the country team should be published at the end of each IMF mission and that all surveillance reports will be published when they are presented to the IMF board. He has advocated greater independence of the country desks that conduct Article IV surveillance from the lending activities of the IMF to ensure that surveillance is objective, rigorous, and consistent. Finally, he has recommended that the IMF institute regular annual reviews of the effectiveness of its surveillance and that IMF management report annually to the IMFC on the IMF's performance.

The argument for greater transparency and accountability, to be achieved through institutional reforms, surely applies as powerfully to the Bretton Woods institutions as to other financial market participants. The IMF has already moved a good way down the road to greater transparency, and there is already considerable peer and market pressure for governments to authorize the publication of Article IV reports. The creation of an Independent Evaluation Office in the IMF provides a framework for the kind of annual assessments the chancellor has in mind.

Whether strengthening the independence of regional departments and country desks from the IMF's management and board would provide a check on political pressure to lend is another matter. In a large organization, be it Enron or the IMF, there are incentives to refrain from circulating analyses, especially in public, that conflict with management's party line, whether or not the staff member in question enjoys bureaucratic autonomy. Dissent and internal promotion are not likely to be compatible, notwithstanding any putative independence of regional departments. These kind of firewalls are not likely to be any more effective in creating firewalls within the IMF than they are in separating the underwriting and trading departments of investment banks. Such firewalls are even more problematic in the case of the IMF precisely because it is not an investment bank. Mixed public messages from staff and management would be counterproductive for an institution whose purpose is to restore market confidence. If the goal is to reduce the pressure on the IMF to lend, my own preference would be to instead concentrate on developing other, less disruptive ways of resolving crises (Eichengreen 2002b) and on enhancing the independence of the IMF executive board as a way of insulating its decision-making from the short-term political agendas of its principal shareholders (De Gregorio et al. 2000).

4   Contagion

Predicting, preventing, and understanding contagion is a trendy subfield of crisis studies. Contagious crises are hard to predict because they are contingent events, i.e., their incidence depends not just on the intrinsic susceptibility of the economy to which the crisis spreads, but is contingent on the outbreak of a crisis in the originating country.

Contagion first appeared on the research community's radar screen with the emergence of the "tequila effect" and became a hot topic with the spread of the "Asian flu." Concern peaked in the aftermath of the Russian crisis, when some 30 percent of the countries considered by IMF (1999a) suffered significant currency market pressures.[50] While the results of conventional tests are superficially consistent with the presence of the phenomenon, such tests suffer from problems of observational equivalence. This is true of the approach taken in the first paper on the subject (Eichengreen et al. 1996b), which asks whether the presence of a crisis in one country increases the likelihood of a crisis in a neighboring country in the same or immediately succeeding period, holding constant the observable country-specific and global determinants of crisis risk.[51] This study finds that a crisis anywhere in the world raises crisis risk elsewhere by 8 percent, other things equal. Given the difficulty of predicting crises, however, it is hard to be too confident that such tests have succeeded in controlling for all of the relevant country-specific determinants of crises. That crises cluster is consistent with the presence of contagion, but it is also consistent with the omission of common fundamentals that heighten crisis risk in all the affected countries.

The logical response is to put more structure on the problem: to model not just contagion but also the channels through which crises spread, since an increase in volatility due to a crisis in a neighbor with which one trades displays macroeco-

---

[50]   Compared to 15–20 percent during the tequila and Asian episodes.

[51]   It is equally true of studies that test for contagion by looking for increases in the cross-country correlation of asset prices in periods of turbulence (Corsetti et al. 2002). The seminal paper taking this approach is Boyer et al. (1999).

nomic and financial similarities, or shares a common creditor, is more convincing evidence of direct economic spillovers. Subsequent studies (e.g., Eichengreen and Rose 1999) thus weighted crises in neighboring countries by the intensity of trade links and the extent of macroeconomic and financial similarities.[52] Their finding that contagion spread more from trading partners than from countries with macroeconomic and financial similarities raised eyebrows. Since this early work focused on Europe and considered the 1970s and 1980s as well as the subsequent recent period, there were suspicions that the result was context specific. However, subsequent research (e.g., Glick and Rose 1999, Forbes 2001) has found the result to be surprisingly robust.[53]

The literature now appears to be moving in a synthetic direction, admitting a role for both trade and common-creditor channels (see, e.g., Calvo 1999). Thus, Van Rijckeghem and Weder (1999) find that countries that compete for funds from common bank creditors were most likely to suffer contagion in the Mexican and Russian crises. Kaminsky and Reinhart (2000) similarly find that the presence of a common creditor increased the likelihood of spillovers in the Asian crisis. Through all this, however, the trade channel remains.

What light does this research shed on why contagion from the crisis in Argentina was initially so mild? One explanation is that Argentina is a relatively closed economy – that it trades so little means that contagion through trade was limited. Exports to Argentina are only 1 percent of GDP for Brazil and Chile, 2 percent for Uruguay, and 4 percent for Paraguay. But it is hard to believe that this is the entire story, and in particular that it is the story of why there was so little fallout for Brazil. Trade between Argentina and Brazil flows both ways, and there is considerable evidence that the devaluation of the *real* some years earlier was a factor in Argentina's subsequent crisis.[54]

---

[52]   To be sure, this does not entirely eliminate the possibility that results are being driven by the omission of common fundamentals. Thus, one of the most careful recent studies (Fratzscher 2002) finds that countries that trade heavily and share common creditors are more likely to be affected by crises elsewhere in the world even after allowing for unobservable shifts in investors' beliefs (which are modeled empirically as a Markov-switching process). Still, this does not rule out the possibility that countries infected by crises in, say, their trading partners share unobserved fundamentals that are correlated with their tendency to trade with one another. This objection is less compelling than the general common-omitted-fundamentals critique insofar as the omitted fundamentals most now take a restrictive form, but the critique retains at least some force.

[53]   De Gregorio and Valdes (2001) find that there is a regional effect above and beyond the trade effect (for which they control). Whether this reflects macroeconomic and financial linkages or something else they cannot determine.

[54]   It is not clear, in other words, why a channel that operated in one direction should not also operate in the other.

Alternatively, it could be that contagion has been limited by the adoption of more flexible exchange rates in other emerging markets, including Argentina's neighbors, Brazil and Chile. No doubt there is something to this observation, although IMF (1998) shows that crises can occur under flexible as well as fixed exchange rates and can spread even to countries whose currencies are unpegged.

Perhaps efforts to improve transparency have enabled investors to better discriminate between countries by creditworthiness. The steepening of the gradient between credit ratings and secondary-market spreads since 1998 is consistent with this view. At the same time, the fact that early studies of contagion did not suggest that volatility tended to spread as a result of superficial macroeconomic and financial similarities makes it hard to attach too much confidence to this interpretation. If future studies show that countries which have done the most to enhance transparency are the least susceptible to contagious crises, it will be possible to be more confident that this is the story.[55]

It could be that the decline in leverage in the international financial system since 1998 has reduced the need for institutional investors hit by crises in one country to sell other securities from the same asset class in the desperate effort to raise liquidity. There is some evidence that the use of credit, especially by the most highly leveraged institutions, has fallen significantly since the Russian crisis and the all but failure of Long-Term Capital Management.[56] This suggests revisiting the literature on the common creditor channel.

It is also possible that contagion from Argentina was limited by the anticipated nature of the country's crisis. Since institutional investors could see the crisis coming, they could provision for it and draw down their exposures. This limited the distress experienced by institutional investors – even those like J.P. Morgan–Chase and Banco Santander with relatively large positions – and hence the tendency to sell into a falling market to raise liquidity.[57] That Brazil's crisis, which was also widely anticipated, did not create significant contagion is similarly consistent with this view.[58] Now that there are enough observations to test the

---

[55]   Unfortunately, the obvious indicators of transparency, like the PriceWaterhouseCoopers "Opacity Index," were developed too recently to permit much retrospective analysis.

[56]   See Eichengreen and Park (2002). The Financial Stability Forum (2002) has claimed that this decline in leverage reflects improved counterparty risk management and strengthened regulatory oversight, but whether these or changes in borrowers' own appetite for risk are the source remains to be seen.

[57]   In other words, this was a second factor limiting the operation of the common creditor channel. Similarly, banks in other Latin American countries had limited exposure to Argentina. The one exception is Uruguay, but the story there is unique: the freeze on bank deposits in Argentina led Argentines with deposits in Uruguay – traditionally held for tax evasion purposes – to draw on their balances there.

[58]   IMF (1999b) provides evidence consistent with this interpretation.

hypothesis – by using reserve losses, interest premia, and the like to date when expectations of a crisis first became widespread – it is worth revisiting this issue.

Doing so is important. If it turns out that contagion from Argentina was limited because the country's crisis was a member of that select subset of such problems that are widely anticipated in advance, there is little reason to be confident that contagion in general has diminished. If, on the other hand, contagion from Argentina was less because transparency has improved, then there is more reason for hope.

5   Conclusion

It is frequently remarked that crisis prediction is more art than science; this paper reviewed a number of reasons why this is so. It has suggested that the point is no less true of crisis prevention. Crises have multiple causes rooted in the interaction of market fundamentals and investor psychology; it is this interaction that makes them difficult to predict and prevent. Their causes vary with time, reflecting changes in market structure but also shifts in investor sentiment.

It is still possible to identify steps to limit the incidence and severity of crises, such as strengthening the supervision and regulation of financial institutions, rationalizing exchange rate regimes, and reforming fiscal and political institutions. But not all initiatives that might limit crises will in fact be implemented. In some cases, resistance reflects rent seeking by special interests adversely affected by regulatory changes. In others, measures to reduce crises have distributional consequences and side effects that are viewed as undesirable by the international community. For example, changes in the Basel risk weights that raise the cost of funding and threaten to slow the growth of poor countries are at best a mixed blessing and will be embraced by their governments only with reluctance.

Most fundamentally, there is the inefficiency of so completely risk proofing the international financial system that crises never occur. Some risk taking is socially productive, and when risks are taken failures will inevitably result. In the same way that some corporations pursuing value-maximizing investment strategies will be felled by unforeseen events, even governments following policy strategies that maximize expected social welfare will experience crises from time to time. A hermit kingdom with no contact with the outside world can have no financial crises, but this does not make isolation the optimal state of affairs.

For all these reasons, there will always be crises, despite our best efforts to predict, prevent, and understand them. Perhaps then, in the end, all the attention devoted to crisis management by the official community is not really so wide of the mark.

Bibliography

Arteta, C. (2002). Dollarization of Banking, Financial Stability and Financial Liberalization. Unpublished dissertation. University of California, Berkeley.

Backus, D., and P. Kehoe (1992). International Evidence of the Historical Properties of Business Cycles. *American Economic Review* 82: 864–888.

Bayoumi, T., and B. Eichengreen (1999). Is Asia an Optimum Currency Area? Can It Become One? Regional, Global and Historical Perspectives on Asian Monetary Relations. In S. Collignon, J. Pisani-Ferry, and Y.C. Park (eds.), *Exchange Rate Policies in Emerging Asian Countries*. London: Routledge.

Berg, A., and C. Pattillo (1999a). Predicting Currency Crises: The Indicators Approach and an Alternative. *Journal of International Money and Finance* 18: 561–586.

Berg, A., and C. Pattillo (1999b). Are Currency Crises Predictable? A Test. *IMF Staff Papers* 46: 107–138.

Bergman, M., M. Bordo, and L. Jonung (1998). Historical Evidence on Business Cycles: International Comparisons. In J. Fuhrer and S. Schuh (eds.), *Beyond Shocks: What Causes Business Cycles?* Boston: Federal Reserve Bank of Boston.

Borensztein, E., A. Berg, G.M. Milesi-Ferretti, and C. Pattillo (2000). Anticipating Balance of Payments Crises – The Role of Early Warning Systems. IMF Occasional Paper 186, Washington, D.C.

Boyer, B.H., M.S. Gibson, and M. Lortan (1999). Pitfalls in Tests for Changes in Correlations. International Finance Discussion Paper 597, Board of Governors of the Federal Reserve System, Washington, D.C.

Brown, G. (2002). Statement. International Monetary and Financial Committee, Fifth Meeting, http://www.imf.org/external/spring/2002/imfc/stm/eng/gbr.htm.

Buiter, W., G. Corsetti, and N. Roubini (1993). Excessive Deficits: Sense and Nonsense in the Treaty of Maastricht. *Economic Policy* 8: 57–100.

Calvo, G. (1999). Contagion in Emerging Markets When Wall Street Is a Carrier. Unpublished manuscript. University of Maryland, College Park.

Calvo, G., L. Leiderman, and C. Reinhart (1992). Capital Inflows to Latin America: The 1970s and the 1990s. Unpublished manuscript. International Monetary Fund, Washington, D.C.

Cespedes, L.F., R. Chang, and A. Velasco (2002). Balance Sheets and Exchange Rate Policy. Unpublished manuscript. Rutgers University and Harvard University, New Brunswick, New Jersey, and Cambridge, Mass.

CFR (Council on Foreign Relations) (1999). *Safeguarding Prosperity in a Global Financial System*. New York: Council on Foreign Relations.

Cohen, D. (1991). *Private Lending to Sovereign States*. Cambridge, Mass.: MIT Press.

Corsetti, G., M. Pericoli, and M. Sbracia (2002). Some Contagion, Some Interdependence: More Pitfalls in Tests of Contagion. CEPR Discussion Paper 3310, London.

De Gregorio, J., and R. Valdes (2001). Crisis Transmission: Evidence from the Debt, Tequila, and Asian Flu Crises. In S. Claessens and K. Forbes (eds.), *International Financial Contagion*. Boston: Kluwer.

De Gregorio, J., B. Eichengreen, T. Ito, and C. Wyplosz (2000). *An Independent and Accountable IMF*. London: CEPR for the International Center for Monetary and Banking Studies.

Eichengreen, B. (2002a). What To Do With the Chiang Mai Agreement. Paper presented to the Asian Economic Panel, Tokyo.

Eichengreen, B. (2002b). *Financial Crises and What to Do About Them*. Oxford: Oxford University Press.

Eichengreen, B., and O. Jeanne (2000). Currency Crisis and Unemployment: Sterling in 1931. In P. Krugman (ed.), *Currency Crises*. Chicago: University of Chicago Press.

Eichengreen, B., and A. Mody (1998). Interest Rates in the North and Capital Flows to the South: Is There a Missing Link? *International Finance* 1: 35–58.

Eichengreen, B., and A. Mody (2000). Lending Booms, Reserves and the Sustainability of Short-Term Debt: Inferences from the Pricing of Syndicated Bank Loans. *Journal of Development Economics* 63: 1–24.

Eichengreen, B., and B. Park (2002). Hedge Fund Leverage Before and After the Crisis. *Journal of Economic Integration* 17: 1–20.

Eichengreen, B., and A. Rose (1999), Contagious Currency Crises: Channels of Conveyance. In T. Ito and A. Krueger (eds.), *Changes in Exchange Rates in Rapidly Developing Countries: Theory, Practice and Policy Issues*. Chicago: University of Chicago Press.

Eichengreen, B., and A. Rose (2001). Staying Afloat When the Wind Shifts: External Factors and Emerging Market Banking Crises. In G. Calvo, R. Dornbusch, and M. Obstfeld (eds.), *Money, Capital Mobility and Trade: Essays in Honor of Robert Mundell*. Cambridge, Mass.: MIT Press.

Eichengreen, B., and A. Taylor (2002). The Monetary Consequences of the Free Trade Area of the Americas. Paper prepared for the Harvard University-IADB Conference on the FTAA, Montevideo.

Eichengreen, B., A. Rose, and C. Wyplosz (1996a). Speculative Attacks on Pegged Exchange Rates: An Empirical Exploration with Special Reference to the European Monetary System. In M. Canzoneri, W. Ethier, and V. Grilli (eds.), *The New Transatlantic Economy*. Cambridge: Cambridge University Press.

Eichengreen, B., A. Rose, and C. Wyplosz (1996b). Contagious Currency Crises: First Tests. *Scandinavian Journal of Economics* 98: 463–484.

Eichengreen, B., A. Rose, and C. Wyplosz (2002). Financial Stability Forum Holds Seventh Meeting. BIS Press Release, http://www.bis.org/press/p020326.htm.

Forbes, K.J. (2001). Are Trade Linkages Important Determinants of Country Vulnerability to Crises? NBER Working Paper 8194, Cambridge, Mass.

Frankel, J., and A.K. Rose (1996). Currency Crashes in Emerging Markets. *Journal of International Economics* 41: 351–366.

Fratzscher, M. (2002). On Currency Crises and Contagion. ECB Working Paper 139, European Central Bank, Frankfurt/Main.

Glick, R., and A. Rose (1999). Contagion and Trade: Why Are Currency Crises Regional? *Journal of International Money and Finance* 18: 603–617.

Goldstein, M. (1998). *The Asian Financial Crisis*. Washington, D.C.: Institute for International Economics.

Goldstein, M. (2002). *Managed Floating Plus*. Washington, D.C.: Institute for International Economics.

Goldstein, M., G. Kaminsky, and C. Reinhart (2000). *Assessing Financial Vulnerability: An Early Warning System for Emerging Markets*. Washington, D.C.: Institute for International Economics.

Goodhart, C., and D. Schoenmaker (1995). Should the Functions of Monetary Policy and Banking Supervision Be Separated? *Oxford Economic Papers* 47: 539–560.

Government of France–Government of Japan (2000). Exchange Rate Regimes for Emerging Market Economies. http://www.mof.go.jp/english/asem/aseme03e.htm.

Hardy, D.C., and C. Pazarbasioglu (1999). Determinants and Leading Indicators of Banking Crises: Further Evidence. *IMF Staff Papers* 46: 247–258.

Haubrich, J.G. (1996). Combining Bank Supervision and Monetary Policy. *Economic Commentary*. Federal Reserve Bank of Cleveland (November), http://www.clev.frb/org/research/com/1196.htm.

Henning, C.R. (2002). *East Asian Financial Cooperation*. Washington, D.C.: Institute for International Economics.

IMF (International Monetary Fund) (1998). *World Economic Outlook*. Washington, D.C.: International Monetary Fund.

IMF (1999a). *World Economic Outlook*. Washington, D.C.: International Monetary Fund.

IMF (1999b). *International Capital Markets*. Washington, D.C.: International Monetary Fund.

IMF (2001). Transcript of an Economic Forum – Anticipating Crises: Model Behavior or Stampeding Herds. http://www.imf.org/external/np/tr/2x–1/tr011101a.htm.

IMF (2002). *Global Financial Stability Report*. Washington, D.C.: International Monetary Fund.

International Financial Institution Advisory Commission (2000). *Report*. Washington, D.C.: GPO.

International Monetary and Financial Committee of the Board of Governors of the International Monetary Fund (2002). Communiqué. http://www.imf.org/external/np/cm/2002/042002.htm.

Institute of International Finance (2002). *Action Plan of the IIF Special Committee on Crisis Prevention and Resolution in Emerging Markets*. Washington, D.C.: IIF.

Kaminsky, G. (1998). Currency and Banking Crises: A Composite Leading Indicator. Unpublished manuscript. Board of Governors of the Federal Reserve System, Washington, D.C.

Kaminsky, G., and C. Reinhart (2000). On Crises, Contagion and Confusion. *Journal of International Economics* 51: 145–168.

Kaminsky, G., S. Lizondo, and C. Reinhart (1998). Leading Indicators of Currency Crises. *IMF Staff Papers* 45: 1–48.

Katzenstein, P.J. (1996). Regionalism in Comparative Perspective. *Cooperation and Conflict* 31: 123–159.

Krugman, P. (2001). Balance Sheets, the Transfer Problem, and Financial Crises. Unpublished manuscript. Princeton University.

Leblang, D. (2001a). The Political Economy of Speculative Attacks in the Developing World. Unpublished manuscript. University of Colorado, Boulder.

Leblang, D. (2001b). Political Uncertainty and Speculative Attacks. Unpublished manuscript. University of Colorado, Boulder.

Leblang, D. (2001c). To Devalue or Defend? The Political Economy of Exchange Rate Policy. Unpublished manuscript. University of Colorado, Boulder.

Manzano, G. (2001). Is There Any Value-Added in the ASEAN Surveillance Process? *ASEAN Economic Bulletin* 18: 94–102.

Martinez, L., and A. Werner (2001). The Exchange Rate Regime and the Currency Composition of Corporate Debt: The Mexican Experience. Unpublished manuscript. Bank of Mexico, Mexico City.

Meese, R., and K. Rogoff (1983). Empirical Exchange Rate Models of the Seventies: Do They Fit Out of Sample? *Journal of International Economics* 14: 3–24.

Meyer, L.H., B.M. Doyle, J.E. Gagnon, and D.W. Henderson (2002). International Coordination of Macroeconomic Policies: Still Alive in the New Millennium? International Finance Discussion Paper 723 Washington, D.C. International Finance Division, Board of Governors of the Federal Reserve System.

Miller, M. (2000). Credit Reporting Systems Around the Globe: The State of the Art in Public and Private Credit Registries. Unpublished manuscript. The World Bank, Washington, D.C.

Mishkin, F.S. (2001). Financial Policies and the Prevention of Financial Crises in Emerging Market Economies. NBER Working Paper 8087, Cambridge, Mass.

Mishkin, F.S., and K. Schmidt-Hebbel (2001). One Decade of Inflation Targeting in the World: What Do We Know and What Do We Need to Know. NBER Working Paper 8497, Cambridge, Mass.

Morris, S., and H.S. Shin (2000). Rethinking Multiple Equilibria in Macroeconomic Modeling. *NBER Macroeconomics Annual* 2000: 139–161.

Mulder, C., R. Perrelli, and M. Rocha (2002). The Role of Corporate, Legal and Macroeconomic Balance Sheet Indicators in Crisis Detection and Prevention. IMF Working Paper WP/02/59, Washington, D.C.

Osband, K., and C. van Rijckeghem (2000). Safety from Currency Crashes. *IMF Staff Papers* 47: 238–258.

Powell, A. (2002). A Capital Accord for Emerging Economies? Unpublished manuscript. Universidad Torcuato Di Tella, Buenos Aires.

Reisen, H. (2001). Will Basel II Contribute to Convergence in International Capital Flows? Unpublished manuscript. OECD Development Centre, Paris.

Rodrik, D. (2000). Development Strategies for the Next Century. Unpublished manuscript. Kennedy School of Government, Harvard University, Cambridge, Mass.

Sachs, J., A. Tornell, and A. Velasco (1996). Financial Crises in Emerging Markets: The Lessons from 1995. *Brookings Papers on Economic Activity* (1): 147–215.

Stiglitz, J. (2002). *Globalization and Its Discontents*. New York: W.W. Norton.

Tornell, A. (1999). Common Fundamentals in the Tequila and Asian Crises. NBER Working Paper 7139, Cambridge, Mass.

Van Rijckeghem, C., and B. Weder (1999). Financial Contagion: Spillovers through Banking Centers. Unpublished manuscript. International Monetary Fund, Washington, D.C.

Comment on Barry Eichengreen

Lukas Menkhoff

Introduction

The frequency and severity of financial crises was the major reason in the late 1990s for the lively debate on a new international financial architecture (see Eichengreen (1999) for an account). Due to several constraints, practical policy making has adjusted the agenda to much more modest goals than had been advanced at the beginning of the discussion. Eichengreen (2003) takes stock of both major efforts made and present concerns. His objective is thus not to float another pathbreaking reform proposal or to dig too deeply into the problems of certain countries or crises. Moreover, he turns attention away from the often pressing day-to-day problems. Instead, he emphasizes the role of crisis prevention and devotes his core section to this topic.

Crisis prevention is a worthy goal, but difficult to reach, as Eichengreen most convincingly shows in the two other sections of his paper, the one on crisis prediction and the other on contagion. What makes progress in this field so difficult to realize is, according to his analysis, that the causes of crisis vary with time. Changes in market structure and investor sentiment make it problematic to draw general lessons and to develop general policy prescriptions. The arguments given, as well as the empirical evidence referred to, lend strong support to this view.

There is, however, another element complicating crisis prediction and prevention, which the following discussion analyzes in more detail, i.e., local knowledge. Local knowledge incorporates the proper understanding of particular characteristics of local institutions and local information in general. The opposite of local knowledge is globally available knowledge and the opposite of local institutions is global – or, to be more precise, globally standardized – institutions. Eichengreen (2003: 179) acknowledges the inherent tension between multilateral crisis prevention and local knowledge: "global standard-setting efforts [are not] obviously consistent with the value of local knowledge."

My comment elaborates on this tension and argues that greater reliance on local knowledge – in comparison to the present plans in international financial institutions – can help to make crisis prevention more effective. The argument consists of three steps: The next section puts the role of local knowledge into perspective, the following section provides empirical evidence for the importance of local knowledge, and the last section discusses consequences of this importance for concrete reform steps. This section is organized according to Eichengreen's reflections on the results of the latest International Monetary and Financial Committee (IMFC) communiqué.

The Role of Local Knowledge in Perspective

It is a fact of life that national economies are becoming more and more integrated into the world economy. As regards financial matters, there is already talk of "financial globalization." In reality, however, this is still an ongoing process. Emerging economies, which are often involved in financial crises, are not fully integrated yet. At the same time, it can be stated that their economic institutions are quite different from those in mature markets. This is not a coincidence, however, but follows from economic logic: the development of markets is the development of institutions and if an economy wants to integrate itself successfully into a new environment, such as international financial markets, it seems to be necessary for it to be in command of the appropriate institutions. Empirical studies tend to support this notion (e.g., Arteta et al. 2001; Edwards 2001).

This relation between financial opening and institution building can be interpreted as a saddle-path relation: both ingredients must fit each other to result in economically optimal outcomes. If any one of the two ingredients is overweighted or develops too fast, disequilibrium occurs. A simple graphical presentation of this relation is given in Figure 1.

Globalization is grasped as the move from a local economy in the bottom left corner of Figure 1 towards a global economy in the top right corner. The two dimensions on the axes are, first, the transformation from local to global institutions and, second, the process of financial opening. The equilibrium saddle-path is marked as the diagonal line for the sake of simplicity. If an economy opens up too fast, that is, if it moves towards point A in the figure, the internationalization creates tough competition and some efficiency gains but at the cost of an unwanted high crisis probability. That is where we stand today and why we are discussing crisis prevention with some urgency. To rebalance this situation, the international financial institutions and the industrialized countries dominating them favor a concept that strongly advises reforming local institutions. Depending on the speed of reform, the objective is to reach a situation as marked in Figure 1 by the area between B and B′, with the "minimum" target being situation B.

There are many alternatives to this presently favored strategy and the seemingly most consistent one might aim for turning the clock of globalization backwards. To clarify any possible misunderstanding: this does not result in being the optimal policy from the framework sketched out above. The optimal policy in-

Figure 1: Relation between Institution Building and Financial Opening

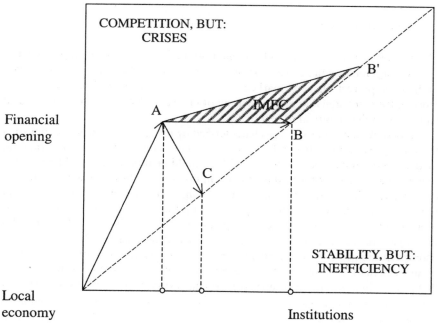

stead aims for a combination of restricting financial opening to some degree and continuing the policy of upgrading local institutions. According to Figure 1, the shortest path towards crisis prevention would be from A to C.

The preferred policy according to this framework neither denies the long-run ambition of fully realizing benefits from international specialization nor does it neglect the advantages accrued by bringing local institutions closer to world standards. The difference in comparison to the presently favored strategy is thus not one of direction but one of speed. The argument, however, is not built on adjusting to equilibrium as fast as possible, as point B might represent a higher welfare level than point C, and this gain might justify temporary instability. The argument is rather that the reform process from A to B would take too much time and is thus unrealistic. Institution building is not only the reforming of formal rules, such as laws or regulations. According to North (1996), institutions are the rules of the game in society and also incorporate informal rules and enforcement mechanisms.

Making markets work efficiently requires first that they are understood as they are and then that the right mix of rules is found and implemented. This complexity and specificity demonstrates exactly the importance of local knowledge.

Local Knowledge Matters

The case of local knowledge has been much strengthened by recent empirical studies. Two arguments will be made in this context: first, local knowledge exists, even in the most perfect financial markets. Thus, second, it can be expected to matter more in the comparatively opaque setting of emerging markets. This is examined and found in the empirical literature.

Modern financial markets are characterized by professional market participants thoroughly examining available information. Due to almost perfect information media and minimal transaction costs, there should be no role for local knowledge in these markets. The observed home bias in investments has been a motivation to dig for any evidence of local knowledge, as this could rationally explain certain preferences for "home investments." Indications that there are such local information advantages are provided, for example, by Coval and Moskowitz (1999), who investigate investment decisions in U.S. stocks, or by Hau (2001), who investigates performance of investments in German stocks. Location does not only matter in stock markets, however; there are also foreign exchange studies that indicate that proximity translates into better performance, studies such as Peiers (1997) on anticipating interventions of the Deutsche Bundesbank, or Ito et al. (1998) on information flows in Japan. In all of these studies, the finding is that information is not equally distributed, but rather that there is a systematic advantage due to proximity indicating the value of local knowledge.

As information heterogeneity depends on market imperfections, such as high transaction costs, it can be expected that the local knowledge identified in mature financial markets has an even higher importance in emerging markets. The empirical approach in studies relating to this expectation usually compares the performance between local and foreign investors. The foreign investors are assumed to have a technological advantage, but are possibly lacking locally relevant information. As empirical studies cannot differentiate between these two factors, they test the combined effect. The benchmark to prove the value of local knowledge is therefore even higher than in the above-mentioned studies on mature markets.

There are several approaches with which to identify whether local investors have a net advantage that outweighs the technological disadvantage. Whether investment performance is examined, or crisis prediction ability, or the proper adjustment of firms to capital inflows (see Table 1), the evidence always indicates that local investors have a significant information advantage, which indicates the

Table 1: Local Knowledge Outweighs Technological Advantage in Emerging Markets

Empirical evidence	Source
Foreign investors trade less profitably on stock markets	Kim and Wei (2002), Choe et al. (2001)
Local investors are better able to predict financial crises	Kaufman et al. (1999)
Foreign investors cause stock revaluation but not investment reallocation after capital inflow	Chari and Henry (2001, 2002)

high value of local knowledge in emerging markets. These results question, in particular, the economic benefit resulting from foreign portfolio investments (see Frenkel and Menkhoff 2002).

In summary, local participants have an advantage in properly interpreting their markets. How does this advantage impact the appropriate course of crisis prevention reforms and how can this be used to improve crisis prevention?

Local Knowledge Impacts the Course of Crisis Prevention Reforms

Eichengreen discusses the present state of crisis prevention reforms by taking reference to the main issues mentioned in the latest IMFC communiqué. He chooses six major subjects which he regards as unresolved issues, discusses the IMFC's view, and substantiates his own recommendations. This section selectively reviews these recommendations assuming that they are relevant from the viewpoint of emphasizing local knowledge. Table 2 gives an overview of five of the six IMFC issues, with Eichengreen's recommendations and my comments assuming that local knowledge matters.

Of central importance for this comment is the sixth issue, i.e., the IMFC's intention to focus more on structural issues and institutional designs in its reform efforts. Eichengreen is cautiously skeptical about this outside approach towards institutional reform as it clearly favors globally standardized institutions over local institutions. As already mentioned above (see Section 2), I assess this approach as ineffective, considering the value of local knowledge. The rapid transition towards global institutions in the same instance heavily depreciates the value of local knowledge. It is not only questionable whether such a depreciation represents a responsible use of human and institutional capital, but it may also be criticized that the depreciation gives a disincentive to invest in local knowledge. However, markets are different, and to work efficiently, markets must find the right mix of formal rules, informal constraints, and appropriate enforcement characteristics (see North 1996). Neglecting that they are different, i.e., neglecting local knowledge, is not efficient.

The issue of bank regulation – number five in Eichengreen's order – is an application of the above-demonstrated principle. Because emerging markets have more opaque information, increasing transparency is important for better functioning markets. The use of publicly accessible credit registries could be one way to increase transparency. However, the Basel II process does not consider emerging markets in particular, but proposes a quite standardized framework of bank regulation that focuses on the internationally active banks in industrialized countries.

Table 2: Local Knowledge Impacts the Course of Institutional Reforms

Unresolved issues on the IMFC agenda[a]	Eichengreen's recommendations (selective review)	Comment, assuming that local knowledge matters
Institutional reform: focus more on structural issues and institutional designs (no. 6)	"advice on ... institutions does not sit easily with the need ... to display ownership of reforms"	ownership requires taking local knowledge seriously; efficient market development builds on local knowledge
Surveillance and regulation of financial markets (no. 5)	install and use public credit registries for rating information	very important to reduce information asymmetries and to increase public information
	pay more attention to banks' problems in emerging markets (Basel II process)	local knowledge has not been considered yet
Impact of large country policies (no. 2)	avoid policies to increase volatility of their own large economies; international policy coordination? → not feasible	asymmetric information makes asymmetric impact more problematic → control capital flows
Exchange rate regimes (no. 3)	more flexible exchange rates plus anchoring (inflating targeting, central bank independence)	less trust in appropriate exchange rate determination by international financial markets
Integration of multilateral, regional, and country surveillance (no. 4)	regional surveillance may substitute multilateral surveillance, but "Europe is sui generis"	regional surveillance gives more importance to local knowledge

[a] Numbers refer to the sequence in Eichengreen (2003).

A possible outcome of neglecting such institutional differences – that is, also the negligence of local knowledge – could be that the new regulatory framework does not improve the situation in emerging economies. One can even imagine that it causes some unwanted changes in risk allocation (see Powell 2002).

Coming to the macroeconomic issues two to four, the view that local knowledge is important may again influence the policy stance. Regarding the impact of large economies on emerging economies (issue 2), the latter not only suffer from this asymmetry but also lack the same level of understanding about foreign economies as industrialized countries do (see Frenkel and Menkhoff 2002). This supports the advisability of detaching to some extent national markets from international financial markets. Similarly, international market participants' limited fundamental understanding of local forces in emerging markets can lower trust in economically sensible exchange rate determination. Thus, the move towards flexible exchange rates appears – keeping everything else equal – less advantageous for emerging economies (issue 3). Finally, multilateral surveillance often implies the use of globally standardized recipes for policy making which may not fit well into an institutionally idiosyncratic environment (issue 4). In this sense, regional surveillance can be more effective.

These considerations do not necessarily lead towards a radical change in policy making, but they may indicate why many policy makers in emerging economies do not feel overly comfortable with the approach presently favored by the international financial institutions and industrialized countries. To put it differently, the present reform agenda does not fully reflect the needs of global governance; rather, it is distorted towards the interests and needs of the major economies in the world. Effective global governance and effective crisis prevention require more than just a reform towards globally standardized institutions. They also require the insight that local knowledge exists, that it matters, and that policy making results can be improved by incorporating this knowledge into decision making processes.

Bibliography

Arteta, C., B. Eichengreen, and C. Wyplosz (2001). When Does Capital Account Liberalization Help More than It Hurts? NBER Working Paper 8414. Cambridge, Mass.

Chari, A., and P.B. Henry (2001). Stock Market Liberalizations and the Repricing of Systematic Risk. NBER Working Paper 8265. Cambridge, Mass.

Chari, A., and P.B. Henry (2002). Capital Account Liberalization: Allocative Efficiency or Animal Spirits? Working Paper, Stanford University.

Choe, H., B.-C. Kho, and R.M. Stulz (2001). Do Domestic Investors Have More Valuable Information about Stocks than Foreign Investors? NBER Working Paper 8073. Cambridge, Mass.

Coval, J., and T. Moskowitz (1999). Home Bias at Home: Local Equity Preferences in Domestic Portfolios. *Journal of Finance* 54(6): 2045–2073.

Edwards, S. (2001). Capital Flows and Economic Performance: Are Emerging Economies Different? NBER Working Paper 8076. Cambridge, Mass.

Eichengreen, B. (1999). *Towards a New International Financial Architecture, A Practical Post-Asia Agenda*. Washington, D.C.: Institute for International Economics.

Eichengreen, B. (2003). Predicting and Preventing Financial Crises: Where Do We Stand? What Have We Learned? In this volume.

Frenkel, M., and L. Menkhoff (2002). Are Foreign Institutional Investors Good for Emerging Markets? Discussion Paper. University of Hannover, Germany.

Hau, H. (2001). Location Matters: An Examination of Trading Profits. *Journal of Finance* 56(5): 1959–1983.

Ito, T., R.K. Lyons, and M. Melvin (1998). Is There Private Information in the FX Market? The Tokyo Experiment. *Journal of Finance* 53(3): 1111–1130.

Kaufman, D., G. Mehrez, and S. Schmukler (1999). Predicting Currency Fluctuations and Crises: Do Resident Firms Have an Informational Advantage? World Bank Working Paper 2259. Washington, D.C.

Kim, W., and S.-J. Wei (2002). Foreign Portfolio Investors before and during a Crisis. *Journal of International Economics* 56(1): 77–96.

North, D.C. (1996). Economic Performance through Time: The Limits to Knowledge. Economics Working Paper Archive 9612004. Washington University, St. Louis.

Peiers, B. (1997). Informed Traders, Intervention, and Price Leadership: A Deeper View of the Microstructure of the Foreign Exchange Market. *Journal of Finance 52*: 1589–1614.

Powell, A. (2002). A Capital Accord for Emerging Economies? World Bank Working Paper 2808. Washington, D.C.

Jason F. Shogren and Stephan Kroll

Globalization & Climate Protection:
Some Microeconomic Foundations for Integration

1   Introduction

An old idea relabeled, *globalization*, has been ongoing since at least the 19th century as international trade advanced global economic integration (see, e.g., O'Rourke and Williamson 2002). The key notions behind globalization are comparative advantage and gains from trade – fewer trade barriers, faster communication, and more global trade reduces the prices of locally scarce resources, which promotes resource price convergence and increases the economic welfare of the trading nations. As stated by Sachs (1997: 24), "global capitalism is surely the most promising institutional arrangement for worldwide prosperity that history has ever seen." Many observers believe that more global trade is the best chance for the world's poor to prosper. These "proponents of trade have always considered that trade is the policy and development the objective" (Bhagwati 2002: 25).

What is relatively recent, however, is the animated fears that globalization puts global environmental integrity at risk, including the global commons like our climate (e.g., Rodrick 1997, Geoffrey 1998). The alarm is that globalization and trade will move the per capita consumption of all people toward the "socially irresponsible" levels witnessed in the industrialized nations (see Dasgupta's (2002) review). If globalization triggers an ever-increasing demand for goods and services, development of land, production of livestock, and use of fossil fuels, such changes could disrupt the planet's climate system, with potentially devastating global consequences. Since fossil fuels are the primary contributor to carbon emissions, our daily actions could induce gradual or abrupt changes in the climate that could affect our well-being. Scientists warn of increased flooding, spreading tropical diseases, shifting gulf streams, and reduced agriculture productivity (e.g., Schelling 1992, Nordhaus 1994, IPCC 2001). A recent illustration is the statement by a committee organized by the U.S. National Research Council (2002: 167): "With growing globalization, adverse impacts [due to abrupt climate change] – although likely to vary from region to region because exposure and sensitivity will vary – are likely to spill across national boundaries, through human and biotic migration, economic shocks, and political aftershocks... The issues are global and it will be important to give attention to the issues faced by poorer countries that are likely to be especially vulnerable to the social and economic impacts of abrupt climate change."

The key question is how to integrate these concerns over the global climate into debates about the world economy and globalization. Climate change policy differs from previous international treaties like the Montreal Protocol for ozone protection and the CITES treaty to protect endangered species. Those risks were immediate, less ambiguous, and in some sense less pervasive than climate change. The insight gained from earlier international treaties can obviously help guide our thinking about integrating climate protection into the world economy. But several characteristics make the climate problem unique. Climate risks are not immediate – most predicted threats will occur decades from now, if not centuries; the primary driver of carbon emissions is fossil fuels, which dominate nearly every aspect of the global economy, and the burden of climate change will be felt by developed nations.

This essay focuses on several microeconomic findings that matter for understanding the benefits of and limits to integrating climate protection into the global economic order. We begin with a brief overview of the question of climate change and the political economy of climate protection. We then review the three main themes that have emerged in the economics literature on climate change – stable international agreements, developing nation participation, and equitable emission reductions. We consider three broad questions that can arise when thinking about assimilating climate protection into the global economic order – how international institutional processes affect integration, how domestic debates over costs and benefits affect integration, and how individual behavior toward risk and risk reduction strategies affects integration.

2   Integrating Climate Protection into the Global Economy

While humanity does not yet have a perfectly integrated global economy, we do have one global climate system – one that makes life on earth possible. Today's arguments for active global policies to protect this climate system is based on two observed trends: (1) the Earth has warmed 0.5 degrees Celsius, or one degree Fahrenheit, over the past 100 years, and (2) atmospheric concentrations of greenhouse gases (GHGs) have increased by about 30 percent over the last 200 years (IPCC 1996). The United Nations Intergovernmental Panel on Climate Change connected these two trends, leading them to conclude in its Second Assessment Report (IPCC 1996) that: "the balance of evidence suggests that there is a discernible human influence on global climate." Five years later, the IPCC deepened its concern in its Third Assessment Report: "[There is] new and stronger evidence that most of the warming observed over the last 50 years is attributable to human activities" (IPCC 2001).

Climate change matters for global economic order because cumulative GHG concentrations are a global public bad – a ton of GHGs released in, say Iceland, has the same effect on the climate as a ton released in South Africa. Climate protection requires global participation in long-run emission reductions aimed at meeting a targeted concentration level (e.g., Schmalensee 1996). According to many scientists and policymakers, the best strategy is a worldwide reduction in the use of fossil fuels (e.g., coal, oil, natural gas) – the primary source of greenhouse gas emissions. But with likely reductions in trade barriers and increases in trade and development, the predicted trend for global energy demand met by fossil fuels is up not down. Energy consumption in Asia, for instance, is predicted to increase to over 170 quadrillion Btus in 2020 from 50 quadrillion Btus in 1990 (USEIA 2000). Total energy consumption is expected to double by 2020 to over 600 quadrillion Btus. If globalization leads to more global per capita energy consumption supplied by coal and oil, the dominant energy resources, carbon emissions and the risks from climate change are projected to rise rather than fall. While the use of coal might be enemy #1 to the environment as a recent issue of *The Economist* claimed, it is estimated that the world has about one trillion metric tons of recoverable coal reserves (USEIA 2000). The pressure to use these carbon-intensive resources to develop and prosper in poorer nations is significant. As pointed out by a Chinese delegate at an international meeting on climate change: "[w]hat they [developed nations] are doing is luxury emissions, what we are doing is survival emissions" (as quoted in Huber and Douglass 1998).

Efforts to bring together these differing international opinions about the need for climate protection within a growing world economy began in earnest in the early 1990s. Held in Rio de Janeiro, the negotiations over the 1992 United Nations Framework Convention on Climate Change (UNFCCC 1999a) were the first major watershed (see Table 1). The convention states that the objective is to stabilize GHG concentrations within a time frame that would prevent "dangerous" human damage to the climate system. Article 4 states that nations should cooperate to improve human adaptation and mitigation of climate change through financial support and low-emission technologies, and the use of cost-effective response measures. Most industrialized countries pledged to voluntarily reduce emissions to 1990 levels by 2000.

Since by the mid-1990s it was obvious that these voluntary pledges were not going to be met, the international community increased the pressure for global climate protection by agreeing to discuss "binding" commitments. After Rio, the 1997 Kyoto Protocol of the Framework Convention (UNFCCC 1999b) was the

Table 1: Milestones in Climate Policy, 1979–2002

1979	• First World Climate Conference
1990	• First Assessment Report of the IPCC; initial evidence that human activities might affect climate, with significant uncertainty
1990	• Second World Climate Conference; agreement to negotiate a "framework treaty"
1992	• UNFCCC established at the UNCED (i.e., the Earth Summit) in Rio de Janeiro, Brazil • Annex I developed countries pledge to return emissions to 1990 levels by 2000 • United States ratifies UNFCCC later in the year
1993	• Clinton Administration publishes its Climate Change Action Plan for voluntary emission-reduction programs
1995	• IPCC Second Assessment Report completed (published in 1996); stronger conviction expressed that human activities could be adversely affecting climate
1995	• Berlin Mandate developed at the first COP (COP1) to the UNFCCC • Agreement to negotiate *legally binding* targets and timetables to limit emissions in Annex I countries
1997	• COP3 held in Kyoto Japan, leading to the Kyoto Protocol • Annex I/Annex B countries agree to binding emission reductions averaging 5% below 1990 levels by 2008–2012, with "flexibility mechanisms" (including emissions trading) for compliance; no commitments for emission limitation by developing countries
1997	• U.S. Senate passes Byrd–Hagel resolution, 95 to 0, stating the United States will reject any climate agreement that did not demand comparable sacrifices of all participants and called for the administration to justify any proposed ratification of the Kyoto Protocol with analysis of benefits and costs
1998	• COP4 held in Buenos Aires, Argentina; emphasis on operationalizing the flexibility mechanisms of the Kyoto Protocol • IPCC Third Assessment begins
1999	• COP5 held in Bonn, Germany; continued emphasis on operationalizing the flexibility mechanisms
2000	• COP6 held at The Hague, The Netherlands, discussions continue on flexibility mechanisms
2001	• COP7 held at Marrakech, Morocco, discussions continue on flexibility mechanisms • IPCC Third Assessment Report published; "new and stronger evidence that most of the warming observed over the last 50 years is attributable to human activities"
2002	• Bush Administration rejected Kyoto protocol, and announced its greenhouse gas intensity approach to climate protection • COP8 to be held in New Delhi, India

IPCC = Intergovernmental Panel on Climate Change; UNFCCC = United Nations Framework Convention on Climate Change; UNCED = United Nations Conference on Environment and Development; COP = Conference of Parties.

next serious advance. The protocol states that the industrialized countries agreed to legally binding reductions in net GHG emissions that average about 5 percent below 1990 levels by 2008–2012. Given expected business-as-usual emission growth between 1990 and 2010, the emission reductions needed for compliance are substantial (Wigley et al. 1996). In the United States, the Clinton Administration's policy to meet Kyoto was based on a conviction that substantial progress toward reducing emissions could be achieved without adverse economic consequences based on a policy of flexibility mechanisms (e.g., international emission trading) and the promotion of cleaner, more climate-friendly technology (e.g., Shogren 1999). For example, the Clinton Administration estimated the impact of Kyoto was an annual GDP decrease of less than 0.5 percent – or $10 billion; no expected negative effect on the trade deficit; increases in gasoline prices of only about $0.05 a gallon; lower electricity rates; and no significant aggregate affect on employment (U.S. Clinton Administration 2000). A critical assumption was a high degree of success in implementing the flexibility mechanisms, especially emissions trading with developing countries and the former Soviet Union.

While developing countries participated in the discussions at Kyoto, they did not agree to any emission targets (see, e.g., Jacoby et al. 1998). The Clinton Administration stated that the Kyoto Protocol would only be sent to the Senate for ratification once there was "meaningful participation" by developing countries, which has yet to come to pass. The post-Kyoto meetings in Bonn, The Hague, and Marrakech have revealed sharp differences in opinion between the United States and other industrialized countries versus the European Union and many developing countries about the technical, legal, and moral foundations of the proposed flexibility mechanisms and developing nation participation. A key issue remains the extent to which reliance on international emissions trading could substitute for, or could only complement, domestic efforts to reduce global energy use and carbon emissions given the developing countries' goal of development.

While some differences have been resolved in post-Kyoto meetings, the ultimate fate of the protocol remains to be seen. In 2001, the Bush Administration officially announced its opposition to Kyoto. Their opposition, like the 1997 Byrd–Hagel resolution, derived from a perception that the costs to meet the targets would be excessive without the global participation of the developing countries. The administration announced its climate policy – a greenhouse gas emission intensity goal. Emission intensity focuses on reducing metric tons of greenhouse gases per million dollars of output (GHGmt/$mo). The administration's stated target is to reduce the U.S. economy to 151 from 180 GHGmt/$mo by 2012, about a 20 percent improvement. The administration's plan promotes voluntary measures to meet a unilateral nonbinding target of about 100 million metric tons GHG abatement, or less if the economy grows faster than expected – about a 2 percent rate of improvement in greenhouse gas emissions intensity over the next decade. While proposed policies to make the Bush plan operational are similar to the Clinton Administration's – tax credits, early emission reduction credits, R&D funding, and voluntary consultations and agreements – the sticking point remains developing country participation.

3   Economics of International Environmental Architecture

The ongoing challenge regarding whether and how humanity can integrate climate protection into the global economy has attracted the attention of many economists. The extant microeconomic literature has focused primarily on whether global participation is possible in any climate protection agreement like the Kyoto Protocol. Consider two areas stressed in the theory behind the micro-foundations of efficient climate treaties – self-enforcing agreements and developing nation participation.

Self-Enforcing Agreements. The first insight is that a climate treaty must have built-in incentive mechanisms to make the agreement self-enforcing. The logic is as follows. Climate protection requires global participation, since climate change is a global public good – every nation contributes to increased carbon concentrations and no nation can be prevented from enjoying a less risky climate, regardless of whether it participates in a treaty (e.g., Kolstad 1996). The responsibility for addressing the problem therefore should ultimately be shared by all countries, both developed and developing countries. Widespread responsibility, however, increases the challenge of creating and maintaining a stable international agreement given weak international enforcement. The incentive problem behind defining an effective and lasting agreement is that while nations have a common interest in responding to the risk of climate change, many are reluctant to reduce GHG emissions voluntarily, especially those that have explicit policies to use coal to develop and prosper. Sovereign countries have an incentive to let other developed nations reduce their emissions, since climate protection is nonrival and nonexcludable in consumption. This incentive challenge is compounded by national differences in current and future wealth, development policies, access to carbon-based energy resources like coal, vulnerability to climate change, and capacities to respond.

A problem with the Kyoto Protocol is it lacks the self-enforcing incentive mechanisms that made other international environmental agreements work (e.g., the Montreal Protocol). No global police organization exists to enforce an international climate agreement. A climate treaty must be self-enforcing – all sovereign parties should have no incentive to deviate unilaterally from the terms of the agreement. A self-enforcing agreement exists when the net benefits of every nation's emission reduction strategy favors climate protection. The problem is that in theory, such agreements are easiest to maintain only when the stakes are either so small as to not matter or so large that no other option exists (see Barrett 1994). Self-enforcing agreements are hardest to achieve in the gray area between low and infinite stakes. The greater the global net benefits of cooperation, the stronger the incentive to free ride (see Hoel 1992, Carraro and Siniscalco 1993, Bac 1996). Theory suggests that while a self-enforcing coalition can be created, the size of the stable coalition is small, and side payments between countries do not increase the size of the coalition.

If the incentive for global self-enforcement is insufficient, signatories who have ongoing relationships can try to alleviate free riding on climate change policy by retaliating with threats such as trade sanctions (Chen 1997). But the force of linkage and deterrence is blunted in several respects. A nation's incentive to refrain to reduce emissions depends on the balance between short-term gains from abstaining relative to the long-term cost related to punishment. Participating nations must see a gain in actually applying punishment, otherwise their threats of retaliation will not be credible. Credibility problems arise when, for example, retaliation through trade sanctions damages both the enforcer and the free rider. Moreover, because many forms of sanctions exist, nations would need to select a mutually agreeable set of approaches – probably another involved international negotiation process (Dockner and van Long 1993).

Developing Country Participation. The second insight is that equitable burden sharing between developed and developing nations is not straightforward. Even if a self-enforcing agreement involved only two or three big emitting markets (e.g., the United States and the European Union) and many small nations refused to agree, total emissions probably would remain higher than global targets. Many policymakers in industrialized countries worry about the self-imposed impact to their economies if developing countries refrain from participation. This situation could adversely affect comparative advantages in the industrialized world, whereas leakage of emissions from controlled to uncontrolled countries would limit the environmental effectiveness of a partial agreement. Estimates of this carbon leakage vary from a few percent to more than one-third of the Annex B reductions, depending on model assumptions regarding the substitutability of different countries' outputs and other factors (Weyant and Hill 1999). Developing nations have many pressing needs, such as potable water and stable food supplies, and less financial and technical capacity than rich nations to mitigate or adapt to climate change. These nations have less incentive to agree to a policy that they see as imposing unacceptable costs. The international policy objective is obvious, but elusive: finding incentives to motivate nations with strong and diverse self-interests to move voluntarily toward a collective goal of reduced GHG emissions.

Equity is a central element of this issue, because differences in perceptions about what constitutes equitable distributions of effort complicate any agreement. No standard exists for establishing the equity of any particular allocation of climate protection. Simple rules of thumb, such as allocating responsibility based on equal per capita rights to emit GHGs – advantageous to developing countries – and allocations that are positively correlated to past and current emissions – advantageous to developed countries – are unlikely to create broad political support internationally. The same holds for various graduation formulas, which seek to increase the control burden of developing countries as they progress (see Burtraw and Toman 1992). Pragmatic distributional agreements will most likely have to emerge endogenously within international negotiations rather than coming from some exogenous consensus philosophical principles.

Direct side payments through financial or low-cost technical assistance are one pragmatic solution. These payments increase the incentive to join the agreement, and, as some contend, might be the only real tool to encourage developing countries to join (Schelling 2002). Incentive-based climate policies can help by reducing the cost of action for all countries. In particular, both buyers and sellers benefit from trade in emission permits. Emissions trading also allows side payments through the international distribution of national emission targets. More reluctant countries can be enticed to join with less stringent targets while other countries meet more stringent targets to achieve the same overall result. These points are lost when critics argue emissions trading weakens the international agreement because a seller country can fail to meet its domestic target and export "phony" emission permits.

Side payments through emissions trading result when countries are given national quotas in excess of their expected emissions, an allocation sometimes called "headroom." Such an allocation was provided to Russia and Ukraine in the Kyoto Protocol and came to be called "hot air" by critics, who feared it would slow international progress by giving advanced industrial countries such as the United States a cheap way out of cutting their own emissions. But had this cost-reducing option not been part of the package, it is unclear whether the United States and other countries would have agreed to the protocol or achieved its goals in practice (see Wiener 1999). International reallocations of wealth in permit trading give rise to broader domestic political debates. Imagine, for instance, the domestic debate if the US administration transferred billions to Russia annually, or perhaps China in a subsequent agreement, for emission permits.

Tradable permits create a Catch-22 that could threaten long-term climate agreements. Without trading, mitigation costs are too high to be politically acceptable; with trading, the distribution of these costs is too unfair to be acceptable. In response, observers have promoted national carbon taxes as the only reasonable option (Cooper 1998, Nordhaus 2002). This approach does not resolve

distributional concerns, however, in that the initial allocation of rights and responsibilities is implicit in *any* international control agreement, including taxes. Moreover, the argument for taxes rests on the willingness of the developing world to
implement substantially higher energy taxes than exist today. Although developing countries theoretically would reap some advantages of increasing energy
taxes (for example, more reliable revenue than from income taxes), it is unclear
whether the advantages are compelling in practice. (See, for example, Wiener
(1999), who offers several efficiency and political economy arguments in favor of
a quantity-based over a tax-based approach.) Without such participation, the tax
approach becomes an inefficient partial agreement like the Kyoto Protocol.

4   Global Links I: The Process of International Integration

The literature on self-enforcing agreements between all nations reflects one key
element to create effective international institutions that help integrate climate
protection with the global economy. We now discuss three additional aspects of
the micro-foundations of global linkages between climate and the world economy
– international integration, domestic debates, and individual reaction to risk. We
begin by considering two elements of international integration – interlinked
games and two-level games. We consider each in turn.

Interlinked Games. As globalization expands, some observers see a natural link
between climate protection and other social issues. Some researchers have proposed linking global environmental issues to other social issues to increase the
likelihood that a country not interested in the environmental issue will nevertheless join an agreement, since it is advantageous for it on other grounds. The
IPCC's Third Assessment Report (2001: 14) makes this explicit: "[climate
change] cannot be addressed or comprehended in isolation of broader social goals
(such as equity or sustainable development), or other existing or probable future
sources of stress." This section presents some of the arguments for and against
such a linkage strategy.

Since no supranational authority exists, countries cannot be coerced into joining an international environmental agreement on climate. Each agreement has to
be voluntary, and countries join them and abstain from free-riding only if it
improves their net welfare. One way to make joining more enticing for reluctant
countries is to offer them "side payments." Actual explicit monetary side payments, however, are hardly encountered in any international agreements, mostly
for political reasons (Kroeze-Gil and Folmer 1998).

An alternative approach is to link two issues that are only marginally or not at
all related. A country with no substantial interest in environmental issues might

still be willing to participate in negotiations if it is promised that an issue about which it is greatly concerned is also on the bargaining table. Examples are the "debt-for-nature swaps" of the late 1980s and early 1990s (Susskind 1994) or the Land of the Sea negotiations a decade earlier (Sebenius 1984). In general, the goal of linking issues is to create "additional value" for those who are reluctant to join and to build or modify coalitions more easily (Susskind 1994).

Game theorists point also out that linking several games to "interconnected games" can widen the strategy space by increasing the punishment possibilities for punishing in repeated games and therefore the stability of an agreement (see, e.g., Folmer et al. 1993, Kroeze-Gil and Folmer 1998, Kroll et al. 1998). If country X does not cooperate in game A (i.e., on issue A), other countries can punish X by not cooperating in game A, game B, or both in the next period. While this "unrelated punishing" is common practice in international trade relations (witness the European retaliation to the U.S. steel tariffs), it is not, at least not explicitly, being used in climate protection.

Economists cite trade and the environment as obvious candidates for linking, but the linkage of these two seems to have become a one-way street – trade agreements like NAFTA incorporate environmental concerns, but environmental negotiations do not address trade issues. Talk about using trade sanctions to punish countries that do not adhere to conditions set forth in a climate change treaty has not been prominent. At this point in the Kyoto process, the major developing countries are unwilling to participate in any greenhouse gas regime that stands alone even though developing countries have the most to lose from global climate change (Schelling 2002). An open question is whether linkages or side payments would provide enough incentive to join. Explicit linkages thus far have been restricted to forms of side payments that are related to global climate change itself – transfers of clean technology or the accounting for forests as sinks. Some believe that climate change is complicated enough even without pulling unrelated issues into the negotiations. The third IPCC assessment report, however, sees this as a challenge to be overcome rather than as an absolute barrier. By linking social issues outside the previous scope of climate change negotiations, one could interpret this as an attempt to create more value-added to climate protection given the worldwide aspiration for sustainable development and north-south equity of opportunity.

Not everybody agrees that linkages are advantageous. Nordhaus (2002), for instance, sees a problem with linking a tradable carbon permit system with unrelated issues. He argues that this is a disadvantage: "it would be tempting to make receipt of any excess emission permits conditional on 'good behavior' with respect to human rights, dolphins and turtles, child and prison labor, and other worthy causes." His statement underlines the biggest disadvantage of linkages: by linking environmental concerns to nonenvironmental issues one invites opposition that might not appear if the environmental issue is negotiated in isolation. The more issues are linked the more countries and domestic groups within countries feel compelled to be against the final agreement even though they might favor some aspects of it. Since global climate change negotiations already include many different issues to begin with, adding more can only increase the complexity and risk of failure. Results from experiments in Kroll et al. (1998) imply another disadvantage of implicit linkage: the more issues are linked the more opportunities for "cheap talk" – nonbinding announcements – are created that eventually prolong the entire process.

Two-Level Games. Another neglected aspect of international integration is that negotiators and politicians who make climate policy still have to report to domestic voters. Consider the consequences when economic models treat countries as single entities without respecting the domestic components in the decision-making process. We consider what one overlooks within the international negotiation arena. The traditional models of international environmental negotiations and agreements assume that countries are "unitary rational actors" – political monoliths that maximize their own welfare when playing the international games. Objective functions are usually given in black box terms like *national interest*. The negotiations leading up to and following the Kyoto Protocol have illustrated several issues neglected by those traditional models: domestic actors are implicitly sitting at the international bargaining table; the international negotiation between the governments is only one part in a sequence of events resulting in a final agreement; and domestic political institutions matter when the preferences between a government and its domestic audience differ.

Putnam (1988) coined the term "two-level game" to describe when a government plays two games at the same time – one on an international level with governments from other countries and one on a national level with a domestic audience. The crucial feature of a two-level game is that even though the government plays *two* games it makes only *one* move that determines its payoff in both of the two games. Therefore preferences and institutions on each level pose a constraint on the other level. In global climate change negotiations, a government plays a bargaining game with its counterparts but, as every observer of the Kyoto process would confirm, faces binding domestic constraints.

The 1997 Byrd–Hagel no-ratification-without-developing-nations resolution is an example. Recall that as negotiations proceeded toward the Kyoto Protocol, the U.S. Senate passed a nonbinding resolution offered by Senators Robert C. Byrd and Chuck Hagel by a vote of 95 to 0 in the summer of 1997. The Byrd–Hagel resolution stated that the United States should accept no climate agreement that did not demand comparable sacrifices of all participants. The resolution was stimulated by concern about the effects of a climate agreement on the U.S. econ-

Figure 1: Two-Level Bargaining Game

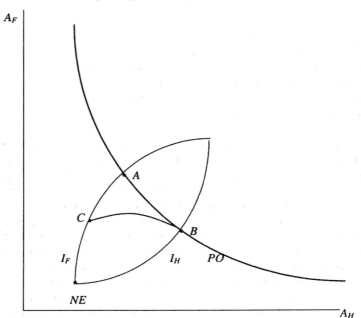

omy, but it conflicted with the idea of common but differentiated responsibilities for developed and developing countries supported by the Climate Convention, which the United States had ratified.

The logic behind Putnam's (1988) two-level game is that a government cannot agree to an international treaty that diverges too far from the preferred outcome of the person who has to ratify this treaty, be this a median voter or median legislator. Kroll and Shogren (2002) extend this idea to a model with two countries, H and F, in which each country, i, has to decide on the level of contribution, A_i, where $i = H, F$, to an international public good, e.g., the abatement of CO_2 emissions, where the contributions are the national abatement measures (see, e.g., Hoel 1991). Each government derives benefits $B_i(A_H + A_F)$ from the total level of the public good, and incurs costs, $C_i(A_i)$, from the economic consequences of its contribution. The payoff function for government i is $U_i(A_H, A_F) = B(A_H + A_F) - C_i(A_i)$, with usual assumptions for the functional forms. Figure 1 shows the relevant bargaining set (between points A and B) if neither government faces a domestic constraint (*NE* is the combination of contribution levels if both countries make their choice noncooperatively). One government, H, faces a domestic constraint – a median voter with a payoff function, $U_V(A_H, A_F) = B(A_H + A_F) - \gamma C_H(A_H)$, with γ as a cost parameter that can differ from unity.

Depending on the interpretation of the game, several explanations exist for the difference between the executive's and the median voter's utility functions. If we interpret the additional actor as a median legislator, then the difference could stem from a divided government – the executive belongs to a different party than the median legislator and therefore views the cost of a contribution to the international public good differently (Milner 1997: 37–42). If the domestic game is a referendum game and the third actor is a "median citizen," then different interpretations are possible. For example, the executive or her advisors could have better knowledge of the public good in question (Portney 1992, Pollak 1998) or the executive could be captured by special-interest groups that do not represent the median voter's interests. If the constraint is not binding (i.e., if the median voter's indifference curve is to the right of I_H), nothing changes. If the constraint is binding, however, the constraint is always "downward" – the agreement the two governments negotiate calls for a combination of contribution levels lower than what they perceive as Pareto optimal (Kroll and Shogren 2002).

A ratification model fits the American system well but cannot explain the domestic mechanics in many European countries in which the ratification process of an international treaty is usually less crucial when there is no divided government of legislature and executive. European negotiators nevertheless face domestic constraints in the form of electoral concerns. These concerns are amplified by the existence of strong green parties that play a major role in government building before and after an election. Political behavior in Germany during the run-up to Kyoto protocol negotiations is one example of how upcoming elections can affect a government's agenda for an international conference. The conservative German government pushed for "greener" outcomes at the Kyoto conference. One could interpret their choices as being based on the belief that the opposition parties (including the Greens) could topple the government in the elections eight months after Kyoto (which they did).

Theoretical explanations of such anecdotal evidence are rare. Recently, economists have developed rational choice models to examine the impact of electoral rules and political regimes on *domestic* public goods (Persson and Tabellini 2000). Results indicate that (a) politicians elected under majoritarian electoral rules tend to underprovide the public good, while those elected under proportional electoral rules tend to overprovide the public good; and (b) a parliamentary regime is better than a presidential-congressional regime in terms of providing the public good, while the presidential regime performs better in terms of accountability. An extension of these models to see whether they hold for the provision of *international* public goods would be interesting since the U.S. system uses majoritarian electoral rules (as does Britain) and a presidential-congressional regime, while most European systems rely on proportional representation and a parliamentary regime.

Kroll and Shogren (2002) include an electoral game into the model from above – the government party (or coalition) has to make a decision on how to bargain with the government from the other country before an election takes place; it knows what the median voter *believes* the opposition would have done if it had been in power. We show that for certain parameters in the payoff functions of the median voter and the opposition party, the possible bargaining outcomes the government will agree to call for contribution levels *above* those considered Pareto optimal by the governments – impossible in the ratification models but consistent with the behavior of the German government.

Understanding international environmental negotiations as part of a two-level game implies that the differences between the observed behavior of U.S. and EU negotiators in the Kyoto process are not only due to vaguely defined cultural differences but also to distinctions in political institutions. Another reason for differences can be domestic reputation and informational cascades that work or have worked in opposite directions for different countries (see Sunstein 2001).

Two-level games shed light on the architectural framework. Schelling (2002) points out that the Kyoto Protocol is focused on "outputs" or results (emission reductions) and not on "inputs" or actions (actual measures to decrease emissions). This focus makes it more difficult for countries to fulfill their own obligations and to monitor, enforce and potentially punish other countries. He cites NATO as an example of an international agreement that has worked better partly because the actual contributions could be monitored better, since they consisted of actions (supply of troops, missiles, etc.) and not of results (level of deterrence). If a focus on inputs, however, potentially works better, why are the negotiations in the Kyoto process so fixated on outputs? Maybe for the same reason that, according to Nordhaus (2002), some observers prefer quantity-based approaches over price-based approaches: the actual costs can be hidden more easily, which relaxes the constraint from the domestic level that is imposed on the international level. Witness the uproar in the United States over Bush's rejection of the Kyoto Protocol when at the same time most people are not willing to accept higher costs for gasoline. A TIME/CNN poll from March 2001 indicates that while 75 percent of Americans believe global warming is a very or fairly serious problem and 67 percent think President Bush should develop a plan to reduce the emission of gases that may contribute to global warming, only 48 percent are willing to pay an extra 25 cents per gallon of gas to reduce pollution and global warming.

5   Global Links II: Domestic Debates over Costs and Benefits

Globalization opens and creates new international markets for trade. International carbon emission trading is one such new market. The promise of international trading is a crucial selling point to domestic audiences because countries could meet their international treaty target cost effectively. Climate protection would be low cost. A well-designed trading policy will lower the cost of achieving any particular targets and thereby make more stringent targets affordable. Nations would be free to find and use the lowest-cost carbon emissions from around the globe. The potential for these markets, however, could have been oversold in the international negotiations for two reasons that we now discuss – carbon trading with institutional lags, and global trading with local pollution goals.

Carbon Trading with Institutional Lags. United States negotiators have long promoted the international carbon trading in climate negotiations. Other countries, notably in Western Europe and the developing world, have reacted cooler toward carbon trading. But while European negotiators advocated trading limits, carbon trading won the day in Kyoto (see Article 17). The international conferences held since Kyoto have tried to work out the institutional details of the trading regime, especially the questions of how to enforce emission commitments and sanction nations that shirk on their emission commitments (Article 18). Demands posed by national sovereignty concerns make the usual organization of emission permit markets problematic in an international setting, particularly with respect to Article 18 (see Nordhaus 2002).

The critical institutional issue is who should be held liable for overselling permits beyond quotas – the seller or buyer country? Weak undercompliance penalties and ineffective monitoring methods create the incentive for selling nations to oversell permits and shirk on their emission responsibilities due to the magnitude of the potential permit revenues. Proceeds from international GHG trading could be significant – the former Soviet Union countries projected emission trading revenues under Kyoto may be as high as $17 billion. Seller liability is the obvious choice if the goal is to minimize transaction costs. Here all permits have the identical value to buyers, and only one market is needed to transact all permits.

But if the social goals of global emission trade are broader, and include both cutting costs to meet the commitments and ensuring "fairness and equity" across the developed and transitional economies, as some people have argued, *buyer liability* is the choice (e.g., Victor 2001). Now the rich buyer nations are responsible for any shortfalls in emission reductions made by the poorer sellers. The appeal of buyer liability arises from the belief that buying implies a commitment by the purchaser to ensure emission compliance, and this commitment creates an incentive for buyers to seek out sellers likely to comply with their emission obligations, thus increasing overall market compliance (see Victor 2001). Buyer liability results in buyers purchasing from those they believe will honor commitments, an outcome to the environment's advantage, and will lead to greater climate protection at fewer costs because markets will form due to the large gains from trade, and that reputation will police market behavior.

Godby and Shogren (2002) reject this notion of *caveat emptor* Kyoto. Using experimental markets, they show that buyer liability under realistic weak international enforcement leads to the worst possible outcome – less climate protection at greater costs. Weak enforcement levels mimic the reality of international emissions trading, in which potential sanctions on sovereign nations are likely to be small (see, e.g., Cooper 1998, Schelling 1997). Buyer liability lowered economic efficiency by increasing risk to buyers and moral hazard to sellers that distorted permit prices and market production patterns. The results suggest such rules worsen environmental performance through greater noncompliance.

This result supports those critics who question whether a quantity-type approach like a tradable permit system is the best way to address climate change. Nordhaus (2002) lists nine advantages of a price-type approach like a harmonized carbon tax, some of which resemble arguments in the buyer-vs.-seller-liability debate. He argues, for example, that rogue governments cannot abuse price-type approaches as easily as quantity-type approaches. Also, liability questions probably also prevent the banking and borrowing of permits, which in turn would result in higher permit price volatility due to inelastic supply and short-run demand curves. In addition, the bureaucracy needed for an international permit trade system is much larger than for price-type approaches (again, at least partly due to liability issues), and price-type approaches do not need a baseline year and therefore avoid the discussion over what constitutes fair benchmarks.

Global Trading with Local Pollution Goals. Another argument that limits the potential of carbon trading to cut net costs is the complementarity between global and local pollution. Free trade in emission permits can lower the welfare of countries that import emission permits – relative to an alternative of regulated trade – because reducing carbon emissions also reduces other emissions that contribute to local air pollution (Lutter and Shogren 2002). If the United States reduces carbon emissions, the emissions of other air pollutants also fall; but if the United States buys carbon permits abroad it foregoes the benefits of these ancillary effects.

Analytically, reducing carbon emission is an activity with joint products: protection from climate change and reduced emissions of local air pollutants. The value of one product, reduced emissions of local air pollutants, varies with the stringency and nature of other local pollution control measures. Optimal controls on carbon emissions also depend on such measures. As a result, the optimal geographic distribution of carbon emission reductions cannot be determined by international markets for carbon emission permits because these reflect only the market cost of reducing carbon, not the extent or value of the ancillary emission reductions.

Lutter and Shogren (2002) assess the impact of global carbon trading on local air pollution policy. They show the costs and gains from international emission trading depend on the flexibility and stringency of local air pollution regulations, and that restricting carbon emission trading can increase the welfare of some countries. Since local air pollution policies in the United States appear to have marginal costs many times greater than marginal benefits, they estimate that the optimal tariff on carbon permits imported into the United States could be several hundred dollars.

The idea that free trade in emission permits can reduce welfare for some countries that trade permits affects how one thinks about linking international agreements with the global economy. National emission quotas are necessary for efficient trade in emission permits. But with ancillary effects, competitive carbon markets do not equate marginal abatement costs. Moreover, countries may impose restrictions on trade in emission permits that are privately advantageous. If permit trade enhances welfare only with regulatory intervention, a key rationale for national emission targets disappears.

6   Global Links III: Individual Behavior toward Risk

Globalization can create both new risks and new markets for risk reduction through adaptation that affects normal people everyday. We consider how people react to these risks, how they invest effort to reduce it, and how this affects our judgment about the integration of climate protection into the world economy – how people and policymakers react to risks like those posed by climate change, and how globalization opens more markets for private adaptation that makes risk endogenous.

Behavior toward Risk. Climate change creates risks for people, regardless of the rate of globalization. Policymakers and modelers interested in effective policy options address how people, both the average citizen and decision makers themselves, actually make choices under risky events. In general, climate change is an ambiguous low-probability, high-severity risk. Whether this risk is founded on science or political scare tactics, fears of catastrophe and our limits on reaction time ultimately frame the debate over climate protection. But in contrast to the benchmark model of expected utility, experimental evidence suggests that people have a bimodal response to low-probability risks – they either ignore the risk completely or overreact.

When the outcome is potentially very bad, experience tells us little about low-probability risks. Many experimental studies of risk perception reveal that people overreact to risk, and commonly overestimate the chance that they will suffer from a risk with low odds and high damage, for example, a nuclear power accident (see Camerer and Kunreuther 1989). People who have low odds of confronting a catastrophe often seek information to help them judge the likelihood that a bad event will actually occur. If the source of that outside information stresses severity without giving some notion of the odds, people tend to bias their risk perceptions upward. Even policymakers are not immune to this tendency. And, while policymakers or at least their advisors should be smarter, evidence suggests that they act "as if" they ignore their superior knowledge – perhaps either because they really do misperceive risk or because they want to get reelected by people with inferior risk perception. In either case, thoughtful people dealing with risk have the tendency to be both conservative and alarmist. They both "plan for the worst, hope for the best" and then over-invest in the worst-case prevention policy rather than balancing the costs and benefits of alternative options.

One explanation of irrational behavior toward risk is that people do not think about odds and consequences simultaneously as expected utility requires. Rather people often seem to separate the two elements and make their decision based on the most attractive element – either certain odds or a big prize (Machina 1987). People use this heuristic to simplify their choices. They separate probability and consequences, and then focus their attention on one element first and then the other. When a player fails to frame the choice problem comprehensively as expected utility presumes, his or her view on the relative importance of probability and consequences will affect the decision.

For example, expected utility theory is the cornerstone of modern decision making under risk, and consequently the cost-benefit analysis of climate protection. The theory presumes that people are fairly sophisticated, such that they can evaluate both old and new gambles consistently. Allais (1953), however, revealed people routinely violate this presumption of rationality. Some people choose both the safer bet and the riskier bet even though it violates the principle of independence. People like certainty but are willing to give up one percentage point to go for the largest prize. The problem the Allais paradox raises for climate policy is that cost-benefit analysis based on expected utility theory might be context-dependent rather than the unbiased measure researchers presume. This means an estimate of net benefits could depend more on how the question of climate protection was asked, or "framed" rather than the question itself. This suggests that one can create any degree of support for or antagonism against a particular climate protection depending on the gambles considered. Inconsistent estimates of net benefits based on expected utility theory suggest that either the behavioral model must be expanded to include likely explanations of the Allais paradox or one must qualify any estimate as incomplete from a behavioral perspective.

Moreover, Ellsberg (1961) demonstrated that people will irrationally avoid a risk when it has ambiguous probabilities. People chose risks with a known distribution even though the ambiguous distribution had a higher expected utility. This violates expected utility theory in that the decision weights assigned to different states of the world should be independent of the origin of the uncertainty. People will pay a premium to avoid participating in such ambiguous lotteries. Irrational aversion to ambiguity is especially relevant for climate change risk, which is as vague as risk gets. Researchers do not have any reasonable estimates of the odds that potential catastrophes will come to pass. The most researchers usually say is that the odds that severe events will come to pass are "uncertain." The basic urge to avoid such ambiguous climate risk puts pressure on policymakers to do something now, which can be costly because strategies that are more cost-effective may take longer to implement. Fear of ambiguous risk, however, makes these cost-effective plans politically hard to implement.

Rational architecture over climate protection depends in part on rational reactions to risk within alternative institutional arrangements. Expected utility theory might be too thin to explain many aspects of behavior under risk. This holds if people simplify their decisions by separating the probability of risk from the potential outcomes, which goes against the presumption that people can deal with both odds and outcomes simultaneously. Policymakers and the news media that stress severity over the odds of climate catastrophe generally endorse more costly immediate protection measures.

Endogenous Risk. While globalization might imply greater climate risk, it also means the expansion of markets. As markets expand, so do national and private opportunities find appropriate methods to adapt to climate change. These expanded adaptation markets matter for international negotiations over mitigation, since societies make climate risk endogenous by protecting themselves through both mitigation and adaptation (Ehrlich and Becker 1972). Greater access to adaptation markets allows people to reduce personal risk by changing production and consumption decisions to reduce the severity of a bad state if it does occur (see, e.g., Mendelsohn and Neumann 1999). A portfolio of mitigation and adaptation jointly determines climate risks and the costs to reduce them. Since private citizens and sovereign nations are free to adapt on their own accord, modelers and policymakers should address these adaptive responses when choosing the optimal degree of public mitigation in international agreements. Otherwise, policy actions are more expensive than need be, with no additional reduction in climate risk.

While most people appreciate that adaptation affects the costs of mitigation, this obvious point is often not addressed in the international architecture of climate change. Policy is fragmented-mitigation for climate hazards, adaptation for natural hazards, and as a consequence, costs are influenced (see Kane and Shogren 2000). Usually mitigation and adaptation are modeled separately as a necessary simplification to gain traction on an immense and complex issue. The questions remain as to how reasonable this presumption is, and the likely consequences that maintaining this assumption has on the estimated costs of mitigation.

Separability presupposes that the overall effectiveness and costs of mitigation do not depend on adaptation. But for this assumption to hold, one must implicitly presume that climate risk is exogenous – a risk beyond people's private or collective ability to reduce. The necessary economic conditions for this to hold, however, are rather restrictive – climate risk is exogenous only if markets are complete. A complete set of markets exists if people can contract all risks from each conceivable state of nature that might be realized. Complete markets would allow for perfect risk-spreading and risk-pooling such that the only remaining risk would be outside the control of human actions. But markets for climate risk are notoriously incomplete or nonexistent due to the high cost of contracting (Chichilnisky and Heal 1993). People make private and collective adaptation decisions through the markets that do exist and through collective policy actions. The economic circumstances that influence these choices matter to the level of risk, and addressing these conditions is essential for well-estimated costs. People choose to create and reduce risk. How people perceive risk, the relative costs and benefits of alternative risk reduction strategies, and relative wealth affect these choices.

Sectoral work in agriculture, forestry, and coastal areas has shown that cost estimates are sensitive to the inclusion of adaptation (see, e.g., Sohngen and Mendelsohn 1997). Greater climate variability, for instance, can influence how adaptation affects mitigation in agriculture. More risk directly induces a nation to adapt more by switching its crop mix and crop varieties to those more tolerant of drier or wetter conditions, and by modifying its weed control strategies. The magnitude of this adaptation depends on how risk affects the perceived marginal productivity of mitigation – e.g., more or less effective soil sequestration per acre; and how mitigation and adaptation work with or against each other. Bouzaher et al. (1995), for example, estimate that winter cover crops can be used to increase soil organic carbon by expanding annual biomass production. They also show that conservation tillage, the Conservation Reserve Program, and the Wetlands Reserve Program can increase soil carbon by minimizing soil disturbance and targeting bottomland for hardwood trees. For nonclimate risk, models that account for mitigation and adaptation risk estimate that benefits were underestimated by 50 percent when adaptation was ignored (e.g., Swallow 1996).

These results suggest that more attention to the interaction of mitigation and adaptation, and its empirical ramifications, seems worthwhile. The challenge is to capture in a reasonable way how mitigation and adaptation interact, and establish how this interaction can impact the estimated costs of climate protection. And even if a complete empirical application of the portfolio of risk avoidance is unreachable today, understanding which unmeasured links might be most valuable to decisionmakers in the future could guide whether we are underestimating the costs of mitigation.

Settle et al. (2002) show how nations adapting to catastrophic climate risk affect how much they devote to mitigation policy for a targeted climate protection budget. Assume a model with two country types: developed (type 1) and developing (type 2); stock of carbon accumulations $= N$, change in carbon stock: $\dot{N} = \dot{N}(S_1, S_2)$, where S_1 are expenditures by developed countries to reduce carbon emissions, and S_2 are expenditures by developing countries to reduce carbon emissions; and level of adaptation $= M_i$, where $i \in (1, 2)$, change in level of adaptation: $\dot{M}_i = \dot{M}_i(X_i)$, where $i \in (1, 2)$, where X_1 are expenditures by developed countries to adapt for the potential catastrophe from global warming and X_2 are expenditures by developing countries to adapt for the potential catastrophe from global warming. Each country type has a fixed annual budget dedicated to fighting the potential damages from global warming, C_i, where $i \in (1, 2)$. Thus $X_1 + S_1 = C_1$ and $X_2 + S_2 = C_2$. The probability of a catastrophe is a function of the stock of carbon, $P(N)$. The severity of a catastrophe is a function of the level of adaptation specific to the country type, $D_1(M_1)$ and $D_2(M_2)$. Expected catastrophic damages for each nation in any given year are $P(N) \times D_i(M_i)$, where $i \in (1, 2)$.

Expenditures to reduce carbon accumulations go toward a public good, while adaptation is a private good. There are two mutually exclusive states of nature for the countries, no catastrophe or catastrophe. Gjerde et al. (1999) examine the survival function $\{1 - Z(N)\}$, which accounts for expected damages in each given year – the probability of avoiding a catastrophe by year t as seen from the present. They ran an integrated simulation model and find that collective adaptation to catastrophe becomes an important policy option when nations are less likely to cooperate, when damages are mainly catastrophic, or the nation's planning horizon increases, e.g., as with the Kyoto perspective.

7   Concluding Remarks

The Kyoto Protocol for climate change established a beachhead from which future negotiations can expand upon. The question remains whether Kyoto was the proper beach given that integrating climate protection into the global economic order remains messy, complex, and inevitable. Climate protection policy is not going to go away. Thus, this review has highlighted several points from the economics literature worth considering as we move forward in this process. First, at the individual level, people either ignore or overreact to the risks of climate change, regardless of whether they are real or perceived. Scientific information that helps pull in rather than push apart these extreme reactions will be vital to integration. Political tactics that stress severity of the risk while ignoring the probability that it could occur do not serve that end. Second, citizens adapt with private protection strategies, which affects their demand for collective risk reduction programs. Not addressing the idea that risk is endogenous at many levels can undercut policy objectives. Third, *cherry-picking* can also undercut political support for more climate protection. Cherry-picking exists when one highlights only the upsides of a policy. Consider international emission trading and local pollution. The idea that climate policy will both reduce local costs through emission trading and increase local benefits through reductions in local air pollution are not mutually exclusive. Emission trading makes it more likely that emission reductions will be done elsewhere, which implies the local population does not receive the ancillary benefits of reduced local air pollution.

Fourth, liability rules and incentives matter when trying to control the costs of climate protection. Neither logic nor evidence supports the notion that using buyer liability because it is "fairer" for poorer countries selling permits could create an effective emission trading market. The exact opposite from what one wanted could happen – less protection at greater costs. Also domestic and international negotiations linking and tradeoffing many social goals reveal the truthfulness of the claim that economists do not necessarily have a comparative advantage in the politics of climate protection. Levels of climate protection have been and will continue to be traded-off at the international level for other domestic policies like national security, education, and health. Domestic political institutions matter for international negotiations. Finally, linking climate protection with all other social problems or agendas might backfire if key players mistrust this top-heavy policy design to cure all of societies ills in one policy package.

Bibliography

Allais, M. (1953). Le Comportement de l'Homme Rationnel devant le Risque: Critique des Postulats et Axiomes de l'École Américaine. *Econometrica* 21(4): 502–546.

Bac, M. (1996). Incomplete Information and Incentives to Free Ride on International Environmental Resources. *Journal of Environmental Economics and Management* 30(3): 301–315.

Barrett, S. (1994). Self-Enforcing International Environmental Agreements. *Oxford Economic Papers* 46(4): 878–894.

Bhagwati, J. (2002). Trading for Development. The Poor's Best Hope. Invited article in *The Economist*, 22 June, 363(8278): 25–27. See also http://economist.com/display-Story.cfm?Story_ID=1188714.

Bouzaher, A., D. Holtkamp, R. Reese, and J. Shogren (1995). Economic and Resource Impacts of Policies to Increase Organic Carbon in Agricultural Soils. In R. Lal, J. Kimble, E. Levine, and B. Stewart (eds.), *Soil Management and Greenhouse Effects*. Boca Raton: CRC Lewis Publishers.

Burtraw, D., and M.A. Toman (1992). Equity and International Agreements for CO_2 Containment. *Journal of Energy Engineering* 118(2): 122–135.

Camerer, C., and H. Kunreuther (1989). Decision Processes for Low Probability Events: Policy Implications. *Journal of Policy Analysis and Management* 8(4): 565–592.

Carraro, C., and D. Siniscalco (1993). Strategies for the International Protection of the Environment. *Journal of Public Economics* 52(3): 309–328.

Chen, Z. (1997). Negotiating an Agreement on Global Warming: A Theoretical Analysis. *Journal of Environmental Economics and Management* 32(2): 170–188.

Chichilnisky, G., and G. Heal (1993). Global Environmental Risks. *Journal of Economic Perspectives* 7(4): 65–86.

Cooper, R. (1998). Toward a Real Global Warming Treaty. *Foreign Affairs* 77(2): 66–79.

Dasgupta, P. (2002). Conflicting Intuitions Regarding Consumption. 12th Economic and Social Research Center Annual Lecture. Available at http://www.esrc.ac.uk/esrccontent/connect/anlec.asp.

Dockner, E., and N. Van Long (1993). International Pollution Control: Cooperative versus Noncooperative Strategies. *Journal of Environmental Economics and Management* 25(1): 13–29.

Ehrlich I., and G.S. Becker (1972). Market Insurance, Self-Insurance and Self-Protection. *Journal of Political Economy* 80(4): 623–648.

Ellsberg, D. (1961). Risk, Ambiguity and the Savage Axioms. *Quarterly Journal of Economics* 75(4): 643–649.

Folmer, H., P. van Mouche, and S. Ragland (1993). Interconnected Games and International Environmental Problems. *Environmental and Resource Economics* 3(4): 313–335.

Geoffrey, G. (1998). Global Markets and National Politics: Collision Course or Virtuous Circle? *International Organization* 52(4): 787–842.

Gjerde, J., S. Grepperud, and S. Kverndokk (1999). Optimal Climate Policy under the Possibility of a Catastrophe. *Resource and Energy Economics* 21(3–4): 289–317.

Godby, R., and J. Shogren (2002). *Caveat Emptor* Kyoto. Working paper, University of Wyoming, Laramie.

Hoel, M. (1991). Global Environmental Problems: The Effects of Unilateral Actions Taken by One Country. *Journal of Environmental Economics and Management* 20(1): 55–70.

Hoel, M. (1992). International Environmental Conventions: The Case of Uniform Reductions of Emissions. *Environmental and Resource Economics* 2(2): 141–159.

Huber, S., and C. Douglass (1998). *Two Perspectives on Global Climate Change. A Briefing Book*. St. Louis: Washington University.

IPCC (Intergovernmental Panel on Climate Change) (1996). *Climate Change 1995: Impacts, Adaptations, and Mitigation of Climate Change: Scientific-Technical Analysis*. Contribution of Working Group II to the Second Assessment Report of the Intergovernmental Panel on Climate Change. New York: Cambridge University Press.

IPCC (2001). *Climate Change 2001: Mitigation. Summary for Policymakers and Technical Summary of the Working Group III Report*. New York: Cambridge University Press.

Jacoby, H., R. Prinn, and R. Schmalensee (1998). Kyoto's Unfinished Business. *Foreign Affairs* 77(4): 54–66.

Kane, S., and J. Shogren (2000). Linking Adaptation and Mitigation in Climate Change Policy. *Climatic Change* 45(1): 75–102.

Kolstad, C. (1996). Learning and Stock Effects in Environmental Regulation: The Case of Greenhouse Gas Emissions. *Journal of Environmental Economics and Management* 31(1): 1–18.

Kroeze-Gil, J., and H. Folmer (1998). Linking Environmental and Non-Environmental Problems in an International Setting: The Interconnected Games Approach. In N. Hanley and H. Folmer (eds.), *Game Theory and the Environment*. Cheltenham: Edward Elgar.

Kroll, S., and J. Shogren (2002). International Public Goods in Two-Level Games. Working paper, St. Lawrence University, Canton, New York.

Kroll, S., C. Mason, and J. Shogren (1998). Environmental Conflicts and Interconnected Games: An Experimental Note on Institutional Design. In N. Hanley and H. Folmer (eds.), *Game Theory and the Environment*. Cheltenham: Edward Elgar.

Lutter, R., and J. Shogren (2002). Tradable Permit Tariffs: How Local Air Pollution Affects Carbon Emissions Permit Trading. *Land Economics* 78(2): 159–170.

Machina, M. (1987). Choice Under Uncertainty: Problems Solved and Unsolved. *Journal of Economic Perspectives* 1(1): 121–154.

Mendelsohn, R., and J. Neumann (eds.) (1999). *The Impact of Climate Change on the United States Economy*. Cambridge: Cambridge University Press.

Milner, H. (1997). *Interests, Institutions, and Information: Domestic Politics and International Relations*. Princeton: Princeton University Press.

National Research Council (2002). *Abrupt Climate Change: Inevitable Surprises*. Washington, D.C.: National Academy of Sciences.

Nordhaus, W. (1994). *Managing the Global Commons: The Economics of Climate Change*. Cambridge, Mass.: MIT Press.

Nordhaus, W. (2002). After Kyoto: Alternative Mechanisms to Control Global Warming. Paper presented at the 2002 joint meetings of the American Economic Association and the Association of Environmental and Resource Economists, Atlanta, Georgia.

O'Rourke, K., and J. Williamson (2002). After Columbus: Explaining the Global Trade Boom 1500–1800. *Journal of Economic History* 62(2): 417–456.

Persson, T., and G. Tabellini (2000). *Political Economics: Explaining Economic Policy*. Cambridge: MIT Press.

Pollak, R. (1998). Imagined Risks and Cost-Benefit Analysis. *American Economic Review* 88(2): 376–380.

Portney, P. (1992). Trouble in Happyville. *Journal of Policy Analysis and Management* 11(1): 131–132.

Putnam, R. (1988). Diplomacy and Domestic Politics: The Logic of Two-Level Games. *International Organization* 42(3): 427–460.

Rodrick, D. (1997). *Has Globalization Gone Too Far?* Washington, D.C.: Institute for International Economics.

Sachs, J. (1997). The Limits of Convergence. Nature, Nurture and Growth. Invited acticle in *The Economist*, 14 June, 343(8021): 19–24. See also http://economist.com/displayStory.cfm?Story_ID=91003

Schelling, T. (1992). Some Economics of Global Warming. *American Economic Review* 82(1): 1–14.

Schelling, T. (1997). The Costs of Combating Global Warming. *Foreign Affairs* 76 (November/December): 8–14.

Schelling, T. (2002). What Makes Greenhouse Sense? Time to Rethink the Kyoto Protocol. *Foreign Affairs* 81(3): 2–9.

Schmalensee, R. (1996). Greenhouse Policy Architectures and Institutions. November 13. Report. Cambridge, Mass.: MIT Joint Program on the Science and Policy of Global Change.

Sebenius, J. (1984). *Negotiating the Law of the Sea.* Cambridge: Harvard University Press.

Settle, C., S. Kane, and J. Shogren (2002). Adapting to Catastrophic Climate Risk, and Its Impact on Mitigation Policy. Working paper, University of Wyoming, Laramie.

Shogren, J. (1999). *The Benefits and Costs of Kyoto.* Washington, D.C.: American Enterprise Institute.

Shogren, J., and M. Toman (2000). Climate Change Policy. In P. Portney and R. Stavins (eds.)., *Public Policies for Environmental Protection.* 2nd ed. Washington, D.C.: Resources for the Future.

Sohngen, B., and R. Mendelsohn (1998). Valuing the Impact of Large-Scale Ecological Change in a Market: The Effect of Climate Change on U.S. Timber. *American Economic Review* 88(4): 686–710.

Sunstein, C. (2001). The Laws of Fear. John M. Olin Law & Economics Working Paper 128, University of Chicago Law School.

Susskind, L.E. (1994). Environmental Diplomacy: Negotiating More Effective Global Agreements. New York: Oxford University Press.

Swallow, S. (1996). Resource Capital Theory and Ecosystem Economics: Developing Nonrenewable Habitats with Heterogeneous Quality. *Southern Economic Journal* 63(1): 106–123.

UNFCCC (United Nations Framework Convention on Climate Change) (1999a). *Convention on Climate Change.* UNEP/IUC/99/2. Geneva, Switzerland: Published for the Climate Change Secretariat by the UNEP's Information Unit for Conventions (IUC). http://www.unfccc.de.

UNFCCC (1999b). *The Kyoto Protocol to the Convention on Climate Change.* UNEP/ IUC/99/10. France: Published by the Climate Change Secretariat with the Support of UNEP's Information Unit for Conventions (IUC). http://www.unfccc.de.

United States Clinton Administration (1998). *The Kyoto Protocol and the Administration's Policies to Address Climate Change: Administration Economic Analysis.* Washington D.C. http://www.whitehouse.gov/WH/New/html/kyoto.pdf

USEIA (United States Energy Information Agency) (2000). *International Energy Outlook 2000.* Washington, D.C.: U.S. Department of Energy.

Victor, D. (2001). *The Collapse of the Kyoto Protocol and the Struggle to Slow Global Warming.* Princeton: Princeton University Press.

Weyant, J., and J. Hill (1999). Introduction and Overview. *Energy Journal,* Special Issue: vii–xiiv.

Wiener, J. (1999). Global Environmental Regulation: Instrument Choice in Legal Context. *Yale Law Journal* 108(4): 677–800.

Wigley, T., R. Richels, and J. Edmonds (1996). Economic and Environmental Choices in the Stabilization of Atmospheric CO_2 Concentrations. *Nature* 379(6562): 240–243.

Comment on Jason F. Shogren and Stephan Kroll

Timothy Swanson

Shogren and Kroll's paper is an excellent survey of the wide range of issues involved in the problem of developing global institutions for environmental problems. Focusing, as requested, on the problem of climate change in particular, they point out the large number of issues remaining to be decided before implementation may proceed: (a) allocation of entitlements; (b) decision on regulatory instruments (taxes, permits, standards); (c) tradability of entitlements; (d) liability for monitoring and ensuring compliance (buyer, seller). Besides these problems of implementation, they mention a number of "differences" that might also get in the way of an agreement: (a) ratification problems (2-level games); (b) discounting differences; (c) linkages with secondary benefits; (d) risk perception differences. Clearly the authors have thought a lot about the various precursors and problems of implementing international agreements, and the paper provides a tremendous amount of thinking on the nature of the problems involved.

Let me commence with the second set of problems identified by the authors. These are problems that derive from the fact that different parties might come to the discussion from very different perspectives on the fundamental issues. For example, the problem of risk perception underlies the question of whether to take action now on climate change. A government charged with treating with urgency small risks of catastrophic harms will respond to climate change very differently from one charged with maximizing aggregate expected value. This is a clear difference in the way that different peoples desire their governments "to govern." Some clearly wish the "precautionary principle" to be a guiding principle of government regulation; others wish things to roughly correspond to basic cost-benefit analysis. Such differences underlie very different approaches to the global environment.

The same might be said about differences in the approach to discounting. There is little question that a significant amount of the total costliness of global warming exists in the future. Today's carbon emissions are expected to have an influence on the climate for the 200 years following their emission. If other countries are expected to increase their emissions dramatically in the future, then it might be incumbent on current emitters to reduce emissions now in order to safeguard the climate of fifty or one hundred years from now. Some countries might believe that the appropriate discount rate to apply to injuries to global public goods such as the climate should be low or virtually zero; others might believe that such costs should be discounted as usual (Broome 1992). A lot of these differences are based on differences in perspectives on the capacity for technological change to allow for substitution away from either carbon emissions or climate change impacts (higher sea levels etc.). Again, it is reasonable to believe that reasonable peoples could disagree on some of these issues, and might instruct their governments accordingly.

The final issue of note is the differences in procedures within different participating states. Some states are able to guarantee ratification once the executive branch approves of an international agreement, others clearly cannot. This is an important difference between the U.S. democratic system and those of the European parliamentary variety. The European executive need not face its electorate on the single issue of climate change, while the U.S. executive must persuade the electorate's representatives to accept the executive's decision regarding an international agreement. This is a difference in form that has quite a lot of impact on substance. It is interesting to see the authors addressing this problem in the context of the United States, and it would be interesting to see others addressing the differences in perspectives that it generates on international environmental agreements. It might also be interesting to see if this explains the relative importance of secondary benefit "linkages" in differing jurisdictions.

These are fundamental issues that address the difficulties that result from attempting to get agreement on the development of governance institutions, especially in relation to a problem such as climate change. These differences in initial perspectives always exist, and the development of some sort of pathway toward agreement from these initial differences is always important, and so they are important subjects for future research.

The first set of issues (regarding implementation) is also always present, and always has been in the problem of implementing international agreements. To some extent our preexisting experience with the development of multilateral environmental agreements is able to inform the practical issues concerning implementation. The Convention on International Trade in Endangered Species (CITES) first adopted a set of standards (Appendix I vs. Appendix II) and a system for their implementation in 1972. The Conference of the Parties was empowered as the standard-setting organ for listings on the appendices. Trading was allowed within the regime, and sometimes only up to agreed quotas. For example, the African Elephant Ivory Quota Management System developed individual quotas for traded ivory for each specified state. This system collapsed precisely on account of the problem of seller vs. buyer liability for monitoring trade (as the sellers were initially authorized to license their own trade). Now CITES has a system that enables "seller liability" for Appendix II trade (less restricted commodities) but "buyer liability" for Appendix I trade (more restricted commodities) (see Swanson 2001). The same sort of appendix I/appendix II system has been developed to aid in the regulation of the international trade in hazardous wastes, the so-called Basel Convention.

So, these problems of implementation are some with which we have some accumulated experience, and we need to bring this experience to bear in the development of a more general and more global environmental regulatory system. At the risk of some relatively futuristic thinking, it might be possible to propose a way forward in the development of effective global environmental institutions. Perhaps we might want to retain some derivative from the multilateral environmental agreement (MEA) system functioning solely as the standard-generating bodies. This would make sense, as the MEAs currently function relatively well as democratic representative bodies, although they could perhaps benefit from some more structure being imposed upon their procedures. Then it might be possible to make use of the quasi-judicial capabilities of the World Trade Organization (WTO) as the dispute settlement organ for the MEAs. In this way the experience from the MEA movement might be grafted upon the existing dispute settlement procedures to generate a more effective organization in total. Then the existing sovereign states would exist as the local implementing governments between the MEA legislative branch and the WTO judicial one.

In general, the problem of generating global environmental institutions is one that is being generated afresh each time that a new and serious global environmental problem arises. This is unnecessary as we now have more than thirty years of accumulated experience with developing and implementing global environmental agreements. Rather than looking at each environmental problem as a reason to build institutions from scratch, it would be better to refine existing approaches and build up from that base of experience.

Bibliography

Broome, J. (1992). *Counting the Costs of Global Warming.* Cambridge: White Horse Press.

Swanson, T. (2001). Developing the CITES Convention. In J. Hutton (ed.), *Endangered Species, Threatened Convention.* London: Earthscan.

Geoffrey Heal

Biodiversity and Globalization

1   What Is the Issue?

There is a general scientific consensus that we are losing biodiversity at a rate greatly in excess of that which has been normal for much of human history. It is also agreed that this loss is largely attributable to human activities. Loss of biodiversity is driven largely by destruction of the habitats of the species that are becoming extinct, a product of the need to clear land for housing, growing food and providing firewood. Behind this increasing pressure on space is of course the great growth of the human population, from about one and a half billion in 1900 to six billion in 2000 and quite possibly to ten billion by 2050. Population growth, habitat loss and biodiversity loss are global problems, in the sense that they are occurring globally and have global consequences. But they are not problems of globalization: they are not driven by the expansion of international trade and capital movements, nor the possible cultural homogenization which we associate as part of the phenomenon called globalization.

Another factor that may already be contributing to the loss of biodiversity, and will probably contribute much more in the future, is climate change. Again, this is a global problem but not really a problem of globalization. It is global in that it occurs at a global level and has to be solved at this level. But it is driven by economic growth and concomitant increases in energy use, which is a distinct issue from the expansion of trade and capital flows.

In the balance of this paper I set out briefly the economic consequences of biodiversity loss, and then argue that as a global problem it needs global solutions, and suggest that further globalization, in the sense of the development of global economic institutions, including markets, is a prerequisite for solving the problems posed by biodiversity loss. The central point here is that the willingness to pay for conservation and for the services that biodiversity provides is located largely in the rich countries, whereas the biodiversity itself is mainly in poor countries. Conservation requires institutions that turn this willingness to pay into cash flows from rich to poor countries, cash flows that are conditional on conservation and provide incentives for conservation. I review several mechanisms that could be important in achieving this.

2   Biodiversity as a Commodity

I have set out elsewhere the characteristics of biodiversity as an economic commodity (Heal 2000). It provides human societies with a number of important services, which include enhancing the productivity and resilience of natural and agricultural ecosystems, providing insurance against attacks on agricultural crops by pathogens, and providing us with valuable knowledge of novel genetic and molecular forms.

The relationship between biodiversity and the productivity and resilience of natural ecosystems has been a topic of intense and sometimes controversial research amongst ecologists over the last decade (see Tilman et al. 1997, Hooper and Vitousek 1997, Grime 1997). The controversy is associated mainly with the mechanisms through which increased diversity affects the resilience of natural ecosystems: there is general agreement that more diverse systems are more resilient in the face of natural and anthropogenic variations in their environment (Walker et al. 2000). Systems that are species-poor relative to their natural state are vulnerable to collapse through predation, through introduced species and through climatic variations.

Biodiversity contributes to the productivity of agricultural ecosystems through a rather different mechanism. Access to the genetic diversity stored in wild races of plants and animals has been critical in raising the productivity of commercially valuable species. Indeed the U.S. Office of Technology Assessment estimated that over $1 billion has been added to the value of U.S. agricultural output alone each year since the Second World War because of plant breeders' access to the biodiversity of wild races. This diversity operates as a source of characteristics that can be used to increase the productivity of commercial crops by cross-breeding or genetic engineering. Historically these characteristics have included heat resistance, short ·stems (which reduce vulnerability to wind damage), and resistance to pathogens. Ultimately biodiversity is the source of all crops and domestic animals, through its role as the raw material in plant and animal breeding, and new and higher-yielding plant and animal varieties are generated from the natural variation in plants and animals. The great increases in grain yields of the "green revolution" of the 1960s and 1970s, which were responsible for keeping food output growing in parallel with population in developing countries, were largely achieved by use of the genetic diversity of plant populations. Specifically, in the last half century we have seen a doubling in yields of rice, barley, soybeans, wheat, cotton, and sugarcane, a threefold increase in tomato yields, and a quadrupling in yields of maize, sorghum, and potato (National Research Council 1999). All of this has been based on and derived from genetic variability in the underlying plant populations. In economic terms, this variability is an asset, and one that has yielded a great return at little cost.

Insurance against attack by pathogens has been one of the most important contributions of biodiversity. An example that illustrates well the issue here is the role of biodiversity in preserving the Asian rice crop in the face of a new virus, the grassy stunt virus, carried by the brown plant hopper. This virus appeared capable of destroying a large fraction of the crop and in some years destroyed as much as one quarter. Rice breeders developed a form of rice resistant to this with the help of the International Rice Research Institute (IRRI) in the Philippines, which conducts research on rice production, and holds a large seed bank of seeds of tens of thousands of different varieties of rice and the near-relatives of rice. In this case the IRRI located a strain of wild rice not used commercially but resistant to the grassy stunt virus. The gene conveying resistance was transferred to commercial rice varieties, yielding commercial rice resistant to the threatening virus. This would not have been possible without genes from a strain of rice apparently of no commercial value. The same story was repeated later in the 1970s, and similar stories have occurred with other food crops, in particular corn in the United States (Myers 1997). We have every reason to expect that events like these will recur regularly: planting large areas with genetically identical plants greatly increases the chances that once a disease starts it will spread with dangerous speed through the entire area and crop.

The third reason I gave above for the importance of biodiversity is that it is a source of knowledge. We can learn from natural organisms how to make chemicals that have important and valuable properties. A good example is provided by the polymerase chain reaction (PCR). This reaction is central to the amplification of DNA specimens for analysis – as in forensic tests used in trials, and in many processes central to the biotechnology industry. Culturing requires an enzyme that is resistant to high temperatures. Enzymes with the right degree of temperature resistance were found in hot springs in Yellowstone National Park, and the heat resistance of these was then used to create an enzyme that could be used to culture DNA specimens. This enzyme is now central to the rapidly growing biotechnology industry. There are many less complex examples. In fact 37 percent by value of the pharmaceuticals sold in the United States are or were originally derived from plants or other living organisms (Carte 1996). Aspirin comes from the bark of willow trees. The bark of Yew trees has been used to derive a drug that is effective against ovarian cancer. A derivative of the Rosy Periwinkle flower is being used to cure childhood leukemia. The key point is that certain plants and animals are known to produce substances that are highly active pharmacologically. Plants that live in insect-infested areas produce substances that are poisonous to insects, and these have been used as the basis for insecticides. Some snakes produce venom that paralyses parts of the nervous system, and others produce venom that reduces blood pressure. Other insects produce anti-coagulants. All of these have been adapted for medical use.

3   Markets and Biodiversity

Given the undoubted economic value of biodiversity, it is natural to ask whether some of this value could be captured by markets. If it could, then this captured value would provide a conservation incentive: some of the services of biodiversity could be sold by those who conserve it and would give a return on conservation. To some degree this is possible and is even happening, but the realization of its full potential requires further development of global markets – requires, that is, further globalization. Good examples of this point are provided by ecotourism, by emerging markets for carbon sequestration, and by the beginnings of a movement that merges conservation with development.

Ecotourism is emerging as a powerful force for combining economic development with environmental conservation in a number of poor countries, particularly in Africa and Latin America. Tourism is one of the world's largest industries, being, according to several estimates, the largest source of employment in the world and also the fastest-growing. Within this whole, one of the fastest-growing subsectors is ecotourism, tourism based on the desire to see and experience some of the world's most unique ecosystems. Within the industrial world there is a substantial willingness to pay for experiencing these ecosystems, and this translates into a high return to their conservation if this is accompanied by successful marketing in rich countries. Figure 1, based on data from Zimbabwe, illustrates this

Figure 1: Returns per Hectare from Cattle and Wildlife in Zimbabwe

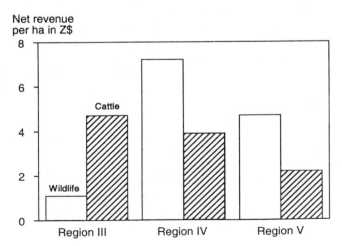

Source: Cumming (1990a).

Figure 2: Land Areas (sq km) for Wildlife Conservation in Zimbabwe

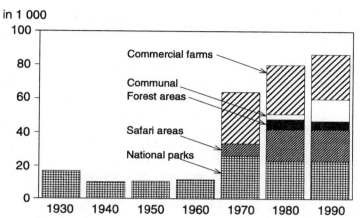

Source: Cumming (1990a).

point. For three of the five ecological regions into which the country is divided (the three which cover the great majority of the country), it shows the returns to two different forms of land use, cattle ranching and game ranching. Cattle ranching is the traditional form of agriculture here, and destroys the native flora and fauna. Game ranching is the term used for reestablishing the original ecosystems and then charging tourists for viewing the animals that are a part of these. This usually involves some initial expenses, restocking the land with the native fauna and fencing it to prevent them from moving away. As the figure shows, for two of the three regions the revenue per hectare per year is greater from game ranching than from cattle ranching, and indeed for all three regions the return on capital is greater from game ranching. Environmental conservation or restoration is competitive with cattle ranching, and because of this we see in Figure 2 that the land area devoted to wildlife conservation has increased dramatically over the last thirty years. Similar stories can be told for other African countries, and indeed for some regions in Central and South America. The growth of ecotourism in southern Africa has been so extensive that about 18 percent of the land area is now given over to wildlife support.

The connection with globalization here is immediate: the great majority of the tourists whose spending supports game ranching are from the United States and Western Europe. Only since the development of a truly global tourist industry has this business taken off. For tourism to both provide good returns to the local population and be sufficiently low-impact to avoid adverse environmental impacts, it has to be low-density and high-price, which means that most of the visitors must be from rich countries. So the existence of global markets is a prerequisite for tourism to support environmental conservation.

Markets for carbon sequestration have the potential to modify greatly the incentives for the conservation of forests, which are home to much of the planet's biodiversity. From an economic perspective the big problem with forest conservation is that the benefits of conservation accrue to people who do not pay the costs, and in particular very few of the benefits of conservation ever reach those who have to pay for it. This is a classic example of external effects and of course results in underconservation relative to what is needed for efficiency. The benefits of forest conservation include biodiversity support, carbon sequestration, and in many cases watershed conservation. In the first two cases, biodiversity and carbon sequestration, the benefits are global. Everyone on the planet benefits from the reduction of greenhouse gases and from the conservation of biodiversity. In the third case, watershed conservation, the benefits accrue to those who live downstream. In no case do the forest owners, who pay for conservation, receive the returns. The only returns that they can usually obtain are from logging, which in general involves destroying the forest. To avoid this mismatch between costs and benefits we need to find ways of bringing returns from conservation home to the owners. Bioprospecting is in principle one way of doing this, though there is some uncertainty about the yields from this (Simpson et al. 1996, Rausser and Small 1998). Another route lies via payment for carbon sequestration. This is possible under the Clean Development Mechanism (CDM) of the Kyoto Protocol, and rough calculations suggest that payments for carbon sequestration could be in excess of the returns from logging followed by cattle ranching (Heal 2000). If this were true, and this provision were implemented, then this would radically change the incentives for the conservation of forests, especially moist tropical forests. Again, a prerequisite for this is the development of global markets for carbon sequestration, through which willingness to pay for climate stabilization could be channeled to developing countries with forests.

4   Markets and Public Goods

Many of the services provided by biodiversity are public goods. Its contributions to productivity, to insurance against pathogen attack, and to the accumulation of knowledge are all essentially public in nature in that they are nonrival in consumption. It is counterintuitive that we should be seeking to use global markets, or indeed any markets, to ensure the adequate provision of public goods. After all, we know that markets will typically underprovide public goods. In fact the examples discussed, ecotourism and carbon sequestration, illustrate situations where markets do have real potential for managing the provision of public goods. Incentives for carbon sequestration under the CDM of the Kyoto Protocol are a by-product of a cap-and-trade regime for greenhouse gases, which is central to the cost-minimization provisions of the Protocol. Cap-and-trade mechanisms are increasingly being used to manage the provision of public goods, particularly those that are privately produced (Heal and Lin 2000). In this case a public bad, greenhouse gas, is produced by every individual and firm on the planet, and only decentralized mechanisms have the potential to provide incentives for reducing this production. This is where cap-and-trade systems match the problem well.

In the case of ecotourism, the connection between public goods and markets is less clear. What is happening in this case is that public and private goods are being bundled. The reason is that public goods can affect willingness to pay for private goods. We have long known that local public goods affect property values. Schools are the canonical example: house prices reflect access to good public schools. This is also true for environmental public goods. Recent econometric studies (Sieg et al. 2000, Chay and Greenstone 2000) indicate that house prices are positively affected by local environmental quality. Lately some property developers, seemingly aware of this, have deliberately conserved environmental assets and provided local public goods as a part of profit-maximizing development strategies.

Two examples capture the key issue well. Spring Island off the coast of South Carolina has long been highly valued as a nature reserve. Zoned for development, it was auctioned in 1990. The State of South Carolina bid, hoping to purchase the land for conservation, but was outbid by a developer. The latter, instead of constructing the 5,500 homes permitted, built only 500 high-value properties and deeded the balance of the land to a land management trust whose objective is to conserve the natural environment. He subsequently explained that this was his most profitable strategy. Proximity to a nature reserve boosted buyers' willingness to pay, so that limiting development in this way raised the value of the homes sufficiently to compensate for the reduced number. (The tax deduction on the donation to a conservation foundation also helped (Thacker 2000).) A similar story relates to hunters in Montana, who had long hunted over many thousands of acres of unspoiled land. Concerned that second-home development might end their hunting, they borrowed money to buy the land and finance the construction of a small number of luxury homes. The hunters placed a conservation easement on the remainder of the land, reserving the right to hunt on it themselves, and sold the houses for more than the total cost of buying the land and building the houses (Heal 2000).

What do these examples suggest? Clearly proximity to a unique and beautiful environmental site (a public good) enhances property values, and some developers believe that this is sufficient to justify conserving such sites even when developing them is an option. In other words, the conflict between development and conservation may not be as sharp as generally thought: there may be cases in which the most profitable development requires some measure of conservation. To put this in more economic terms, bundling an environmental public good with homes may be a profitable strategy. An interesting recent study by Taylor and Smith (2000) confirms more generally that access to environmental amenities can be a source of market power and product differentiation. In fact this point is now widely known: developers and urban planners now refer to this strategy as smart growth. An early illustration emerges from the history of New York's Central Park. When the designer Frederick Law Olmsted was asked how the city could pay for the park, he responded that its presence would raise property values and the extra tax revenues would easily repay the construction costs. History shows that was correct (Lerner and Poole 1999).

These observations naturally prompt us to examine in more detail the incentives for bundling environmental public goods with private goods. It would be interesting if there were conditions under which a profit-maximizing supplier of a private good would provide an associated public good at the economically optimal level. Given our normal skepticism about the ability of markets to provide public goods optimally, this appears at first sight an unlikely outcome. But I show (Heal 2001) that there are in fact reasonable and robust conditions under which this occurs. When viewed from the appropriate perspective, this result is intuitive.

The precise result proven is the following. A price-discriminating monopolist provides a private good and can also provide a public good. The latter can be bundled with the former, affecting buyers' willingness to pay for the private good. Then the monopolist will provide the public good at its economically efficient level. I also establish various generalizations of this: the central feature of the argument is not the public nature of the good bundled with the private good but the fact that there is no market for it. The same result holds when we replace public goods by untraded goods.

This result has some connections to earlier results on price discrimination in markets with private goods and increasing returns. There is also a close connection with the literature on the provision of local public goods in competing jurisdictions, especially with a result due to Scotchmer (1994). There are also references in the recent literature to the bundling of public and private goods – both Holm-Müller (1999) and Henderson and Thisse (1999) address this issue.

Although this research was motivated initially by environmental examples, the results are more general. There are many examples of sellers bundling public or other nontraded goods with private goods. Security is often bundled with other products, as in gated communities: the security of the community is a local public good that contributes to the value that its inhabitants place on the private goods it contains, houses.[1] And in a post-9/11 world, all airlines are to some degree bundling security with transportation. Going further afield, Reuters and other securities information sellers have long realized that information, being nonrival in consumption, has some of the aspects of a public good, and have relied in their business models on bundling it with private goods such·as analytical capabilities and access to proprietary networks. One reason for the greater profitability of AOL relative to other Web portals has been their bundling the private good internet access (as an ISP) with the information gateway function of a portal. Returning to the environmental area, another illustration is the activity of the Forest Stewardship Council (FSC).[2] FSC certifies tropical hardwoods as having been sustainably logged. Many timber retailers and furniture makers now sell only imported hardwoods certified by the FSC. Their customers are willing to pay extra for this type of wood. When purchasing certified timber, customers are again buying two commodities – the timber itself and also the preservation of tropical forests, a public good.

5   Bundling Public and Private Goods

Next I summarize a formal model that justifies the statements made above about bundling public and private goods. The full development of this model can be found in Heal (2001). We assume that a developer owns the exclusive right to develop a site that is an environmental asset valued by local population. Maximum development of this will destroy its environmental value totally, but is permitted by current zoning regulations. More development means more houses but less of the environmental public good, which may affect population's willingness to pay for houses. The developer has to find the most profitable tradeoff here. House buyers' preferences are represented by $u_i(y_i, h_i, e)$, where y_i is i's income or wealth, h_i is the level of housing consumed by i in the area to be developed and e, a local public good, is the quantity of a local environmental asset preserved. We assume that u_i is strictly concave and that buyers have initial endowments given by $(y_{i,0}, h_{i,0}, e_0)$. As a result of development of the area the amounts of housing and public good change to $(h_{i,0} + \Delta h_i, e_0 + \Delta e)$.

Define agent i's willingness to pay for a change as the value w_i that solves

$$u_i(y_{i0}, h_0, e_0) = u_i(y_{i0} - w_i, h_{i0} + \Delta h_i, e_0 + \Delta e).$$

---

[1]   We could also think of this as a club. However, in general, clubs do not operate by bundling public and private goods but by collectively providing an excludable public good. Many of the bundling examples cited below can clearly not be interpreted as clubs.

[2]   http://www.fscoax.org/principal.htm.

The problem facing the developer is to choose levels of housing development Δh_i and conservation Δe so as to maximize profits, which are given by

$$\max \sum w_i - c(\Delta h_1, \ldots, \Delta h_N, \Delta e),$$

where $c(\ )$ is the cost of development and conservation. It is now straightforward to prove:

Proposition: *If utility functions are strictly concave and the cost function strictly convex, a profit-maximizing developer who has exclusive development rights and can practice first-order price discrimination will provide an economically efficient combination of the private goods involved in housing and the public goods involved in environmental conservation.*

In Heal (2001) this basic model is extended in several ways. One extension is to discrete choices, describing situations where the public good is either provided or not provided. An area is either conserved or not – there are no intermediate possibilities. This is relevant to the ecotourism cases mentioned above: in Africa one can either ranch cattle or restore the original animal populations. But as lions and leopards will eat cattle, combinations are not readily possible. In this case the same results carry over: the profit-maximizing outcome is efficient.

Another extension is to the important case of imperfect ability to extract the willingness to pay for conservation of the environmental asset. Again this is important in the case of ecotourism, as tourist sites in Africa can only capture the willingness to pay of those who actually travel there. There are surely many others who are willing to pay for conservation but who will never actually visit southern Africa. In this case I show in Heal (2001) that for discrete conservation projects there is a fraction f, $0 < f < 1$, such that if a developer can extract more than fraction f of willingness to pay, then the profit-maximizing outcome is efficient.

6   Globalization and the Environment

I have argued above that globalization, of a specific type, has the potential to help the conservation of biodiversity. Are there other relationships between globalization and the environment? There have been suggestions that globalization will provide corporations with the opportunity to avoid environmental regulations by moving to countries with low environmental standards. The idea here is that meeting the environmental standards of the United States or the European Union is costly and places companies at a disadvantage relative to their competitors located in countries without such standards. Conceptually this is clearly possible: whether it matters is an empirical question. The evidence available to date suggests that it does not (Eskeland and Harrison 2002). This is perhaps not surprising: as Eskeland and Harrison note, the costs of environmental compliance are usually a small part of a plant's total costs and rarely sufficient to justify relocation to a different country. Even if it were the case that corporations relocate to take advantage of lower environmental standards, it is not clear that this would affect the conservation of biodiversity: this is a rather different problem from pollution control, which is what is at issue in the arguments about footloose industries.

It is also possible that globalization leads to incentives to clear land for agricultural production for export, and through this mechanism accelerates deforestation and the loss of biodiversity. Opening up overseas markets for timber may also accelerate deforestation for timber. My impression is that, at least currently, most forest clearing for food production is for domestic consumption rather than for export, although this was probably not always true. It is hard to find firm numbers on this issue. But opening up export markets undoubtedly has contributed to logging and so to deforestation, and this is an aspect of global trade that we need to address. Mechanisms such as the Forest Stewardship Council mentioned above are a part of the solution, though are not on their own sufficient to provide a solution. Recently there have been moves to have some of the trees most threatened by logging declared as endangered species and brought within the scope of CITES, the Convention on International Trade in Endangered Species. This could also be a move in the right direction, but again is at best a partial solution. Non-endangered trees may support endangered animals. Ultimately the solution lies in more, not less, globalization, but perhaps of a different type – in the development of the mechanisms discussed earlier for transferring willingness to pay for conservation from rich to poor countries. Then there would be adequate returns to the conservation of forests.

7   Conclusions

Biodiversity loss is a global problem, and needs global solutions. It is not caused by the globalization of trade and capital markets, but by the growth of the world's population and by the desire for higher stands of living, particularly with respect to food consumption. The solution must involve internalizing some of the external effects associated with biodiversity conservation, and these external effects are often global in scope. Another way of looking at the same phenomenon is as channeling some of the willingness to pay for conservation of the rich countries to the poor countries. Ecotourism and markets for carbon sequestration are two very different mechanisms for doing this, but we need more. The fact that many of the services of biodiversity are public in nature does not necessarily rule out the use of market mechanisms for its support.

Bibliography

Carte, B.K. (1996). The Biomedical Potential of Marine Natural Products. *BioScience* 46(4): 271–286.

Chay, K., and M. Greenstone (2000). Does Air Quality Matter? Evidence from the Housing Market. Revised December 2000. Available at http://elsa.berkeley.edu/~kenchay

Cumming, D.H.M. (1990a). Developments in Game Ranching and Wildlife Utilization in East and Southern Africa. WWF Multispecies Animal Production Systems Project, Project paper no. 13, June 1990. WWF program Office, Zimbabwe, P.O. Box CY 1409, Causeway, Harare, Zimbabwe.

Cumming, D.H.M. (1990b). Wildlife and the Market Place: A View from Southern Africa. WWF Multispecies Animal Production Systems Project, Project paper no. 12, June 1990. WWF program Office, Zimbabwe, P.O. Box CY 1409, Causeway, Harare, Zimbabwe.

Cumming, D.H.M., and I. Bond (1991). Animal Production in Southern Africa: Present Practices and Opportunities for Peasant Farmers in Arid Lands. WWF Multispecies Animal Production Systems Project, Project paper no. 22, July 1991. WWF program Office, Zimbabwe, P.O. Box CY 1409, Causeway, Harare, Zimbabwe.

Eskeland, G.A., and A.E. Harrison (2002). Moving to Greener Pastures: Multinationals and the Pollution Haven Hypothesis. NBER Working Paper 8888. Available at http://papers.nber.org/papers/W8888

Grime, J.P. (1997). Biodiversity and Ecosystem Function: The Debate Deepens. *Science* 277: 1260–1261.

Heal, G. (2000). *Nature and the Marketplace*. Washington, D.C.: Island Press.

Heal, G. (2001). Bundling Public and Private Goods. Columbia Business School Working Paper 2001. Available at www.gsb.columbia.edu/faculty/gheal

Heal, G., and Y. Lin (2000). Strategic Behavior in Permit Markets. In G.M. Heal (ed.), *Environmental Markets*. New York: Columbia University Press.

Henderson, J.V., and J.-F. Thisse (1999). On the Pricing Strategy of a Land Developer. *Journal of Urban Economics* 45(1): 1–16.

Holm-Müller, K. (1999). Finanzierung von Naturschutz über Komplementärgüter. *Konjunkturpolitik* 45(1): 24–39.

Hooper, D.U., and P.M. Vitousek (1997). The Effect of Plant Composition and Diversity on Ecosystem Processes. *Science* 277: 1302–1305.

Lerner, S., and W. Poole (1999). The Economic Benefits of Parks and Open Spaces. The Trust for Public Lands. See http://www.tpl.org

Myers, N. (1997). Biodiversity's Genetic Library. In G.C. Daily (ed.), *Nature's Services: Societal Dependence on Natural Ecosystems*. Washington, D.C.: Island Press.

National Research Council (1999). *A Framework for Managing Biodiversity*. Report of the Committee on the Economic and Non-Economic Value of Biodiversity. Washington, D.C.: National Academies Press.

Rausser, G.C., and A.A. Small (1998). Valuing Research Leads: Bioprospecting and the Conservation of Genetic Resources. Paper presented at the Conference on Managing Human-Dominated Ecosystems at the Missouri Botanical Gardens, March 1998. *Journal of Political Economy* 108(1): 173–206.

Scotchmer, S. (1994). Public Goods and the Invisible Hand. In J. Quigley and E. Smolensky (eds.), *Modern Public Finance*. Cambridge, Mass.: Harvard University Press.

Sieg, H., V.K. Smith, H.S. Banzhaf, and R. Walsh (2000). Estimating the General Equilibrium Benefits of Large Policy Changes: The Clean Air Act Revisited. NBER Working Paper 7744. Available at http://papers.nber.org/papers/W7744

Simpson, R.D., R.A. Sedjo, and J.W. Reid (1996). Valuing Biodiversity for Use in Pharmaceutical Research. *Journal of Political Economy* 104 (February): 163–185.

Taylor, L.O., and V.K. Smith (2000). Environmental Amenities as a Source of Market Power. *Land Economics* 76(4): 550–568.

Thacker, P. (2000). Spring Island Developers Go Green. Environmental News Network. Available at www.enn.com/features/2000/06/06012000/island_11964.asp\

Tilman, D., J. Knops, D. Wedin, P. Reich, M. Ritchie, and E. Siemann (1997). The Influence of Functional Diversity and Composition on Ecosystem Processes. *Science* 277: 1300–1302.

Walker, B., A.P. Kinzig, and J. Langridge (2000). Plant Attribute Diversity, Resilience, and Ecosystem Function: The Nature and Significance of Dominant and Minor Species. *Ecosystems* 2(3): 24–30.

Comment on Geoffrey Heal

R. David Simpson

Geoffrey Heal offers a number of insightful and, in my judgment, perfectly valid observations in his contribution on "Biodiversity and Globalization." Yet Professor Heal has not addressed some core issues. I agree entirely with what I take to be his main points. First, as he writes on p. 227, "Conservation requires institutions that turn [rich nations'] willingness to pay into cash flows from rich to poor countries." Second, "globalization" does not necessarily cause biodiversity loss, but is, rather, potentially a mechanism for solving the problem. Finally, various existing and proposed market mechanisms can help, at least in part. My reservations are captured in the qualification "at least in part." Because the nature of the problem is that *local* actions generate *global* public goods, however, we have to assume that efforts to internalize *local* public goods will not generate *globally* optimal outcomes. Thus, while I certainly agree with Professor Heal as far as he goes, I'm curious as to the guidance he would offer in resolving the thornier problems of how to assure the adequate supply of the global public good, biodiversity.

A strident debate has arisen among international conservation advocates. For most of history, protected areas have been established and either actively managed with a "fences and fines" approach under which almost all commercial uses are prohibited, or allowed to degenerate into mere "paper parks" (for a history of protected areas, see Davenport and Rao [2002]; Bruner et al. [2001], argue that even "paper parks" may not be as futile as is often alleged). For a variety of political and economic reasons, the fashion in international biodiversity conservation policy over most of the last two decades has shifted toward a "sustainable use" approach (IUCN et al. 1981, 1991). The battle has now been joined by those who feel that this new approach must be perfected (e.g., Wilshusen et al. 2002) and those who maintain that it has failed utterly, and a return to strictly protected areas is the only effective option (Terborgh 1999; van Schaik et al. 2002).

Professor Heal seems to side with those who believe that sustainable use is the key to biodiversity preservation. In a sense, there can be no argument with advocating sustainable use. Surely, no one can object to mechanisms by which land developers, pharmaceutical product researchers, tour operators, and so forth "do well by doing good." If biodiversity can be preserved while employing the habitats on which it depends in ecologically benign ways, it is surely a "win-win" situation. Yet if the solution to the problem were this easy, there would be no "problem."

One community believes that there is not, in fact, any problem. Consider, for example, Anderson and Leal's (1991: 172) view that "Expanding [market] processes to include natural resources and environmental amenities offers the only possibility for improving environmental quality, raising living standards, and ... expanding individual liberty." In short, government need only unfetter private enterprise. Daily and Ellison (2002) offer a very different perspective in noting that "Private enterprise cannot substitute for governments ... government regulation is called for to kick-start and supervise the profound economic transformation needed ..." Commentators from both the political left and the right seem to agree that market mechanisms and incentives can help solve difficult environmental problems. They part company on the issue of whether market incentives provide complete or partial solutions.

This is the issue on which Professor Heal might have shed more light. He does provide examples of instances in which private parties might fully "internalize the externalities." Are such instances important in biodiversity conservation? Things like existence values – the moral satisfaction people feel from knowing that certain of God's creatures remain in the world, regardless of any instrumental use they might make of them – are global public goods. One must, then, think either that the social benefits realized from bundling public and private goods are necessarily limited, or that purported global values are overstated.

I do not believe that Professor Heal and I differ in our general views on these matters. We may have more fundamental differences concerning the policy implications of the observation that "eco-entrepreneurs" can both "do good and do well." There is a spectrum of possible policy responses to global biodiversity loss. At one extreme one might say "markets do well enough," and suppose that whatever further gains in biodiversity conservation might be achieved by additional intervention do not compensate the political and economic compromises required to initiate further collective action. At the other, one might say "markets will never be effective in preserving truly global public goods; we should rely instead on massive public funding of conservation interventions." As with most things, the best policy is likely to be found in the middle ground. Markets undoubtedly "work" for, e.g., promoting tourism in beautiful natural environments or allocating access to truly unique troves of genetic resources, but public intervention may be required to prevent would-be eco-tourists from "loving an area to death" or to provide incentives over and above those afforded by purely private agents.

This brings us again to the question of how biodiversity conservation might best be accomplished, particularly in the nations of the developing tropics in which it is both richest and most imperiled. It seems clear that the sustainable development approach is not providing as much protection for biodiversity as many conservation advocates desire. This then begs the question of how best to structure further support. Some organizations subsidize "ecofriendly" ventures of the type

Professor Heal has described in order to expand the scope of their operations and with it, the area preserved. Other conservation advocates have called for strengthening institutions in developing countries in the hope that, for example, establishing more secure land tenure will induce local people to devote the lands under their control to their "highest and best use" – presuming that that use is consistent with preserving indigenous biodiversity.

My own experience in countries of the developing world has led me to embrace the sentiment of a friend with more experience in such areas: "The surprising thing is often not how poorly simple economics explains things in the developing world, but rather, how well." Opportunities for realizing profits do not often go wanting. I fully agree with Professor Heal's observations that game ranches in Southern Africa comprise the most lucrative use of the marginal agricultural lands there. I would even expand upon it by noting the increasing prevalence of private nature reserves in other spectacular regions of the world (see, e.g., Langholz et al. [2000] on private reserves in Costa Rica). These developments are heartening. Yet such private ventures are far from sufficient to achieve biodiversity conservation in the magnitude that many advocates desire (see, e.g., James et al. 2001) who estimate the yearly costs of worldwide biodiversity conservation as being in the order of a third of a trillion dollars.

Such estimates of the magnitude of the task lead some advocates to despair and others to wishful thinking. It would be both unfair and inaccurate to blame Professor Heal for the excesses of wishful thinkers. Yet there are those who may infer from his work that we can generate biodiversity protection on the cheap by subsidizing ecofriendly ventures or simply waiting for the world fully to appreciate their potential. My own work on valuing the market potential of certain aspects of biodiversity leads me to believe it is simply not great (Simpson et al. 1996).[1] Moreover, existing biodiversity conservation approaches that call for subsidizing ecofriendly activities of the kind Professor Heal describes even when they are not privately profitable can be extremely inefficient means to achieve conservation objectives (Simpson and Sedjo 1996; Ferraro 2001; Ferraro and Simpson 2002). There is, then, a danger that overly optimistic assessment of the prospects of ecofriendly ventures can lead to a view that our problems will solve themselves, or can be solved more cheaply than they can.

---

[1]   I should also note, however, that some selected areas may present more optimistic scenarios (Rausser and Small 2000), and private agents may not capture all, or even an appreciable share, of social values (Craft and Simpson 2001).

Bibliography

Anderson, T.L., and D. Leal (1991). *Free Market Environmentalism.* San Francisco: Pacific Research Institute for Public Policy.

Bruner, A., R.E. Gullison, R.E. Rice, and G.A.B. da Fonseca (2001). The Effectiveness of Parks in Protecting Tropical Biodiversity. *Science* 291(January 5): 125–128.

Craft, A.B., and R.D. Simpson (2001). The Social Value of Biodiversity in New Pharmaceutical Product Research. *Environmental and Resource Economics* 18(1): 1–17.

Daily, G., and K. Ellison (2002). *The New Economy of Nature: The Quest to Make Conservation Profitable.* Washington: Island Press.

Davenport, L., and M. Rao (2002). The History of Protection: Paradoxes of the Past and Challenges for the Future. In J. Terborgh, C. van Schaik, L. Davenport, and M. Rao (eds.), *Making Parks Work: Strategies for Preserving Tropical Nature.* Washington: Island Press.

Ferraro, P.J. (2001). Global Habitat Protection: Limitations of Development Interventions and a Role for Conservation Performance Payments. *Conservation Biology* 15(4): 990–1000.

Ferraro, P.J., and R.D. Simpson (2002). The Cost-Effectiveness of Conservation Payments. *Land Economics* 78(3): 339–353.

IUCN (International Union for the Conservation of Nature), United Nations Environment Program (UNEP), and World Wildlife Fund (WWF) (1981). *World Conservation Strategy: Living Resource Conservation for Sustainable Development.* Gland (Switzerland): IUCN, UNEP, WWF.

IUCN (International Union for the Conservation of Nature), United Nations Environment Program (UNEP), and World Wildlife Fund (WWF) (1991). *Caring for the Earth: A Strategy for Sustainable Living.* Gland (Switzerland): IUCN, UNEP, WWF.

James, A., K.J. Gaston, and A. Balmford (2001). Can We Afford to Conserve Biodiversity? *BioScience* 51(1): 43–52.

Langholz, J.A., J.P. Lassoie, D. Lee, and D. Chapman (2000). Economic Considerations of Privately Owned Parks. *Ecological Economics* 33(2): 173–183.

Rausser, G.C., and A.A. Small (2000). Valuing Research Leads: Bioprospecting and the Conservation of Genetic Resources. *Journal of Political Economy* 108(1): 173–206.

van Schaik, C., J. Terborgh, L. Davenport, and M. Rao (2002). Making Parks Work: Past, Present, and Future. In J. Terborgh, C. van Schaik, L. Davenport, and M. Rao (eds.), *Making Parks Work: Strategies for Preserving Tropical Nature.* Washington: Island Press.

Simpson, R.D., and R.A. Sedjo (1996). Paying for the Conservation of Endangered Ecosystems: A Comparison of Direct and Indirect Approaches. *Environment and Development Economics* 1(May): 241–257.

Simpson, R.D., R.A. Sedjo, and J.W. Reid (1996). Valuing Biodiversity for Use in Pharmaceutical Research. *Journal of Political Economy* 104(1): 163–185.

Terborgh, J. (1999). *Requiem for Nature.* Washington: Island Press.

Wilshusen, P.R., S.R. Brechin, C.L. Fortwangler, and P.C. West (2002). Reinventing the Square Wheel: Critique of a Resurgent "Protection Paradigm" in International Biodiversity Conservation. *Society and Natural Resources* 15(1): 17–40.

Gary C. Hufbauer

Looking 30 Years Ahead in Global Governance

1 Looking Backward

Professor Dr. Herbert Giersch first invited me to a Kiel Week conference in 1973. That memorable event was nearly 30 years ago. Let me begin my speculations on global governance 30 years hence by reflecting on the decades since Kiel Week 1973.

That was an era when the direction of the world economy was hotly contested. Foremost was the challenge of the communist economic model. My professors from Harvard and Cambridge were impressed by Soviet growth.[1] Then, and for the next 15 years, the CIA also calculated high growth rates. None of these professors or analysts admired the Soviet political model, but they conceded the attraction of command economics.

Meanwhile, many third world nations practiced their own version of command economics, loosely identified with Raul Prebisch and Hans Singer. The core ingredients were forced savings and investment, import substitution, export promotion, allocation of credit, and state guidance over the heights, and even lesser ridges, of the economy. Several countries, especially in East Asia, prospered using economic models that mixed and matched these ingredients, giving a decidedly smaller role to the price system than in capitalist countries (but considerably more than in communist countries).

In that same era, the capitalist system was having a rough time. The United States suffered from the high costs of conducting the Vietnam War and maintaining garrison defenses against the Soviet Union.[2] The end of fixed exchange rates in 1971, the oil shocks in 1973/74, a decade of easy money, coupled with contin-

Remark: The views expressed are the opinions of the author, and do not necessarily reflect the views of the Board, Advisors, Director, or Fellows of the Institute for International Economics. James W. Harris of Centra Technology gave valuable comments.

[1] In that era, Rostow's Stages of Economic Growth (1960), with its emphasis on high investment, amounted to conventional wisdom. The Stages thesis, subtitled A Non-Communist Manifesto, lent credence to the communist economic model. As I recall, both Gottfried Haberler and Herbert Giersch were vocal skeptics.

[2] During this era, defense outlays consumed around 5 percent of GDP annually.

ued high defense outlays – all culminated in a sharp rise in inflation. Productivity growth was low, average real wages in the United States barely increased for two decades, unemployment rose in Europe, and stock markets did poorly for most of the 1970s and early 1980s.

With three horses in the race for prize economic model, it is perhaps surprising that the era was characterized by considerable agreement on matters of world economic governance. The OECD and the G-7 Summits were acknowledged locales for sorting out global macroeconomics, especially in the wake of the oil shocks. Trade ministers conducted the Tokyo Round of GATT negotiations with decorum (measured by today's rhetorical standards), and the U.S. Congress ratified the Multilateral Agreement with little dissent. While a large number of regional trade agreements were on the books, only a few (centered in Europe) had economic substance, and they posed no challenge to the multilateral trading system. The International Monetary Fund and the World Bank were masters of their respective universes. The Fund's role as arbiter of macroeconomic policy among G-7 powers effectively disappeared at the Smithsonian Institution in 1971; but in the 1970s and 1980s, when the Fund told lesser powers how to shape up, Washington's advice was received with respect. Equally important, G-7 legislatures rarely criticized the Fund. Robert McNamara, meanwhile, transformed the World Bank into godfather of development, almost as popular in Washington, European capitals, and Tokyo as in Latin America and Asia.

In terms of macroeconomic governance, the era of the 1970s and 1980s harbored a sharp contrast: on the one hand, a vigorous horse race between economic models; on the other hand, international institutions harmoniously working from Olympian heights. The explanation is part control, part tolerance, part competition. The capitalist camp controlled all the international economic institutions. In their daily operations, however, the institutions tolerated command models practiced in Africa, Asia, and Latin America. The Tokyo Round negotiations, for example, required few tariff concessions from developing countries; and neither the IMF nor the World Bank conditioned its loans on progress towards privatizing state enterprises, liberalizing capital markets, or curtailing corruption. Perhaps the biggest reason for harmonious governance was competition – competition between capitalist countries and communist countries that colored every aspect of international economic and political life. The United States, Europe, and Japan submerged their economic disagreements to the imperatives of a common alliance against the Soviet Union and China.

That era began to crumble in the late 1980s with Deng's transformation of China, and it decisively collapsed alongside the Berlin Wall in 1990. Soviet economic triumphs were unmasked as a sham.[3] China's dedication to communism

---

[3]   The sham had been argued for some years by CIA Team B, led by Charles Wolf of the Rand Corporation.

was revealed as a political prop, not as an economic doctrine. The United States prospered thanks to a fortuitous combination of falling defense expenditures, a flexible and competitive economy, and the diffusion of information technology. Meanwhile, command economies faltered in Latin America and Asia, and erstwhile practitioners of state guidance gradually embraced the Washington consensus and Anglo-Saxon capitalism. By the year 2000, the accepted economic model entailed monetary and fiscal discipline, a market economy safeguarded by independent regulators, and flexible social safety nets. This model had local flavors and was not universally practiced, but significant deviations could be attributed to entrenched interests (state enterprises, local cartels, cultures of corruption), rather than ideological advocacy of an alternative.

The horse race may have ended for economic models, but disarray in global economic governance was just beginning. Wrapping up the Uruguay Round of Multilateral Trade Negotiations in 1995 required enormous political energy from Washington, Brussels, and other capitals – far more energy than the previous Tokyo Round, which ended in 1979.[4] The International Monetary Fund was pilloried by the right and the left for its handling of the Asian, Russian, and Argentine crises. Under James Wolfenson's leadership, the World Bank raced from one trendy mission to the next. The OECD and the G-7 Summits became less relevant in sorting out macroeconomic policy differences between the major powers. They came to be seen instead as "photo-ops," both by cynical press observers and jaded participants.

Reviewing this history, it is evident that the extent of consensus or discord on the economic model did not correlate with the degree of consensus or discord on global economic governance. In retrospect, competition from the Sino-Soviet model in the 1960s and 1970s was a major force for cohesion in governance. When the competition vanished, discord appeared. Individual European countries, as well as the European Union, grew more assertive. Sharp disagreements over the scope of the WTO's agenda at Seattle in 1999, and the choice of a successor to Michel Camdessus at the helm of the IMF in 2000, symbolized storm clouds over the Atlantic. Meanwhile, with prodding from the United States, the international institutions less gladly tolerated local deviations from the precepts of the Washington consensus and Anglo-Saxon capitalism. Many developing and transition economies demanded time and sympathy for the task of implementing reform. Yet the United States grew more critical of corruption, oppression, and incompetence; it wanted faster implementation, not more excuses. Finally, during the 1990s, powerful new players emerged with their own governance agendas:

---

[4]   The WTO endured a major political setback at Seattle in 1999, and barely got to its feet at the Doha Ministerial in 2001. The U.S. farm subsidy bill further clouded WTO prospects in 2002.

NGOs like the Sierra Club, Greenpeace, and Oxfam; rock stars like Bono;[5] and the super-rich like George Soros and Bill Gates. Meanwhile, the multinational corporations continued to press their views.

Outside of India and China (admittedly two huge exceptions), poor countries had a dismal decade in the 1990s.[6] The East Asian model of state-sponsored capitalism, successful at reconstruction and early development, faltered when economies reached a more mature stage, and the East Asian image of miracle growth was swept away by bad banks at home and abroad. The growth record in Latin America – which embraced the Washington consensus and Anglo-Saxon capitalism – was particularly discouraging. Chile and Mexico are star pupils, but other Latin countries are at best C students. The health record in Africa, Russia, and Central Asia went from bad to worse, with the spread of HIV, tuberculosis, malaria, and alcoholism. Meanwhile, in the industrial world, European economic performance was mediocre and the Japanese show was abysmal. Only North America and Australia gave outstanding performances.

Looking at economic outcomes from the 1990s, there is reason to argue that new forms of global governance are urgently required. My essay, however, is devoted to positive forecasts: how I think global economic governance will *actually* evolve, not how I think it *ought* to evolve.[7] Only in conclusion do I offer a few paragraphs on doing things differently.

Experience during and after the Cold War illustrates the overriding importance of the security context. A similar lesson can be drawn from the 19th century: *Pax Britannica* was an era of progressively freer trade – thanks more to British naval ascendancy than the compelling analysis of David Ricardo. When *Pax Britannica* ended in 1914, so did free trade. Because security dominates economics, I start my forecast by speculating on the security context over the next thirty years. In the final paragraphs of this paper, I sketch an alternative and more pessimistic security scenario, and what it might mean for global economic governance.

The central economic forecast is divided into three segments. It starts with my own guess as to five global economic issues that will compel the greatest attention over the next thirty years; it follows with an explanation why several important issues did not make the short list; and it wraps up with a prognosis of institutional frameworks for handling the most compelling issues.

---

[5]   For an illustration of Bono's persuasive powers, see *Financial Times*, 13 May 2002: 14.

[6]   Easterly (2002) documents the dismal record of economic growth among many poor countries over most of the last 50 years.

[7]   Prescriptions as to how global governance *ought* to be organized usually have a utopian aroma. Among the most readable expositions is Soros (2002).

2   The Security Context

The biggest surprise to me, were I so fortunate to attend Kiel Week in 2030, would be looking back on three decades of global tranquility. A surprise almost as big would be the sort of traumatic conflict between the great powers that fathered a new regime of international organizations, akin to the League of Nations after the First World War and the United Nations institutions after the Second World War. But I would not be surprised by thirty years of corrupt and oppressive governance, civil war, killer disease, and general disorder in the outer corners of the globe. For these places, Hobbes had it right. Moreover, I expect recurring terrorist attacks to become a dreaded feature of life within the great powers.

For all that, the security context of the early 21st century will likely resemble the Concert of Europe following the Congress of Vienna of 1815. Once Napoleon was defeated, the imperial powers – Britain, France, Austria, Russia and the Ottoman Empire – agreed on three security principles: respect for monarchy, sovereign rule within state borders, and avoidance of major wars within the European heartland. These principles did not preclude imperial expansion, competitive skirmishes outside of Europe, nor, as the century wore on, battles to adjust borders (not overthrow states) within Europe – notably the Crimean War and the Franco-Prussian War.

At the outset of the 21st century, while the United States ranks far above others in military dominance, this is not the era of an omnipotent super-power, any more than the 19th century was an era of uncontested British dominance. The United States is reluctant to lose troops in battle – a painful legacy from Vietnam that has colored the conduct of subsequent U.S. engagements in Lebanon, Iraq, Somalia, Yugoslavia, and Afghanistan. Moreover, only under the most extreme circumstances would the United States deploy its high-tech weaponry to inflict massive casualties abroad. On the economic field, the United States finds its match in Europe, and significant rivals in Japan and China. Given these constraints, the United States must necessarily share global power with other contenders.[8]

Over the next thirty years, China is certain to be a global power, and the European Union is almost certain. The qualification "almost" comes into play because the backlash against Brussels is running strong. Centralized EU authority could be stopped cold at its current stage – trade and monetary affairs – and not reach fiscal or security matters. In that scenario, the European Union would still qualify as a global economic power, but not as a global security power. Russia and Japan may rejoin the rank of global powers – if they overhaul their economies. India is

---

[8]   See Nye (2002). Even in the purely military sphere, global security cannot be ensured solely with the U.S. brand of high-tech skills. Low-level fighting in Afghanistan and Pakistan is proof.

an outside contender, but only if it fuels the economy with high-octane policies, akin to China's unhesitating embrace of capitalism.

Agreed security principles. These great and near-great global powers appear to agree on three security principles: no military conflict between them, deference (not overriding respect) to the established political order within the global powers, and recognition that rogue states and terrorist movements must somehow be disciplined.

The agreed principles appear to preclude the sort of sustained confrontation that cemented global economic cooperation in the capitalist camp during the Cold War. Episodes of confrontation will occur when a global power (most likely the United States) plays a shadow role during the messy transitions from single party rule in Japan or China, transitions sure to happen in the next thirty years. These episodes are likely to be brief, resembling the tensions that characterized the transition from Gorbachev to Yeltsin to Putin. By themselves, short confrontations will not redraw the map of global economic governance. More disturbing are other events: wars between secondary powers and terrorist attacks.

War between secondary powers. The security principles still allow secondary powers to enter into ferocious battles with one another, akin to the Iran–Iraq war of the 1980s. Some of these battles will provoke intercession by the global powers. The United States will certainly intercede if Israel appears to be losing a war with its neighbors; and more than one global power will intercede if India or Pakistan launches a nuclear attack on the other.[9] Russia will intercede in Central Asian battles. Intercession by the global powers will, at the very least, disrupt cooperation on economic issues. More troubling, however, will be the impact of terrorist attacks aimed at one or more global powers.

Terrorist attacks. The hardest question for the 21st century is how the security principles will stand up in the face of terrorist attacks that, in individual assaults, kill between 1,000 and 100,000 civilians. Warren Buffet believes that a chemical, nuclear, or biological attack is so likely that his reinsurance companies no longer cover these risks. It is hard to disagree with the most successful investor of the 20th century.[10] Buffet's forecast was underlined by Vice President Cheney and Defense Secretary Rumsfeld, who solemnly told the American public, in the

---

[9] According to press reports, Pakistan was preparing to fire nuclear weapons on India during the 1999 border conflict. See *Washington Post*, 15 May 2002: A1.

[10] If the chance of one of these terrorist attacks is only 2 percent annually, then the prospective likelihood of a single attack over a span of thirty years approaches 50 percent. Given the enormous financial damage of a single episode, this is more risk than Buffet wants to bear.

week of May 20, 2002, that the next terror attack was a question of "when," not "if." Shortly after, President Bush announced a strategic doctrine of preemptive strikes. This is a dramatic shift in policy, because preemptive strikes may lack the compelling moral justification of retaliatory strikes, and because preemptive strikes will sometimes be launched on the basis of faulty intelligence.

The systemic danger, as Harris (2002) has explained, is not a single terrorist attack on the scale of September 11, but recurring attacks perpetrated by different groups for different purposes. The terrorist groups of the future will be self-organized, with considerable skill at morphing their internal organization and destructive techniques. From time to time, the terrorists will succeed at inflicting mass death, destroying landmark structures, and disabling vital networks. None of the great powers are exempt – India, China, Japan, Russia, the United States, and even Europe are all targets.

If, as this outlook suggests, September 11 marks the dawn of a new style of warfare – with parallels, as Brad DeLong has argued, to the 30 Years War – much will change. Most importantly, security concerns will shape the attention given to the economic questions raised in this essay. Priority will be assigned to preventive intelligence, preemptive strikes, and search-and-destroy missions. International cooperation in fighting the long war will not spring automatically from the nature of the attacks. Security cooperation will be limited by the fact that terrorist groups have idiosyncratic targets – they will not simultaneously attack several great powers in a single campaign (see Doran 2002). Since security alliances will not spring automatically from the fact of terrorism, to some extent, clubs and agreements on economic governance will be shaped to foster those alliances.

Security and economics. The security principles agreed upon (in my view) among the global powers allow ample room for them to skirmish in secondary theaters – what rogue states to overthrow; how to combat terrorism; what civil wars to quell; how to attack drug trafficking; how to cope with HIV and TB. We have seen such skirmishes over Cambodia and Iraq, Hizbollah and al-Qaeda, Rwanda and Yugoslavia, Colombia and Burma, and South Africa and Thailand.[11] Many more skirmishes will occur in the decades ahead.

Since great power skirmishes are bound to recur, the question to my mind is whether they will interfere with global economic governance. On this question, I am mildly optimistic. The United States will play a leading role in spotlighting security theaters, and in supplying combat materiel and manpower. In the process, attention to economic issues will be subordinated. Moreover, U.S. disappointment over the extent of support from other great powers will erode cooperation in the

---

[11]   A recent example: Jiang Zemin's cordial visit with Muammar Qaddafi in April 2002. See *The Economist*, 27 April 2002: 39–40.

economic realm. The operative verbs in my forecast are "erode" and "subordinate," not "derail" and "forget." Cooperation would be derailed if, for example, the European Union actually assisted Iraq while the United States was seeking to overthrow Saddam. But the European Union is not about to provide opposing assistance, even though it may question an overthrow strategy.[12] Indeed, there are few secondary theaters where great powers will openly oppose one another – an event that would push the economic agenda almost out of sight. Instead, great power skirmishes will take the form of diplomatic protest, indifference, or tepid support.

3   Five Compelling Issues

There is no shortage of demanding economic issues. The challenge is to identify the most compelling issues. Here is my short list of five, with no particular priority among them.

3.1   Global Warming

The case for global warming will, I think, become *politically* persuasive in the next twenty years. Shogren and Kroll (2003) make an astute observation: when presented with an event with low but uncertain probability (substantial global warming caused by greenhouse emissions) and very high but uncertain costs (droughts, floods, hurricanes), people find it very difficult to combine the probable risk and the probable cost into a single estimate that dictates action. Instead, people divide into two groups: those that fixate on the low probability and correspondingly ignore the problem, and those that fixate on the high costs and demand extraordinary sacrifice.

Right now, the low probability school is shaping policy – namely, inaction. When evidence of global warming meets the Missouri test ("show me"), and patterns of winners and losers begin to emerge, the political balance will shift to the high cost school. The big continental nations – the European Union, Russia, China, Canada, Brazil, and the United States – will have important winners and losers *within* their borders. Other countries will score themselves entirely in the winner or loser column. While gains and losses may partly net out, it seems certain that losses will be more concentrated and therefore attract far more attention than gains. Just as winners from urban congestion are seldom heard, so winners from global warming will seek to avoid notice.

---

[12]   For a sharp example of this type of dissent, see Patten (2002) and the press reports surrounding President Bush's speech to the German Reichstag on 24 May 2002.

But economists, at least, should recognize that global warming could improve living conditions in large areas. People living in those areas may form a sort of "silent minority" against the major sacrifices needed to halt the warming process. For this reason, the political tilt will have to be sharp before global action is taken.

Even with lots of action, reasonably cheap technological fixes will not, in my opinion, be found. I am impressed by J. Craig Venter's investigation of deep-sea microbes that would voraciously consume CO_2.[13] I am impressed by the search for alternatives to petroleum-powered vehicles. But I am also impressed by costly and so far unsuccessful technological searches in other areas – a cure for HIV, controlled nuclear fusion, and cheap seawater conversion. Controlling greenhouse gases will, in my opinion, prove more elusive and expensive.

Climate change that creates huge concentrated losses, highly differentiated across countries, no quick remedy, and very costly long-term measures – these are ingredients for global economic conflict that will compel some sort of cooperative governance.

3.2   Poverty

International altruism – measured by the ratio of foreign assistance to the GDP of donor countries – becomes increasingly scarce following the Marshall Plan in the 1950s and the burst of development aid in the 1960s. Not coincidentally, assistance budgets declined as the attractions of communism diminished. Bauer's (1972) well-founded skepticism about the economic merits of development aid was recently given fresh vitality by Easterly (2002). To be blunt, we do not have a reliable recipe for economic growth,[14] and we do not have a compelling security rationale for foreign assistance. Nevertheless, Third World poverty earns a place on my short list for two reasons. First, as Florini (2003) has stressed at this Conference, the combined forces of Oxfam, Bono, and CNN will assuredly thrust the face of appalling misery into the daily consciousness of Europe and America. Second, a certain amount of Third World poverty will actually spill over into the First World through immigration, disease, and terrorism.[15]

---

[13]   See *Science*, 3 May 2002: 824. Another imaginative approach involves salting the oceans with iron to absorb CO_2. See *Science*, 19 April 2002: 467.

[14]   To be more precise, we do not have a recipe that can persuade all those who feast on a predatory economy – the corrupt leaders, the mercenary officials, and the monopoly firms – to change their ways. As long as those ways persist, it is very hard for an economy to grow.

[15]   Such spillovers could just as easily isolate the affected poor countries as accelerate their integration into the world economy. Indeed, one prominent "spillover" already has this effect: widespread fears that "social dumping," conveyed via merchandise imports from the Third World, will depress living standards in the United States and Europe.

3.3   Oil and Culture

According to conventional wisdom, oil prices should remain relatively stable in the range of $20 to $35/bbl, in real terms, for the foreseeable future. This, after all, was the story of the 20th century, interrupted by short-lived spikes up and down – spikes up in the 1970s, spikes down in the 1930s and the mid-1990s. OPEC pricing power is said to be waning, with new fields coming on stream in Russia and Central Asia, better technology to extract petroleum from tar sands in northern Canada, Colombia, and Venezuela, and large deep-sea gas reservoirs waiting to be discovered.

While I am optimistic about petroleum and gas technology, I am pessimistic about culture in North Africa, the Middle East, and Central Asia. In a benign world, nations in these regions would gradually transform themselves into secular democracies. In a benign world these nations would steadily export oil to finance their own development.

Malign is a better guess than benign. Regimes in these regions have a knack for combining kleptocracy with theocracy and autocracy. They have increasingly added anti-Western xenophobia to this mix. In economic terms, petroleum breeds kleptocracy. The ratio of rent to output is very high, and the higher this ratio the more easily those in power can dedicate national wealth to personal goals – whether those goals are sumptuous pleasure or weapons of mass destruction. Why should those in power – either as theocrats or autocrats – hasten their own demise by welcoming democracy? Instead, why not embrace radical Muslim hatred of Western culture as a device for maintaining power in the midst of economic privation? Such calculations are increasingly common – reinforced by the Israel–Palestine conflict.

The danger, of course, is that radical theology will successfully insist that the oil weapon be deployed against the West – not just for a few years, but for a decade. Bargains may be struck with China, Japan, and other sympathetic countries to create a two-tier oil market – cheap oil for friends, costly oil for enemies – in a half-successful attempt to defy the logic of fungible commodities and integrated markets. The possibilities in this scenario for sowing discord between the global powers are substantial.

3.4   Financial Crises

Financial crises exacted a toll on developing nations that added up to about $400 billion in the 1990s, averaging about 0.7 percent of GDP annually for developing countries as a group (see Dobson and Hufbauer 2001: Table 1.11). The cost was highly concentrated on a few countries. East Asia, Russia, Brazil, and Argentina were big losers. When the Nasdaq bubble burst, unhappy investors quickly lost more than $2 trillion. The brewing Japanese banking crisis will cost $1 trillion to clean up.

Talk of a "new financial architecture" has been mostly that – talk.[16] There is only limited evidence of new attitudes on the part of financial markets and their regulators. Some progress has been made on transparency, standstills, and collective action clauses. Numerous "clubs" have been formed, bringing together financial regulators and practitioners, and many of them have adopted "best practice" codes. So far, this effort has had little impact on practices that corrode financial markets. In developing countries, too many banks have unscrupulous connections with their corporate borrowers. Nor is the problem confined to emerging markets: as the Enron scandal revealed, many U.S. corporations had unsavory dealings with their accountants and investment bankers.

Banks and corporations everywhere have become adept at hiding losses. Financial architecture efforts have yet made little difference to surveillance or enforcement – not in emerging markets, not in the OECD. Financial regulators still do not collect real time information on the top financial players – banks, insurance companies, portfolio investors, and nonfinancial corporations. Consequently financial regulators are in no position to sound a precautionary warning when the collapse of Argentina or Enron looms in the mist.

Since the world economy has acquired no lasting immunity to the viruses that bred financial crises in the 1980s and 1990s, there is every reason to anticipate that they will continue to erupt. Sophisticated capital markets are inseparable from economic progress. As currently regulated, they are also inseparable from recurring crises.

3.5   Trade and Investment

Trade and investment seem sure bets for the short list, for three reasons. First, while trade and investment growth have outpaced and indeed powered GDP growth for the past half century, the scope for further trade and investment growth remains very large. Interregional commerce within major nations, such as the United States and Germany, exceeds international commerce by a factor of at least five, after allowing for distance and income. If international commerce grows to cover half the gap, trade will more than double (relative to GDP) in the next three decades.

The second reason is that barriers are responsible for at least part of the gap between interregional and international commerce. Merchandise trade barriers are generally straightforward: tariffs, quotas, discriminatory standards, and restrictive procurement regulations. The most important investment regulations are those

---

[16]   For an incisive review, see Posen (2002).

that limit foreign competition in service markets, ranging from transportation to insurance. The CGE model constructed by Brown et al. (2001) suggests that complete liberalization of identified barriers would increase world trade by about 20 percent, and it would probably boost world direct investment at least as much.

The third reason is econometric evidence showing that denser trade and investment relations between countries can help close the astounding gaps in income per capita that characterize the world economy. Bilateral and multilateral assistance, if it makes any difference at all, pales by comparison as a vehicle for narrowing income gaps. Many developing countries – importantly including China, India, Eastern Europe, and most of Latin America – have grasped this essential proposition. So has Oxfam (2002). In coming decades, they will push for greater liberalization.

As explicit barriers are dismantled, and as transportation and communication costs fall, business firms search for new ways to preserve their market domains. Evenett et al. (2001) argue, for example, that market integration fosters collusion, citing the 1990s boom in horizontal cartels. It was no accident that, as trade and investment boomed in the 1990s, mergers and acquisitions also took off. The steady rise in antidumping actions is widely known, and trade experts appreciate that, as tariffs and quotas fall, antidumping remedies have become the safeguard of choice. To summarize, the underlying forces that drove cartels, mergers, and antidumping actions in the 1990s look like persisting, ensuring a place for competition policy alongside traditional trade and investment questions.

3.6   Not on the Short List

Important issues are not on my short list, and a word of explanation is in order for three worthy contenders.

Immigration. The world economy is within sight of achieving the free movement of goods and capital. The free movement of services is more distant, but the real laggard is the free movement of people.[17] Industrial countries will strain their pension and health care systems as they grow older. Demographic aging thus reinforces the basic argument for allowing more immigrants to enter the rich OECD nations.[18]

---

[17]   Immigration politics are centered on people moving to the rich OECD nations from poorer places. However, Indians and Pakistanis have long sought employment in the Middle East, Thai immigrants are numerous in Malaysia, and millions of Africans migrate across their national borders each year.

[18]   It is widely known that, in demographic terms, many European countries are beginning to look like Florida. Not so widely known is that life expectancy is regularly increasing at 2 to 3 months per year in the healthiest OECD countries, with no evidence of reaching an upper limit. What this means is that health burdens will be much larger than currently assumed in official financial projections. See Peterson (1999) and Oeppen and Vaupel (2002).

Years ago, Goldberg and Kindleberger (1970) advocated a "GATT for Investment."[19] The closest the world got was an ill-starred effort to create a Multilateral Agreement on Investment (see Graham 2000). Is a "GATT for Immigration" more likely? The short answer has to be "no:" It is not just the political following of Patrick Buchanan in the United States, Jean-Marie Le Pen in France, Joerg Haider in Austria, Pim Fortuyn in the Netherlands, and John Howard in Australia. More fundamentally, nations regard domestic control of immigration questions as a quintessential dimension of sovereignty, on par with national security and taxation. To no significant extent will they consign this topic to an international institution. For immigration, my forecast is immense international concern and quite limited international cooperation.

Unlike national security, where survival compels countries to form alliances with friends and to negotiate with enemies, no overriding rationale requires international agreement on the terms and quantity of immigration.[20] Does the handbook of *realeconomik* leave no room for international cooperation? That would be too pessimistic. What can be done is to create an international center for realistic studies of the costs and benefits of migration. But an international study center, however distinguished, does not put an issue on the short list of international governance questions.[21]

Disease. If a disease as deadly as Ebola *and* as communicable as influenza erupted from nature or the laboratory, the awful combination would reenact the devastation visited on Europe by the Black Death. An event of that magnitude would dominate politics and economics throughout the 21st century. According to current estimates, HIV will kill 70 million people by the year 2020. But HIV is not nearly so contagious as influenza, and the victims are not evenly spread over rich and poor countries. In other words, for all its horrors, HIV is not a modern version of bubonic plague. Right now, a smallpox epidemic triggered by terrorists seems the most likely plague – and the public health and intelligence services appear to be devising plans that would curtail an outbreak to a single urban area. My forecast for the next three decades allows ample room for *local* deadly dis-

---

[19] In their landmark study, Bergsten et al. (1978) advocated the same idea.

[20] At most, bilateral agreements may be negotiated, addressing the rough edges of immigration between close partners, such as Mexico and the United States, or Turkey and the European Union, just as bilateral tax treaties smooth out the problems of overlapping tax jurisdiction.

[21] To make a useful impact, the center must be politically incorrect. Unlike World Bank studies of development assistance – which for years glossed over acute problems of corruption and governance – the international migration center must honestly address hard questions. How much social welfare do different categories of immigrants absorb? How much tax do they pay? What is their crime rate?

ease,[22] especially among poor countries, but it does not contemplate *global* deadly disease.

Exchange rates. Since the Second World War, exchange rates have been a staple of global economic governance. The International Monetary Fund was founded on exchange rate issues, and some of the most prominent economists of the 20th century built their careers on analyzing and advocating exchange rate regimes. Yet exchange rates are not on my short list of top issues for the next thirty years. Why not? Only once, in its long history, has the Fund criticized a member country for manipulating its exchange rate to achieve a trade advantage. Far more often, the Fund has insisted that member countries devalue (or float) to help resolve their balance of payments crises.

That observation brings me to the primary reason for relegating exchange rates to the second tier of governance issues: the financial crisis agenda will, in my opinion, subsume exchange rate problems. Balance of payments crises were a 20th century phenomenon; financial crises are the 21st century analogue. Financial crises will more often originate from misdeeds by financial institutions and from bloated public deficits than from misaligned exchange rates. Argentina will be seen as the exception, Indonesia as the rule. International financial crises will come to be viewed as parallel to the New York City crisis of the 1970s and the Japanese banking crisis of the 1990s. Even Argentina's recent collapse owed more to its fiscal posture and reckless operation of a *faux* currency board than to the dollar peg.

4   Global Economic Governance

If top issues have been correctly identified – a big "if" – then speculation as to which institutions will prove central to global economic governance becomes more manageable. The term "institution" conjures up a centralized body, akin to the European Commission, with considerable authority over member governments. This is not what I have in mind. In my forecast, the global powers – the European Union, China, and the United States, possibly joined by Japan, Russia, and India – will call the shots. Global economic governance will resemble the U.N. Security Council, where each permanent member retains a veto. In practice, the International Monetary Fund, the World Bank, and the World Trade Organization are similarly governed today. This will remain true for key global economic institutions thirty years hence. When global institutions speak, they will be voic-

---

[22]   For an example of a local disease, poliomyelitis, see Nathanson and Fine (2002).

ing the sentiments of their six principal masters. When the masters disagree, the institutions will be silent.

4.1   A Greenhouse Club?

It would be truly surprising if anything like the Kyoto Convention became an operational component of global governance. The huge costs of meeting Kyoto targets, the imbalance between obligations contemplated for the United States and China (to take extreme cases), and the formulistic approach were all fatal flaws. Equally improbable is a global system of tradable emission rights – beloved by economists, but distrusted by nearly everyone else.[23]

More likely than the Kyoto or tradable rights approach is a "greenhouse club" convened by the great powers – an idea promoted by Schelling (2002). Following the pattern of burden sharing arrangements within NATO, the global powers will invoke peer pressure to elicit mutual pledges. They will persuade smaller countries to cooperate, using economic sanctions as needed.[24] Such informality may seem inadequate to the dangers posed by global warming. But in my forecast, as the political balance shifts towards a fixation on high costs rather than low probabilities, domestic constituencies and the media will insist, and the global powers will act in closer concert. The concession I see to more formal institutional cooperation is an international organization with a substantial research budget, a mandate to monitor all aspects of greenhouse warming, and a mission to report on "bad actors."

Measures taken in the next thirty years may lower the rate of greenhouse gas accumulation, but they will not reverse the upward trajectory. The "greenhouse club" will thus need to assist countries (especially small countries, like the Maldives) that are severe losers from global warming. Since resources will be limited, available funds will be targeted on the most desperate nations – those beset by flood, drought, and hurricanes.

4.2   A New World Bank?

Poverty will get attention – the question is how much and in what form. NGOs and rock stars will be hard at work. Sooner rather than later, as Florini (2003) has predicted, these new forces will call the tune for official development assistance.

---

[23]   The success of power producers at gaming California's wholesale electric market indicates that distrust is not entirely misplaced. See *Wall Street Journal*, 13 May 2002: A1.

[24]   This is a very large-scale version of the political model used by big powers to induce cooperation from small states in the fight against money laundering.

Accordingly a much larger share of World Bank activity will be directly targeted on the very poor – for example, ensuring water, sewage, and basic roads.[25] The pleasant fiction that the World Bank can bring economic growth to misgoverned countries will be quietly shelved for more visible "made-for-media" attention on the wretched of the earth.[26] When added up, this attention might eventually reach $50 per person per year for the nearly 3 billion people who survive on less than $2 a day. Even spent in the most productive way, $50 per person per year would probably not deliver much economic growth.[27] But it could alleviate a good deal of grinding poverty.

NGOs, media stars, and the World Bank will also be hard at work on disease – especially since poverty and disease are twins in most countries.[28] Health expenditures of $10 per person per year in the poorest countries could make an enormous difference in combating many debilitating diseases, even if it will not do much for HIV.

4.3   A Revitalized IEA?

A possible response to oil-and-culture shocks is to revitalize the International Energy Association, the organization created in the 1970s in response to the first oil shock. The twin ideas in that era were to distribute energy supplies so that oil-importing nations shared the pain, and to promote energy efficiency throughout the OECD. The IEA partly succeeded, because the "seven sisters" dominated oil distribution, because the United States, Europe, and Japan were tightly linked in their military alliance, and because OECD nations could roughly agree on the goal of energy efficiency. Background circumstances have since changed: not only have new players crowded into world oil distribution and consumption, but also the military alliance is far less cohesive. Major energy consumers in Asia –

---

[25]   The focus on direct poverty reduction will probably spread to the regional development banks. See, for example, pledges by the Asian Development Bank, as reported in the *Financial Times*, 13 May 2002: 3.

[26]   See Easterly (2002). For a cautious assessment of the links between poverty and globalization, see Bardhan (2003).

[27]   Poor countries are already coming to realize that economic growth is delivered not by aid, but by functioning economic incentives. In terms of external economic contacts, international trade and investment deliver growth far more reliably than aid.

[28]   See, for example, the description of the Global Fund to Fight AIDS, Tuberculosis and Malaria, *Science*, 3 May 2002: 841. Likewise, in May 2002, the World Bank pledged $42 million to help Zambia fight AIDS. *World Bank Press Review*, 7 May 2002. These are harbingers of future trends.

notably China and India – are neither part of the alliance nor do they see energy efficiency in the same light as OECD nations.

In the wake of future oil-and-culture shocks, my forecast calls for a fragmented response. Put starkly, Japan, China, and India will bend their diplomacy to ensure continued oil supplies from major suppliers in the Middle East and Central Asia. The European Union will look to Russia and secular Middle Eastern states, such as Libya and Iraq. The United States will seek energy security foremost in the Western Hemisphere, even at high exploration and pumping costs. Beyond that, the United States may extend security protection to Islamic states that fight the cultural tide – potentially small oil-rich countries such as Kuwait, Bahrain, the UAE, Brunei, and breakaway parts of Indonesia (Aceh).

Oil-and-culture shocks will be so divisive in both political and economic terms that global economic institutions, such as the IEA, can at best paper over the differences between great powers. The proper measure of achievement will not be unified response to the Islamic states, but sufficient respect between the great powers that differing oil policies do not erupt into major security conflicts.

4.4   New Life for the IMF and BIS?

Depending on the diagnosis, financial crisis is either a systemic feature of capitalism or an outgrowth of failed regulation. Optimistically, I favor the second explanation, with a small twist. The financial markets continuously innovate, some of the innovations create fragile structures, and some of those structures eventually collapse: Pyramid corporate structures in the 1930s; S&L deposit guarantees in the 1980s; mismatched assets and liabilities in the 1990s; off-balance sheet debt in the 2000s. Until regulators embrace a philosophy of proactive rules, financial crises will recur in tandem with financial innovation.[29]

The International Monetary Fund and the Bank for International Settlements are positioned to fill the role of proactive regulators overseeing portfolio capital flows to emerging markets. Their oversight role critically depends on the concurrence of Washington and Brussels, specifically on the concurrence of the Federal Reserve and the European Central Bank. In my forecast, the United States, the European Union, and powerful central bankers will agree that the IMF and the

---

[29]   Judging from the assessment offered by Eichengreen (2003), it will take several more crises before regulators would voluntarily shoulder their responsibility for proactive measures. Instead, they would rather fall back on the time-worn defense that the next crisis is impossible to predict. If President Lincoln had accepted this sort of excuse, he would have allowed General McClellan to lead the Union to defeat in the Civil War. At some point in the next decade, "Lincoln-style" leadership from the United States and Europe will, I think, force financial regulators to do a better job of anticipating and preventing financial crises.

BIS can help in averting financial crises, and demand a proactive stance from reluctant regulators.

There are strong reasons for vastly expanding capital flows to poor countries. OECD demographics point to less demand for housing and infrastructure in rich countries. If aging OECD populations save responsibly, they will save more; and their pension and mutual funds, searching for higher returns, will push capital to younger but poorer countries. The scope is enormous for mortgage-backed securities and infrastructure investment in developing nations. Additionally, well-run corporations based in emerging markets will issue debt and equity securities, and many of those securities will find their way to OECD portfolio investors. Virtuous capital flows of the kind described require proactive regulation on both the demand and supply side of world capital markets. The IMF is positioned to foster demand-side regulation; the BIS is structured to provide for supply-side oversight.

On the *demand side*, the IMF will assist and certify financial rectitude in emerging countries. As world financial challenges have evolved, the Fund has made an art form of rewriting its mission statement, so it seems likely that the Fund can (with prodding) rise to its newest challenge. First Deputy Managing Director Anne Krueger has already proposed a Fund role in international bankruptcy proceedings, a controversial role at the "back end" of financial crises (see Miller 2002). To get on the "front end" of the financial crisis curve, the Fund will need to publicly expose weak oversight practices in emerging countries – practices that abet excessive leverage, undercapitalized institutions, connected lending, misleading accounting, mismatched assets and liabilities (currency or maturity), undue debtor rights, and other financial diseases.

Looking at the historical record, there is less reason to predict that the BIS will oversee the supply side of world capital markets. Under BIS auspices, two Basel capital accords have been negotiated, but both are timid and backward looking. To cite a few shortcomings: the accords do not establish real-time reporting between banks and G-10 regulators; they do not require large G-10 banks to monitor their financial counter-parties; they do nothing to improve disclosure by nonbank portfolio investors; they make no attempt at creating an early warning system (see Dobson and Hufbauer 2001). But when future financial crises drag down major G-10 banks, mutual funds, and pension funds, as I expect will happen under current relaxed oversight practices, the call for anticipatory regulation will escalate.

The impact of emerging country crises on financial regulators will resemble the impact of Arthur Andersen on the U.S. Securities and Exchange Commission. In the case of the SEC, the Arthur Andersen debacle, and associated corporate failures, has altered the regulatory mission statement from a search for "lone-wolf" offenders (insider trades and the like) to a systemic emphasis on the corrupted U.S. accounting industry. When a big enough crisis occurs, the IMF and the BIS will lift their gaze from individual country problems and capital adequacy standards to systemic reform of financial oversight.

Stiglitz (2002) hungers for a world monetary system in which SDRs would be issued more freely to developing countries. Poor nations would then have less need to run current account surpluses as a means of building precautionary foreign exchange reserves. The chances of something like this happening are, in my view, close to zero. The Federal Reserve and the European Central Bank are not about to share their powers to create money; and the U.S. Congress and European parliaments would fiercely resist a monetary end-run around their legislative prerogatives.

Instead of a world currency issued under the auspices of the Fund, my forecast contemplates wide adoption of the euro or the dollar, not merely for reserves, but as the domestic currency in many countries. The scenario of wider dollar and euro zones will gradually emerge as countries affiliate their trade and investment regimes with NAFTA and the European Union. Currency choices will be decided nationally, but future trade agreements between rich and poor countries will contain a chapter on financial regulation. In effect, EU trading partners will come under the prudential guidance of the European Central Bank, while U.S. trading partners will come under the guidance of the Federal Reserve (see Posen 2002).

If the euro and dollar acquire wide usage, then thirty years from now today's debates over currency boards, target zones, and floating rates will seem as quaint as the 19th century debates over "free silver" and the "cross of gold." Small and middle-sized countries outside the euro and dollar zones will make their sovereign decisions whether to fix, to manage, or to float – but no one else will much care.

Outside the dollar and euro zones, the remaining currency question of global significance is whether China or Japan forms the core of a third currency bloc. The Chiang Mai Initiative marks the beginning of the "third bloc," and my forecast is that it will be anchored on China (see Henning 2002). Whether grouped into two currency blocs or three, the pulse of the world economy will beat to the monetary decisions of the dominant central banks. As now, a G-2 or a G-3 will deliberate on world economic conditions, but with an important difference. Central bankers will occupy the main seats, and finance ministers will take the back row.

4.5   Super-RTAs Ascendant?

The most effective international policy for stimulating economic growth in emerging countries is free trade and investment. As this lesson has become conventional wisdom, many countries are trying to join two central poles: the United States and the European Union. The limiting factor is not the willingness of poor nations to join, but rather the willingness of rich nations to open the club doors. Political elites in Europe and the United States now face strident resistance to the agenda of free trade. Optimistically, I forecast that the elites will prevail – partly because of economic arguments (new markets, new places to invest), but more because of security arguments (drugs, crime, terrorism).

While terrorist attacks are sure to provoke tighter border security, they will not reverse the progressive integration of markets. My argument is that intrusive security measures will be built into production and assembly plants, before goods are sealed in high-tech, tamper-proof shipping containers. This will entail costs, perhaps equivalent to a 5 percent *ad valorem* tariff. In the face of higher security costs, investment rather than trade will play a larger role in integrating markets. But security costs, in my view, will slow rather than arrest the progressive rise in the ratio between merchandise imports and world GDP.

Within this context, some of the political geography of super regional trade arrangements (RTAs) seems clear: a Western Hemisphere group anchored on the United States, with branches elsewhere; and a Eurasian/North African group anchored on the European Union, again with branches elsewhere. The economic geography of Asia is less clear: a single super-RTA anchored on China, or two super-RTAs, with the second anchored on a Japan-India core (driven by shared fears of China)? My guess is two super-RTAs, rather than one.

Within the super-RTAs, tiers are inevitable – both because the newer members will not instantly meet all the club conditions, and because the richer members will not accept total integration with the newer members. Some recent illustrations may be cited. Farmers in new applicants to the European Union (Poland, Czech Republic, Hungary, etc.) are slated to receive sharply lower "blue box" agricultural support payments than farmers in existing member states. Meanwhile, the United States has taken agricultural liberalization off the table in FTAA talks, even though free agricultural trade between the United States and Mexico was an essential chapter of NAFTA. Free migration is not part of EU free trade agreements with Turkey and North Africa; nor is it part of NAFTA. Neither free agricultural trade nor free migration seems a plausible component of super-RTAs in Asia. Moreover, fiscal transfers will remain small. The EU budget, now capped at 1.27 percent of GDP, might conceivably triple to 4 percent of GDP, but fiscal transfers within the Western Hemisphere or Asia will not likely reach 1 percent of GDP. For poorer members of super-RTAs, the economic benefits will almost entirely take the form of enhanced trade and investment opportunities, not fiscal transfers.

In the super-RTA scenario, what is left for the World Trade Organization (WTO)? As Ostry (2003) has argued at this conference, the WTO suffers from its own success. "Mission creep" is the problem: various constituencies demand that the WTO address labor, environment, and development issues – all well beyond its core competence. In time, wiser heads will prevail, and the WTO will again focus on what it does best – stabilizing and liberalizing the world trading system. Two agenda items will be paramount: first, mediating trade and investment relations between the super-RTAs, and, second, providing a club for nonmembers. The second mission will shrink as more countries adhere to the super-RTAs, just as EFTA withered as the EU prospered. But the first mission will grow in importance.

5   What Would I Change?

To summarize my central forecast: even in a security scenario of recurring terrorist attacks, global economic cooperation does not wither. The world economy does not retreat to walled cities. Globalization marches forward. But economic governance is conducted by shifting clubs rather than permanent organizations. To a considerable extent, economic cooperation is shaped by security concerns. For those who lived through the Cold War, this might seem like *déjà vu* all over again – but without the hard frontiers that separated capitalist and communist camps.

My forecast for global governance is far removed from the universal institutions envisaged (but never attained) by the Holy Roman Empire, *Pax Britannica*, the League of Nations, or the United Nations. Instead I foresee quasi-cooperative governance through loose arrangements between the global powers. I envisage a great power club to cope with global warming, polite respect to deal with oil politics, World Bank attention on poverty and disease, while the IMF, BIS, super-RTAs, and the WTO continue to address finance, trade, and investment questions.

For many people – those who live within the borders of the great and near-great global powers, and those who live in countries that associate with the global powers through currency clubs and super-RTAs – this portrait of global economic governance conveys several essentials of the good life: no world wars, no deadly epidemics, and growing economies. Even for those lucky people, recurring terrorist attacks mar the picture, killing thousands of civilians at a time. For those living outside the charmed borders, however, life will often be far more brutal – corrupt governments, vicious wars, persistent disease, hazards to person and property, meager economic growth.

With a magic brush, I would brighten the portrait of global governance in many ways. But let me concentrate on the feature that bothers me most. My forecast leaves too much room for small and mid-sized criminal states – those that make life especially miserable for people living outside the charmed circle. By criminal states, I mean countries that harbor some combination of genocide, terrorism, weapons of mass destruction, kleptocracy, and grinding poverty. To be specific, a list of criminal states in recent years would include Afghanistan, Burma, Congo, Haiti, Kenya, Libya, North Korea, Palestine, Rwanda, Somalia, Sudan, and Zimbabwe. While state sponsorship of terrorism is waning (Harris 2002), the other attributes of criminal states are in full flower.

For these states – not all at once, but one at a time – I would urge the great powers to revive the concept of "trusteeship," with these elements:

- Criminal states would become trustees of the United Nations, upon the concurrent determination of the great powers. Soldiers and civilians would be disarmed; culpable leaders would be exiled. Normally the trusteeship would last for five years, with a possible extension to ten years.
- Trustee states would be governed by international civil servants, judges, and police. Preferably these officials would be drawn from Asia, Latin America, and Africa. Along with governing the country, the foreign officials would be responsible for training a corps of successors drawn from the local population.
- During its trustee period, the trustee state would receive substantial aid to help fund normal government operations, and to alleviate poverty and disease. The funds would be administered by the international civil servants.
- To promote growth, the trustee state would be internally organized around the concept of economic incentives. Inward foreign investment would be fully guaranteed, and exports would have free access to the markets of the great powers.

"Trusteeship" is a drastic solution with multiple disadvantages, among them a distasteful flavor of colonialism, an assault on self-governance, and no guarantee of success. Even so, some states so endanger their own citizens and the outside world that, in my view, they compel drastic action. In early 2003, President Bush was toying with this approach for Iraq, but with little support from other great powers. Coordinated U.N. supervision of other criminal states is, at best, a distant prospect.

6   Governance in a Pessimistic World

One truly pessimistic, but not far-fetched, security scenario is Sino–U.S. conflict. The most likely spark is Taiwan.[30] Other potentially severe irritants to U.S.–China relations include the unification of Korea and wars between secondary powers in Indochina. In the very worst case, conflict between the United States and China would culminate in nuclear disaster and occupation. Short of nuclear disaster, Sino–U.S. conflict would set the stage for a new Cold War, permeating all international relations. Japan and India would ally themselves with the United States, but what about Russia and Europe?

Sino–U.S. conflict, whether hot war or cold war, would alter the map of global economic governance. World War III, like its predecessors, would be so destructive that it would spawn a new international order – replete with political and economic institutions designed to banish World War IV to the realm of science fiction. Fortunately, World War III is a very low-probability event. More likely is Cold War II, and this too would have enormous consequences.

Chinese leaders have proven their talent at adapting capitalism to Chinese society and, in the process, creating a powerful growth machine. In a run-up to Cold War II – if that's what Chinese leaders plan – they will not abandon a highly successful economic formula. But they may add some twists to strengthen their security position.

One twist would be aggressive Chinese liberalization to jump-start a super-RTA, centered on China, embracing all of Southeast and East Asia (except Japan), and possibly Russia. A second twist would be Chinese sponsorship of an Asian Monetary Fund (distinct from the IMF) and an Asian Development Fund (distinct from the Asian Development Bank). A third twist would be a Chinese decision to move substantial reserves out of dollars and into euros. In an extreme form, China might link the yuan to gold, thereby declaring "monetary independence." In response to such Chinese initiatives, the United States, Japan, and India would find common cause in closer economic cooperation. Europe and Russia, however, are question mark powers in a Cold War II scenario.

To summarize, Cold War II would spawn parallel institutions in the two camps, with similar purposes but different governing coalitions, to cope with classic trade, investment and finance issues. Despite the Cold War frontier, these institutions might well cooperate in areas of mutual advantage – and there are many such areas within the domain of classic economics. But cooperation on global warming and other issues that require mutual sacrifice would be exceedingly difficult.

---

[30] Chinese leaders, whatever their age, see unification with Taiwan as a paramount national goal. China's military force will soon be strong enough to conquer Taiwan – unless the United States resolutely defends the island. No U.S. political leader can acquiesce in Chinese military conquest and hope to stay in office. Here we have the makings of a great power conflict.

Bibliography

Bardhan, P. (2003). International Economic Integration and the Poor. This volume.

Bauer, P.T. (1972). *Dissent on Development: Studies and Debates in Development Economics.* Cambridge, Mass.: Harvard University Press.

Bergsten, C.F., T. Horst, and T.H. Moran (1978). *American Multinationals and American Interests.* Washington D.C.: Brookings Institution.

Brown, D.K., A.V. Deardorff, and R.M. Stern (2001). CGE Modeling and Analysis of Multilateral and Regional Negotiating Options. Discussion Paper 468. Research Seminar in International Economics, University of Michigan.

Dobson, W., and G.C. Hufbauer (2001). *World Capital Markets: Challenge to the G-10.* Washington D.C.: Institute for International Economics.

Doran, M. (2002). Somebody Else's Civil War. *Foreign Affairs* 81(1): 22–42.

Easterly, W. (2002). The *Elusive Quest for Economic Growth: Economists' Adventures and Misadventures in the Tropics.* Cambridge, Mass.: MIT Press.

Eichengreen, B. (2003). Predicting and Preventing Financial Crises: Where Do We Stand? What Have We Learned? This volume.

Evenett, S.J., M.C. Levenstein, and V.Y. Suslow (2001). International Cartel Enforcement: Lessons from the 1990s. *The World Economy* 24 (9): 1221–1245.

Florini, A.M. (2003). From Protest to Participation: The Role of Civil Society in Global Governance. This volume.

Goldberg, P.M., and C.P. Kindleberger (1970). Toward a GATT for Investment: A Proposal for Supervision of the International Corporation. *Law and Policy in International Business* 2 (Summer): 295–325.

Graham, E.M. (2000). *Fighting the Wrong Enemy: Antiglobal Activists and Multinational Enterprises.* Washington D.C.: Institute for International Economics.

Harris, J.W. (2002). Building Leverage in the Long War: Ensuring Intelligence Community Creativity in the Fight Against Terrorism. Cato Policy Analysis 439. Washington, D.C.

Henning, C.R. (2002). East Asian Financial Cooperation after the Chiang Mai Initiative. Working draft. Institute for International Economics, Washington, D.C.

Miller, M. (2002). Sovereign Debt Restructuring: New Articles, New Contracts – Or No Change? Policy Brief Number PB02-03. Institute for International Economics, Washington, D.C.

Nathanson, N., and P. Fine (2002). Poliomyelitis Eradication – A Dangerous Endgame. *Science,* 12 April 2002: 269–270.

Nye, J. (2002). *The Paradox of American Power: Why the World's Only Superpower Can't Go It Alone.* London: Oxford University Press.

Oeppen, J., and J.W. Vaupel (2002). Broken Limits to Life Expectancy. *Science,* 10 May 2002: 1029–1031.

Ostry, S. (2003). What Are the Necessary Ingredients for the World Trading Order? This volume.

Oxfam International (2002). *Rigged Rules and Double Standards: Trade, Globalisation, and the Fight Against Poverty.* Oxford: Oxfam GB.

Patten, C. (2002). Jaw-jaw, not war-war. *Financial Times,* 15 February 2002: 12.

Peterson, P.G. (1999). *Gray Dawn: How the Coming Age Wave Will Transform America – And the World.* New York: Times Books.

Posen, A.S. (2002). U.S. and E.U. Views on Financial Architecture: From the Lesson of Deep Integration to a Neighborhood Watch? Paper presented at the Conference, sponsored by the Center for Business and Government, Harvard University, *et alia,* on "Transatlantic Perspectives on US-EU Economic Relations." 11–12 April 2002, Cambridge, Mass.

Rostow, W.W. (1960). *The Stages of Economic Growth: A Non-Communist Manifesto.* Cambridge: Cambridge University Press.

Schelling, T. (2002). What Makes Greenhouse Sense: Time to Rethink the Kyoto Protocol. *Foreign Affairs* 81(3): 2–9.

Shogren, J.F., and S. Kroll (2003). Globalization & Climate Protection: Some Microeconomic Foundations for Integration. This volume.

Soros, G. (2002). *George Soros on Globalization.* New York: Public Affairs.

Stiglitz, J.E. (2002). A Fair Deal for the World. *New York Review of Books,* 23 May 2002.

Comment on Gary C. Hufbauer

Robert Z. Lawrence

Gary Hufbauer has given us a splendid and imaginative paper. It provides us with a very interesting historical perspective, a basic forecast of the most important challenges for international governance in the future and some brief prescriptions. In my comments I will first summarize what I see as the paper's main points and then offer some reflections.

By looking back thirty years, Gary teaches us to be humble about our ability to predict accurately. As the immortal baseball manager Yogi Berra remarked, "the future is not what it used to be." And what seems to be a powerful trend often turns out to be part of a cycle. This is a useful starting point for any discussion of this nature.

Gary contrasts the harmony and relatively uncontroversial position of international institutions during much of the postwar period with the controversy and turmoil they have faced over the past decade. He perceptively ascribes an important role to the security situation. The cold war context was important in facilitating this harmony in international economic organizations, despite strong disagreements over the right economic model. It encouraged moderation. The United States, in particular, could not press as hard for conformity to capitalist norms as it might have wanted to because of its competition with the Soviet Union. Gary might have added, that in the United States, those on the right who were prone to isolationism were forced to take an interest in international relations. Meanwhile, capitalist developed countries had strong security incentives to cooperate with the United States. The paradoxical result was that despite the differences over economics, international organizations actually could do their work in relative harmony, since the security situation served to keep the lid on economic conflicts.

The end of the cold war, by contrast, has brought about a consensus over the right economic model. Yet it has been associated with international turmoil: (a) a protracted Uruguay Round, (b) a World Bank that "lost its way," (c) an IMF unpopular and unsuccessful in dealing with international financial crises, and (d) G7 meetings that are photo opportunities (and protest opportunities). He might have added the eruption of trade conflicts between the United States and the European Union.

Gary then turns to the future. Overall he predicts that global governace will be centered on and dominated by a few powerful nation states, with international organizations playing minor roles. He argues there are five big international issues on the short list: climate change, poverty, oil and "culture"(Islam), financial crisis, trade and investment. He is overwhelmingly skeptical about the potential role that the leading global institutions can play to deal with the issues. On global warming, he discounts Kyoto and foresees a greenhouse club of large countries that take minor steps and mainly bale out island economies like the Maldives that are most seriously affected. On poverty, he sees the World Bank in dispensing aid that is unlikely to be very effective in alleviating poverty. On oil and culture, the International Energy Agency will simply paper over the cracks. On financial crisis, the IMF and BIS will help regulate financial markets but inevitably remain behind the curve of financial innovation. And finally, on trade, he foresees the emergence of major super-regional trading blocs with the WTO's role reduced primarily to settling disputes between them and helping countries outside these arrangements. He also sees little chance of much liberalization on freer immigration, no massive efforts on disease, and dollarization and euroization render the need for exchange rate coordination moot.

In the rest of this comment I would like to deal with two important elements I feel are underplayed in the paper. First, the broad nature of international governance and, second, the fundamental reason for the problems facing official international organizations.

Broad Nature of International Governance

In his forecast, Gary implicitly presents us with a rather narrow conception of international governance. He concentrates on nation states and official organizations. I believe that today, global governance has a far broader reality. Gary compares the security regime over the next thirty years to the system after the Congress of Vienna. But a crucial development he mentions, but does not really incorporate, is the development of international networks of international civil and uncivil society. (NGOs, multinational firms, criminal and terrorist organizations.) These organizations all create systems of governance outside the purview of national governments. International governance at its most basic entails providing international public goods. These can involve the determination and enforcement of rules and the provision of public goods and services. To be sure, many issues still require governments and governmental procedures but many others can be decided and provided outside government, and I expect this trend to continue to increase dramatically (examples include international standards-setting bodies, international charitable organizations, and international arbitrators). There is also a vital, softer element that involves the media and international public opinion, because governance is as much about establishing norms and molding opinions as about enacting rules.

Problems Facing International Organizations

I would like now to build on Gary's comments about the origins of the governance problems facing international organizations. What lies behind the recent conflicts over international institutions? I think the lack of "security glue" is only part of the story. What else? Effective government organizations must do three things. They must be given the right missions, they must be given the means to carry out these missions, and they must be perceived as legitimate. In the 1990s, the institutions' problems are related to inadequacies on each of these elements.

First, mission. I think Gary is onto something. The inward- looking orientation of many developing countries in the early period paradoxically freed the World Bank and IMF from responsibilities for their development. Countries were more isolated from each other and from international capital markets, so their crises tended to be localized. Their overall policy stances were often determined independently of World Bank and IMF advice and thus these institutions were not held responsible for their performance.

Once developing countries actually implemented outward-oriented policies advocated by these institutions, they became more dependent on and exposed to global markets and the institutions. The large number of countries that have joined or are seeking to join the WTO, for example, is indicative of the centrality of the organization to their strategies.

This has meant much larger missions for these institutions. The IMF was asked to manage major global financial crises and the transition to capitalism rather than simply provide global liquidity and supervise exchange rates, the World Bank to supply good governance, to help attract foreign investors, and promote exports, rather than good roads and dams, the WTO to achieve a trading system that ensures sustainable development rather than reduce border barriers.

I would also point to the much more powerful drivers coming from the complex nature of globalization itself that Hufbauer seems to downplay. These have contributed to expanding missions and placed strains on international governmental institutions that would have been present even if the cold war had continued. These strains reflect functional and political pressures.

As the world economy becomes more integrated, there is a growing functional demand for greater governance. The trading and financial relationships have deepened and there are great benefits from deepening the rules and making enforcement more effective. This is most evident in the area of trade. Not only has the scope of trade agreements expanded to cover rules for intellectual property, services, agriculture, and investment but there are pressures for even more items to be added to the agenda: competition policies, investment, labor standards, and environment. The second driver is political. The most important forces in our societies, business, labor, and environmentalists each find themselves competing with their counterparts in other countries and they all claim to seek level playing fields and to have their issues subject to international rules.

There is "a problem of the commons" associated with international organizations, since their members have huge temptations to free ride. If an international organization can get others to devote resources to a goal, my country may have to spend less. In addition, the Peter principle operates and organizations that are successful are loaded with missions until they are bound to fail. Paradoxically, the more effective an international organization becomes in enforcing rules, the more rules it will be asked to enforce.

Second, means. International organizations are rarely given adequate means to achieve their missions. Thus the IMF is expected to solve financial crises, but it has no prior power to regulate and has inadequate resources to serve as a lender of last resort. The United Nations sends in forces to keep peace, with strict instructions not to fire their weapons. The WTO is responsible for implementing a system based on the rule of law but its findings do not have any direct effect in national laws and it cannot impose sanctions on violators. The World Bank gives countries policy advice, but is often required to provide them loans even when they do not take it.

Third, legitimacy. And here is the rub. Were these institutions actually to be given the means to carry out these missions effectively, they would inevitably be regarded as illegitimate. The missions are so ambitious, that the means required to implement them may require overriding norms of national sovereignty and democracy. If the IMF subjected its members to regulation, if the United Nations forces fired their weapons, if the World Bank strictly enforced conditionality, if the WTO could change domestic regulations, they would be met with accusations of suffering from democratic deficits. As indeed they all do. In addition, even if supported by a majority of domestic citizens, they will often threaten actors with an interest in other policies. As international issues occupy more importance, they disturb domestic political equilibria and this provides those who lose from the policies with a reason to complain about the process by which policy was made. Finally, international organizations serve as lightening rods, often taking the heat. Governments like to take the credit themselves when their countries do well, but in tough times of crises, it is more convenient to blame the international organizations. Over time, however, this erodes their support.

Now there are two simple approaches to providing democratic decision-making. Nation states or global federalism. But acting alone, Westphalian sovereign states cannot increasingly provide us with the international public goods we require to benefit from a global economy. Acting alone they cannot meet the functional or political requirements asked of global governance.

Global federalism would allow us to eliminate the nation state and to have mass democratic politics, combined with an integrated global economy, but it comes at the expense of diversity and identity. Few seem ready for this outcome, although Europe seems furthest on this path.

So if the nation state is inadequate to some tasks, and we do not want global federalism, we need to craft intermediate approaches that reflect compromises. The great challenge for these institutions is to achieve a balance between mission, means, and legitimacy. It requires intermediate approaches in which nation states and international institutions share power.

Success requires understanding the basic vulnerabilities in this system. It requires carefully circumscribing the missions: respecting the principle of subsidiarity and selecting only those missions that are strictly necessary (e.g., genuinely global public goods) and for which the institution has adequate means. It also requires remaining lean and flexible, for example, by using private operators and NGOs to carry out missions when they have an advantage in doing so. Success also requires not overreaching, by operating through consensus and in a transparent and open manner. It is also important, wherever possible to avoid sanctions, penalties, and fines and to build in "opt out" mechanisms and safety valves.

In sum, therefore, in my view the most important item on the agenda for global governance is aligning the mission, means, and legitimacy of international organizations in a world in which international governance has become increasingly complex because the central players are no longer organized neatly within the borders of nation states.

LIST OF CONTRIBUTORS

PRANAB KUMAR BARDHAN
University of California, Economics Department, Berkeley, California, United States

JAGDISH BHAGWATI
Columbia University, School of International & Public Affairs, New York, N.Y., United States

THILO BODE
Former Chief Executive of Greenpeace International, Berlin, Germany

BARRY EICHENGREEN
University of California, Economics Department, Berkeley, California, United States

ANN FLORINI
The Brookings Institution, Governance Studies Program, Washington, D.C., United States

GEOFFREY HEAL
Columbia University, Columbia Business School, New York, N.Y., United States

MEINHARD HILF
Universität Hamburg, Seminar für Öffentliches Recht und Staatslehre, Abteilung Europäisches Gemeinschaftsrecht, Hamburg, Germany

GARY C. HUFBAUER
Institute for International Economics, Washington, D.C., United States

RAINER KLUMP
Universität Frankfurt, Lehrstuhl für wirtschaftliche Entwicklung und Integration, Frankfurt/Main, Germany

STEPHAN KROLL
St. Lawrance University, Canton, N.Y., United States

ROBERT Z. LAWRENCE
Harvard University, John F. Kennedy School of Government, Cambridge, Mass., United States

OLIVER LORZ
Universität zu Kiel, Institut für Volkswirtschaftslehre, Kiel, Germany

LUKAS MENKHOFF
Universität Hannover, Fachbereich Wirtschaftswissenschaften, Hannover, Germany

SYLVIA OSTRY
University of Toronto, Munk Centre for International Studies, Toronto, Canada

HORST RAFF
Universität zu Kiel, Institut für Volkswirtschaftslehre, Kiel, Germany

JASON F. SHOGREN
University of Wyoming, Department of Economics & Finance, Laramie, Wyo., United States

HORST SIEBERT
Institute for World Economics, Kiel, Germany

R. DAVID SIMPSON
Resources for the Future, Energy and Natural Resources Division, Washington, D.C., United States

TIMOTHY SWANSON
University College London, Chair of Law and Economics, London, United Kingdom

KEVIN WATKINS
Oxfam UK, Oxford, United Kingdom

KIELER STUDIEN · KIEL STUDIES

Kiel Institute for World Economics

Editor: *Horst Siebert* · Managing Editor: *Harmen Lehment*

311. **Bildungspolitik für den Standort D,** *Federico Foders*
Berlin · Heidelberg 2001. 125 pp. Hardcover.

312. **Der Euro als Ankerwährung. Die mittel- und osteuropäischen Beitritts-**
länder zwischen Transformation und Integration, *Rainer Schweickert*
Berlin · Heidelberg 2001. 123 pp. Hardcover.

313. **Noise Trading, Central Bank Interventions, and the Informational Con-**
tent of Foreign Currency Options, *Christian Pierdzioch*
Berlin · Heidelberg 2001. 207 pp. Hardcover.

314. **Internationale Diversifikation in den Portfolios deutscher Kapitalan-**
leger. Theorie und Empirie, *Susanne Lapp*
Berlin · Heidelberg 2001. 176 pp. Hardcover.

315. **Subsidization and Structural Change in Eastern Germany,** *Katja*
Gerling
Berlin · Heidelberg 2002. 208 pp. Hardcover.

316. **Complementarities in Corporate Governance,** *Ralph P. Heinrich*
Berlin · Heidelberg 2002. 234 pp. Hardcover.

317. **Globalisierung der Automobilindustrie. Wettbewerbsdruck, Arbeits-**
markteffekte und Anpassungsreaktionen, *Julius Spatz, Peter Nunnenkamp*
Berlin · Heidelberg 2002. 117 pp. Hardcover.

318. **Sozialhilfe, Lohnabstand und Leistungsanreize. Empirische Analyse für**
Haushaltstypen und Branchen in West- und Ostdeutschland, *Alfred Boss*
Berlin · Heidelberg 2002. 201 pp. Hardcover.

319. **Schooling and the Quality of Human Capital,** *Ludger Wößmann*
Berlin · Heidelberg 2002. 228 pp. Hardcover.

320. **Climate Policy in a Globalizing World. A CGE Model with Capital**
Mobility and Trade, *Katrin Springer*
Berlin · Heidelberg 2002. 293 pp. Hardcover.

321. **Die neue Ökonomie: Erscheinungsformen, Ursachen und Auswirkungen,**
Henning Klodt et al.
Berlin · Heidelberg 2003. 248 pp. Hardcover.

More information on publications by the Kiel Institute at http://www. uni-kiel.de/ifw/pub/
pub.htm, more information on the Kiel Institute at http://www.uni-kiel.de/ifw/

Berlin · Heidelberg: Springer-Verlag (http://www.springer.de)

Kieler Diskussionsbeiträge

Kiel Discussion Papers

389./ Fit für die EU? Indikatoren zum Stand der Wirtschaftsreformen in den Kandida-
390. tenländern. Von Federico Foders, Daniel Piazolo und Rainer Schweickert. Kiel, Juni 2002. 69 S. 16 Euro.

391. Fortschritte beim Aufbau Ost. Forschungsbericht wirtschaftswissenschaftlicher Forschungsinstitute über die wirtschaftliche Entwicklung in Ostdeutschland. Kiel, Juni 2002. 53 S. 8 Euro.

392./ Subventionen in Deutschland. Von Alfred Boss und Astrid Rosenschon. Kiel,
393. August 2002. 71 S. 16 Euro.

394. 75 Punkte gegen die Arbeitslosigkeit. Von Horst Siebert. Kiel, August 2002. 23 S. 8 Euro.

395. Vom Mangel zum Überfluss – der ostdeutsche Wohnungsmarkt in der Subventionsfalle. Von Dirk Dohse, Christiane Krieger-Boden, Birgit Sander und Rüdiger Soltwedel. Kiel, September 2002. 52 S. 8 Euro.

396. Euroland: Upswing Postponed. By Kai Carstensen, Klaus-Jürgen Gern, Christophe Kamps and Joachim Scheide. Kiel, Oktober 2002. 19 S. 8 Euro.

397. Central Exams Improve Educational Performance: International Evidence. By Ludger Wößmann. Kiel, Oktober 2002. 45 S. 8 Euro.

398. Makroökonomische Reformen und Armutsbekämpfung in Bolivien: Ebnet die HIPC-Initiative den Weg zu sozialverträglicher Anpassung? Von Rainer Schweickert, Rainer Thiele und Manfred Wiebelt. Kiel, Februar 2003. 41 S. 9 Euro.

399. Higher Economic Growth through Macroeconomic Policy Coordination? The Combination of Wage Policy and Monetary Policy. By Klaus-Jürgen Gern, Carsten-Patrick Meier and Joachim Scheide. Kiel, Februar 2003. 29 S. 9 Euro.

400. Why the Case for a Multilateral Agreement on Investment Is Weak. By Peter Nunnenkamp and Manoj Pant. Kiel, März 2003. 41 S. 9 Euro.

401. Evidence of the New Economy at the Macroeconomic Level and Implications for Monetary Policy. By Klaus-Jürgen Gern, Carsten-Patrick Meier and Joachim Scheide. Kiel, März 2003. 21 S. 9 Euro.

402. Lohnt sich die private Bereitstellung von Infrastruktur? Das Beispiel der Fehmarnbelt-Querung. Von Henning Sichelschmidt. Kiel, April 2003. 29 S. 9 Euro.

403. Euroland: Recovery Will Slowly Gain Momentum. By Klaus-Jürgen Gern, Christophe Kamps, Carsten-Patrick Meier, Frank Oskamp, and Joachim Scheide. Kiel, April 2003. 29 S. 9 Euro.

Current information on the Institute's publications is available in World Wide Web under: http://www.uni-kiel.de/ifw/pub/pub.htm, further information about the Kiel Institute under http://www.uni-kiel.de/ifw/

Institut für Weltwirtschaft an der Universität Kiel, 24100 Kiel

Kiel Institute for World Economics

Kiel Institute for World Economics

Symposia and Conference Proceedings

Horst Siebert, Editor

Quo Vadis Europe?
Tübingen 1997. 343 pages. Hardcover.

Structural Change and Labor Market Flexibility
Experience in Selected OECD Economies
Tübingen 1997. 292 pages. Hardcover.

Redesigning Social Security
Tübingen 1998. 387 pages. Hardcover.

Globalization and Labor
Tübingen 1999. 320 pages. Hardcover.

The Economics of International Environmental Problems
Tübingen 2000. 274 pages. Hardcover.

The World's New Financial Landscape: Challenges for Economic Policy
Berlin . Heidelberg 2001. 324 pages. Hardcover.

Economic Policy for Aging Societies
Berlin . Heidelberg 2002. 305 pages. Hardcover.

Economic Policy Issues of the New Economy
Berlin · Heidelberg 2002. 251 pages. Hardcover.

Global Governance: An Architecture for the World Economy
Berlin · Heidelberg . 276 pages. Hardcover.

Berlin · Heidelberg: Springer-Verlag (http://www.springer.de)
Tübingen: Mohr Siebeck (http://www.mohr.de)